D1095240

Officially Withdrawn

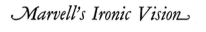

Marvell's Ironic Vision

Marvell's Ironic Vision

BY HAROLD E. TOLIVER

New Haven and London, Yale University Press

1965

Copyright © 1965 by Yale University.
Designed by Crimilda Pontes,
set in Garamond type,
and printed in the United States of America by
Connecticut Printers, Inc., Hartford, Conn.
All rights reserved. This book may not be
reproduced, in whole or in part, in any form
(except by reviewers for the public press),
without written permission from the publishers.
Library of Congress catalog card number: 65–11188

To Mary
and my mother and father

tant professor of English
California at Los Angeles.

48727

The fiction of the leaves is the icon

Of the poem, the figuration of blessedness,
And the icon is the man. The pearled chaplet of spring,
The magnum wreath of summer, time's autumn snood,

Its copy of the sun, these cover the rock.
These leaves are the poem, the icon and the man.
These are a cure of the ground and of ourselves.
(Wallace Stevens, "The Poem as Icon")

Preface

SINCE THE PRIMARY OBJECT of a single-author study of this kind is to explore the boundaries of the poet's particular world, I have tried to allow Marvell's poems to illuminate one another as far as possible, concentrating on the lyrics. In order to indicate something of the full curve of Marvell's range, however, I have also discussed the political poems briefly. The difference between Marvell the lyricist and Marvell the apologist and satirist explains a good deal not only about Marvell's development as a poet but also about the movement of seventeenth-century poetic in general. Hence, though the inner working of the lyrics is the main concern, my aim has been in a sense twofold, to explicate particular poems and to look at the times in a perspective sufficiently deep to give some sense of the context of those poems. After the many years of skirmishes between "historical" and "new" critics, no one could have failed to be aware of the risks involved in such divided interests, but Marvell, I believed, left no alternative. For whatever comfort it may afford, historical discussion is quarantined in the first chapter, except for local outbreaks.

I am especially grateful to Arnold Stein, whose comments have been encouraging and generous. William Matchett, D. C. Allen, Edward Bostetter, James Calderwood, Douglas Peterson, John Wallace, Ed Robbins, John Harold Wilson, and Howard Babb have read parts or all of the manuscript and offered helpful suggestions. To them and to Marvell scholars and critics I extend thanks, knowing that prefaces are not the best of currency with which to pay such debts.

PREFACE

I should like to thank also the librarians of the Johns Hopkins library, the Ohio State University library, the Library of Congress, and especially the Padelford branch and interlibrary loan office of the University of Washington library for their courtesy and assistance. Parts of three chapters are revisions of articles originally published in *Texas Studies in Literature and Language, Studies in English Literature,* and the *Bucknell Review*.

H. E. T.

Columbus, Ohio
March 1964

Contents

Abbreviations

BNYPL   *Bulletin of the New York Public Library*
CQ   *Critical Quarterly*
ES   *English Studies*
HLQ   *Huntington Library Quarterly*
HR   *Hudson Review*
JEGP   *Journal of English and Germanic Philology*
JHI   *Journal of the History of Ideas*
KR   *Kenyon Review*
Migne   *Patrologiae Cursus Completus, Series Latina,*
        ed. J. P. Migne
MLN   *Modern Language Notes*
MLQ   *Modern Language Quarterly*
MLR   *Modern Language Review*
MP   *Modern Philology*
N&Q   *Notes and Queries*
PQ   *Philological Quarterly*
RES   *Review of English Studies*
SP   *Studies in Philology*
SR   *Sewanee Review*
UTQ   *University of Toronto Quarterly*

1. A Grammar of Seventeenth-Century Platonism

Above the forest of the parakeets,
A parakeet of parakeets prevails,
A pip of life amid a mort of tails.
. . . .
 though the turbulent tinges undulate
As his pure intellect applies its laws,
He moves not on his coppery, keen claws.

He munches a dry shell while he exerts
His will, yet never ceases, perfect cock,
To flare, in the sun-pallor of his rock.

> (Wallace Stevens, "The Bird
> with the Coppery, Keen Claws")

IF POETS WHO WRITE large risk devaluation in skeptical, anti-heroic times, those who set tight restrictions for themselves risk something as undesirable: having their restrictions become a definitive indication of their achievement. Until the last few years, Marvell's reputation suffered from just such a reduction. The comparatively slight regard in which all but three or four of his lyrics were held was undoubtedly due in part to the infrequent use of the microscope in literary criticism, but perhaps also to the Aristotelian impulse of critics to classify poets in schools. As minor products from the school of Donne, Marvell's lyrics were not considered quite in their own terms. Since the mid-1950s, however, closer examination of the dozen or so best lyrics has revealed something both different from and in most cases better and more unique than curious pre-Wordsworthian or Donnelike specimens. It is becoming clear that Marvell's discipline resulted not simply in comparatively modest poems but also in an extremely fine articulation—and paradoxically, perhaps, an embodiment of infinity in a grain of sand at a time when nothing larger would hold it. Thus Marvell's original share in the Donne revival, slow to mature as it has been, shows increasing signs of leading to an independent and expanded study of his poetry for its own sake. (And it seems unlikely to bring in its train a share in the mild reaction against the species of Donne.) The present essay is intended as a contribution to that study.

Despite the injustice of the term "school," Marvell is like Donne in some ways: he is concerned with many of the same themes, metaphysical in the primary sense of the word, and attempts in exploring them to avoid "dissociation"[1]—which is to say, tries to hold head and heart together and maintain a balance between certain prevailing polarities. But unlike Donne, and unlike Milton as well, he is inclined to leave opposites carefully balanced rather than fusing them or subordinating them to a higher unity. He encompasses a wide intellectual range, but loosely, and with a disarmingly humorous *sprezzatura*. A hierarchical integration of nature and grace, for example, will not ordinarily resolve the pervasive dualisms of body and soul,

---

1. Despite its troublesome history, the word "dissociation" can serve some useful functions. It would not do to go into that history here since, as Montaigne observes, "it is more of a job to interpret the interpretations than to interpret the things, and there are more books upon books than upon any other subject: we do nothing but write glosses upon one another." By "dissociation" I mean simply the divisive tendency of a range of seventeenth-century oppositions, such as spirit and matter, body and soul, fact and value, religion and science.

eternity and time, the ideal and the real. The dialectic between these poles generally ends in compromise, a period of rest between hostilities, or perhaps resignation finely tempered with tension. Whereas Donne often arrives at some kind of resolution—in the oneness of lovers, for instance ("so we shall / Be one, and one another's All")—and Milton eventually cashiers discordant elements (having Eve submit to Adam), Marvell avoids both hierarchy and identity. In "The Definition of Love," he insists that the essence of love is a tension between identity (the conjunction of minds) and separation. In "The Garden," the unity of the wanderer depends upon a preliminary rejection of "Eve"; the moment for taking "longer flight" is left to the future, though the intervening time is "wholesome." Likewise, in "An Horatian Ode" Marvell looks forward to Cromwell's next campaign and watches the future ominously coming on; like the microcosm of the individual soul, the state is under continual siege. Marvell's humor and irony, important tonal elements both in poems spoken by mask figures such as the Mower and in straightforward lyrics, are an indication of his prevalent sense of the incongruous; his typical perspective is a "perspective by incongruity." The incongruous cannot be purged by reason or converted into motives for action. If Milton's protagonists are defined by action in "trial by what is contrary," Marvell's demonstrate (or lose) their internal harmony in combat against pressures from outside. Were they parakeets like Stevens', they too would simply "prevail," a "pip of life amid a mort of tails." Irony and humor provide the ballast for Marvell's contemplative performance; they enable him to "flare" and "move not."

His distancing and diminishing techniques, however, are counterbalanced by serious philosophical concerns which are not characteristic of witty poets of the seventeenth century outside of Donne and Herbert. Like the Puritan-Platonists of his time, he found the self, at least when its potential was fully realized, to be no less than a mirror and epitome of the macrocosm, which is to say, integrated with nature. The incongruity between self and scene was paradoxically part of an encompassing general harmony. (He was not willing, at least in the lyrics, to abandon entirely the old emblematic universe with its multi-leveled correspondences for a rational, deistic universe.) Though his preoccupation with dichotomies of one kind or another suggests a Manichean dualism, the attempt to avoid dissociation is often successful in peculiarly Marvellian ways that undoubtedly owe a good deal to the intellectual tradition he shares with Donne. Both Marvell and Donne explore it critically but reaffirm it in their own ways. To make history (the total process of becoming in time, in the Platonist framework) or nature meaningful in terms of divine order and purpose required a greater effort by Marvell's time, a leap across the gulf, like that of a spark between distant poles; but like Donne, Marvell at his best has the intellectual agility and disciplined spiritual force to bring it off—irony and vision together, not separately.

Since Marvell chooses to work within restrictive modes and tries out contradictory positions in successive poems, it is tempting to ignore the coherence of that intellectual and spiritual tradition when reading individual poems. But we need to be aware of the parts of his mind that are *not* engaged by a particular work as well as what does appear. For Marvell experiments with limited perspectives; he does not think of the lyric as a medium for intense self-expression. In "The Definition of Love" he talks jokingly about his own despair, though the poem is serious in its levity; for his Coy Mistress (no belle dame sans merci) he sprinkles the path to seduction not with languishing gestures or primroses but with incisive ironies, and an awareness of the expense of winning her.

My first concern, then, will be with some of Marvell's typical polarities in as encompassing a context as possible, and with contemporary thought about them, especially themes of art, nature, grace, and political issues, and especially in the form in which these were articulated by the Cambridge Platonists. And a secondary concern will be with the development of a lyric style capable of embracing the intense levity and the ironic self-exploration that characterize his poetry and allow him to play off certain small dramas against the greater context of his traditions. After exploring Marvell's intellectual range, I shall turn to particular groups of poems to consider matters of structure, recurrent image patterns, and, not least urgent in a study of Marvell's lyrics, texture and tone.

Self and Scene: Interplay of Art and Nature

Even without explicit temptation and dialogue poems such as "A Dialogue between the Resolved Soul and Created Pleasure" and "A Dialogue between the Soul and Body," we would be justified in stressing the importance in Marvell's lyrics of dialectical contests, usually between the soul and an aspect of nature partly but not totally hostile. It is a contest of opposites that are somehow much alike—fencing partners rather than *moral* opposites like Milton's Christ and his adversary. The ambivalence Marvell feels toward the opponent, if not sharper than that of other seventeenth-century poets, is at least more prevalent and structurally operative. Kenneth Burke's concept of the shift in "grammar" from medieval to modern times is one way of accounting for that ambivalence:

> The humanistic emphasis that arose with the secularization of middle class culture was new not in the sense that humanism itself was new but in the sense that humanism began to undergo a strategic transformation. We might describe this as a change from a "consistent" humanism to a "compensatory" humanism. "Consistent" humanism had placed human personality as the lineal descendant of a "principle of personality" [that is, God] felt to be present in the universal

5

ground. But with the increasingly secular emphasis, the motivations of the universal ground were viewed not in terms of a superhuman personality but in terms of naturalistic impersonality. And human personality was affirmed in dialectical opposition to the quality of the ground. . . .

At this point a calculus of "therefore" was supplanted by a calculus of "nevertheless." By a change in the tactics of grammar, men ceased to think, "God's personality, *therefore* human personality" and began to think, "Nature's impersonality, *nevertheless* human personality," the first pair related consistently, the second oppositionally.[2]

In the seventeenth-century phase of this movement toward secularization, it became more difficult for the poet to consider nature a reflection of the self, either as a collection of revelatory symbols or as a "macrocosm" corresponding in detail to the physical and spiritual structure of the microcosm. The subject-object dichotomy of later nature poetry began to replace the old system of "integrative" or "consistent" analogues. It is Marvell, part lyricist and part satirist, who perhaps more than any other poet of the mid-century reveals the difficulty of making the transition from one to the other. In the lyric he looks two ways, backward toward Herbert and forward toward Keats and Wordsworth. By and large, however, his pre-Wordsworthian and pre-Keatsian nature poetry is not an attempt to absorb the self into nature or even nature into the self; rather, it maintains clear distinctions between the human and the natural in order to preserve the ground of personality in a personal God. These distinctions can take the form of an apparently complete denial of commerce with nature, as in "A Dialogue between the Resolved Soul and Created Pleasure" and "On a Drop of Dew" or they can be simply an assertion of the mind's control over na-

2. *A Grammar of Motives* (New York, Prentice-Hall, 1945), pp. 112–13. I have used several of Kenneth Burke's terms as a shorthand way of making certain broad distinctions.

ture through art or through annihilation of "all that's made" to green thought.

In either case, Marvell stresses, along with the need to transcend the scene, the difficulty of doing so, especially if human love is allowed to complicate the dialectic. The plight of Damon the Mower, the Nymph, and the speakers of "The Fair Singer" and "The Picture of Little T. C. in a Prospect of Flowers" is aggravated by a commitment to someone in the "prospect." Passion entangles the soul in nature so that its retraction becomes difficult or impossible; the contest ceases to be mere sport. At these points, however, Marvell is generally distinguishable from the speaker of the poem; the speaker's confusion merely feeds Marvell's sense of the incongruous. The tension of the poem is that of an oppositional calculus, but it is the speaker who fails to see beyond it. In terms of rhetoric and poetic style, the distinction is important. The Platonist's rage for order is still reflected in the logical clarity of the poem; it is simply made to embrace a denser texture and sharper ambivalence than an unironic Platonist would tolerate. Many of Marvell's poems are thus characterized by a peculiarly *distilled* feeling, by the imagery of violence in a regular syntax, meter, and logical structure.

Perhaps the central paradox of Marvell's poetry, in fact, is its apparent rejection of (or at least detachment from) nature, which is nevertheless sensuous and engaging, the soul's fair enemy. Where Donne is explicitly paradoxical and rational in arguing for the unity of body and soul, for instance, Marvell's "unity" is denied logically but affirmed implicitly in such poems as "Dialogue between the Resolved Soul and Created Pleasure," "On a Drop of Dew," and others. The senses are not "explained" by metaphysical riddle but embraced warmly as they are ushered out. Though comparatively simple in their statement of the soul's independence, these poems are rich in

7

oblique movement; nature is engaged on the periphery, around a fixed, inviolable intellectual center. Hence Marvell avoids the dilemma of Platonist poetic that John Crowe Ransom once posed in this way: if "things" are useful only insofar as they can be translated "at every point into ideas," the Platonist can be positive only when he "believes in the efficacy of the idea"; he will be negative when the idea has "conspicuously failed to take care of him." And either way he is really a variety of philosopher rather than a poet.[3] Marvell's poetry, however, is sensuous and still manages to reaffirm the otherworldly elements of traditional Platonism. The interplay of self and scene is complex and variable. Marvell's Resolved Soul confronts nature as opposition-within-integration. The complexity of his poetry is thus the complexity of a mixed calculus: both Platonism and the alien, existential fact are vital to the individual poem—or perhaps I should say, to the poet exploring the possibility of wholeness in the complex strategies that poetry encourages.

Another way of approaching this mixed calculus historically is to say that Marvell is aware both of the contemporary conditions in which his poetry takes shape and of the Christian Platonist traditions which help him interpret those conditions and assimilate them into a larger, timeless context. His poetry is a verbal enactment of order in, and transformation of, a given "scene"—the civil wars, the pervasive threat of "femininity," the distractions of created pleasure—with the aid of the Platonist's cosmic order. But only a partial transformation: the force of time in "To His Coy Mistress," the violence of historical change in "An Horatian Ode," the wanton slaying of the Nymph's fawn, the documented folly of the satires, the death wish of Damon the Mower, testify to the residual stubbornness of nature that Marvell insisted upon making an essential part of poetry. As a Puritan of sorts and later as a practicing poli-

3. *The World's Body* (New York, Scribner's, 1938), p. 123.

tician, he could not accept symbolic gardens of ideas having no contact with the impolite world outside, any more than he could write escapist pastorals in the manner of Victorian scene painting. He inherited a long tradition of Platonist faith in the essential order of things and the non-being of evil, but it came to him at a crucial moment in its history. The tradition and the moment intensified his awareness of each other. In fact, Marvell would conceivably have endorsed Eliot's statement that a historical sense "which is a sense of the timeless as well as of the temporal and of the timeless and temporal together, is what makes a writer most acutely conscious of his place in time, and of his own contemporaneity."[4]

The tension between rational order and existential nature is reflected in a parallel tension, between contemplative and active lives. For the Puritan-Platonist the difficulty lay in deciding whether to surrender nature to science and isolate the important matters of the soul or to endorse the Reformation, which would make isolation impossible. His most typical attempts to resolve the tension between the self and the scene—in "The Garden," "Upon Appleton House," and "An Horatian Ode"—are versions of what we would have to hyphenate as a Puritan-Platonist motive, prominent until at least the Restoration: retreat and attack at the same time; renounce and *thus* control the world. It is another aspect of the fusion of "consistent" and "compensatory" humanism. Hence the puzzling mixture in Marvell of withdrawal, into forests, gardens, places "beyond the Pole," into irony, and so forth—"annihilation" of nature in green thought—and yet, subsequently or simultaneously, emergence into the world, in satire, political commitment, and enjoyment of the "annihilated" garden. Hence also the masochistic impulse that critics have noticed, as Marvell forces himself into and out of the world; the contemplative life may become the

4. "Tradition and the Individual Talent," in *Selected Essays* (New York, Harcourt, Brace, and World, 1950), p. 4.

most active kind of life. In a sense, Marvell is destroyed with Charles and the old protective "pallaces and temples" and is reborn with Cromwell. His dewdrop-soul lies restless and insecure, "congeal'd and chill" in the human "flower," but "recollects" itself for the dynamic ascent "Into the Glories of th' Almighty Sun." The passive victim of time in "To His Coy Mistress" emerges to tear pleasure with rough strife and make the sun "run." The active verb in Marvell will bear watching because, like Cromwell's "three-fork'd Lightning," it breaks the protective clouds that nurture it and emerges in aggressive action. His poetry is luminous with patterns of constriction and release, and at times, as "The Garden" illustrates, of simultaneous withdrawal and emergence.

Withdrawal is thus often a form of meditative exercise in Marvell and a preparation for emergence. In "An Horatian Ode," for example, the speaker celebrates the changes in social and economic institutions only after he has prepared his audience and (apparently) himself adequately with acknowledgment of their cost to the peaceful retiring poet and his subject. To wander "solitary" in the garden is the highest of pleasures and finds a mythic expression in the androgynous Adam, who contains both active and passive principles within himself and hence can safely enjoy nature. In contrast, Milton, more Protestant and less Platonist, thinks of solitude as deficiency. To avoid it is Adam's strongest motivation in accepting the apple; in *his* "solitary way" he walks eventually "hand in hand" with Eve, both of them guided by providence in the active struggle of good and evil they are to enter beyond paradise. Marvell awaits the time when the "almighty Sun" will draw back the soul, sometimes enduring time in the pleasure of "fruits and flow'rs," sometimes threatened by time's encircling decay, but always aware of change and the mazes of contemporary life which force him to retire. The speaker of "To His Coy Mistress," in exploring the opposite strategy, is aware not only of time's chariot at his back but also of the unlimited expanse of eternity's desert that lies before him—which means that, overturning the Platonist faith, he has no place to retreat *to*. To cheer his mistress and to surmount their isolation, he has only the consolation that together they can make the sun run faster, though only thus to burn up more quickly. The integrative humanist's concept of time as a process of continuous spiritual development is destroyed along with the idyllic pleasantness of the mistress' leisurely scene.[5]

The pattern of withdrawal and emergence so prominent in Marvell is also an important element in the thought of contemporary Christian Platonists, who in some ways provide a better commentary on his poetry than the more distant intellectual traditions of Plotinus, Richard of St. Victor, and the Stoics, normally associated with him. With them, however, it is an indication of philosophical uncertainty, due in part to the dangers of the new empiricism and Calvinist theology, rather than a conscious strategy for uniting the active Protestant life and the Platonist's emphasis upon contemplative illumination. By mid-century, empiricism had already made nature appear mechanistic; Calvinist thought, of course, made it appear depraved. And either view undermined the "consistent" calculus of the humanism of Ficino and earlier renaissance Platonists. For the Platonist of the preceding century, cosmic structure and universal moral law were more or less automatically taken to be mediaries between an absolute, unknowable source and the sensory world. As Ficino writes, it is not

> possible for the mind to strive, both by nature and by plan, to
> give diverse and single things an order in relation to one

5. The humanistic view of time is reflected in Hooker's remark that "God's own eternity is the hand which leadeth Angels in the course of their perpetuity; their perpetuity the hand that draweth out celestial motion, the line of which motion and the thread of time are spun together." *Laws of Ecclesiastical Polity*, V.69.2, Vol. 2 of *Works*, ed. Rev. John Keble (Oxford, 1887).

thing, without the mind itself having an order. . . . Further-
more, the ultimate common end moves the rest everywhere
(for all other things are desired for the sake of that which is
desired first). Therefore, it would not be extraordinary if, the
ultimate and common end itself being absent, the rest could
not be present at all. In the same way, unless the perfect form
of an edifice is prescribed by the architect, the different workman will never be moved to particular tasks which accord
with the plan of the whole itself.[6]

This view obviously cannot survive either an absolutism that
denies the worth of the exterior world or a nominalism that
denies the existence of universals;[7] neither can it survive a doctrine of election that denies the instrumental function of moral
action, so that the "workmen" are not moved to their "particular tasks" by the "plan of the whole." Such a doctrine calls into
question the entire structure of created correspondences upon
which Elizabethan concepts of order and action depend. The
temporal life does not "correspond" either actually or symbolically to the divine pattern, which is inscrutable. The "whole"
becomes an unknowable absolute rather than an architectural
plan such as Ficino describes. Though Calvin does not reject
nature or moral law as categorically as one might expect, he
does move them to a peripheral and precariously balanced position; active moral and political life becomes a *sign* of inner
health and possible election rather than a temporal pattern
uniting nature to grace.

6. Quoted from Josephine L. Burroughs' translation in *The Renaissance
Philosophy of Man*, ed. Ernst Cassirer et al. (Chicago, 1948), pp. 197–98.
7. As Rudolf Aller points out in his description of "microcosmus from
Anaximandros to Paracelsus," *Traditio*, 2 (1944), 323: "Whether it be
the κόσμος αἰσθητός [order sensible], or the νοητός [perceptible], or the
πολιτικός [political or social], these κοσμοι correspond to one another not
only in the general and formal sense that they are, all of them, ordered in
some way, but in the strict sense that they are, each in its particular manner, representatives or, better, manifestations, concretizations of the one
selfsame order."

The Cambridge Platonists were unwilling to abandon nature either to Calvinist dogma or to a scientific rationalism which enthusiastically measured, weighed, and labeled everything in a causal grammer. They vacillated between forms of Latitudinarianism and a relatively strict Puritanism and in both extremes found it difficult to relate the inner life to the dynamic attack on nature of the empirical and religious enthusiasts. And without some kind of outward confirmation in the macrocosm, without some manifestation of the ground of being in nature, the integrity of the soul itself was called into doubt. As Shakespeare's Troilus illustrates, when the bonds of moral order collapse, the inner world also disintegrates:

> Instance, O instance! strong as heaven itself;
> The bonds of heaven are slipp'd, dissolv'd, and loos'd;
> And with another knot, five-finger tied,
> The fractions of her faith, orts of her love,
> The fragments, scraps, the bits and greasy relics
> Of her o'er-eaten faith, are bound to Diomed.
> (*Troilus and Cressida*, V.2.155)

For Troilus the arch-idealist, a single existential "instance," a mere fragment of time, becomes as strong as heaven. "Unity" is whatever five fingers can make of the fractions and relics of an "o'er-eaten faith." And as Ulysses, the sad remnant of reason, argues to Achilles, nothing can remain aloof from nature; continual heroic effort and a disciplined civil hierarchy are the only weapons against the ravages of time:

> For Beauty, wit,
> High birth, vigour of bone, desert in service,
> Love, friendship, charity, are subjects all
> To envious and calumniating Time.
> One touch of nature makes the whole world kin.
> (III.3.171)

The education of the Platonist Troilus is thus an initiation into "universal" nature redefined, a depraved nature as difficult to assimilate into a Platonist system as the empirical nature of a Hobbes or Bacon.

Ostensibly, however, the Cambridge Platonists were troubled more by what they called the materialism and atheism of Hobbes and by the new science than by Calvinistic theology and the depravity of nature. It was clear to them that in both Bacon and Hobbes reliance upon sensation and independence from grace or any form of spiritual insight, whatever verbal tribute might be paid to it, involved an unpalatable dissociation of the spiritual and the temporal. For Bacon's Calvinistic concept of an inscrutable deity did not significantly qualify his confidence in the accuracy and independence of the senses. He had little of the epistemological skepticism of Descartes or Locke. His order of nature, however, was not compatible with what Cudworth (1617–88) labeled "the true intellectual system of the universe" (with approximately equal emphasis on "true," "intellectual," and "system"). Though Bacon believed the mind to be a "mirror or glass, capable of the image of the universal world, and joyful to receive the impression thereof," by impression he meant simply "the variety of things and vicissitude of times." If the Pateresque curse would have it that we have sold our birthright for a mess of facts, he was thoroughly convinced that he had the best of the bargain. As Bacon remarked in the *Novum Organum*, he had "purged and swept and leveled the floor of the mind" (CXV), being equally effective in all three operations. The mind's idols were nothing but "arbitrary abstractions" (CXXIV), whereas in the new science truth and utility are to be the "very same things" (CXXIV).

Since increasing awareness of the separation of natural, human, and divine law together with the Calvinist emphasis upon individual isolation and depravity thus made the humanizing of nature more difficult, the problem of self-definition received new emphasis in the Platonists. The Cambridge group looks inward rather than outward for the manifestation of the divine ground. Henry More (1614–87), for instance, though deeply influenced by the *Theologia Germanica*, conceives of the individual ego not as something that can be shed in the process of discovering God but as a necessary repository of one's share of the divine ground. While the medieval mystic, "the residuary legatee of Platonism" in J. S. Whale's phrase,[8] removed the last taint of selfhood in the purgative way, leaving a total vacuum which divinity could fill,[9] More moves divine light inward—and like Benjamin Whichcote (1609–83) makes it much smaller and more personal, a "candle" of the Lord. The relationship of inner and outer takes on overtones of the subject-object polarity; the Lockian inclosed consciousness begins to replace the microcosm as a description of the self. The philosopher as well as the poet is thus conscious of the self acting within a given scene and hence must explore the grounds of the contemplative life before he can emerge.[10]

8. *The Protestant Tradition* (Cambridge, Cambridge University Press, 1959), p. 26.

9. Since the "cloud of unknowing is above thee," a fourteenth-century mystic writes, "betwixt thee and thy God, right so put a cloud of forgetting beneath thee, betwixt thee and all the creatures that ever be made": *The Cloud of Unknowing*, ed. Dom Justin McCann (London, 1941), p. 21. "The more completely thou art able to in-draw thy faculties and forget those things and their images which thou hast taken in," Eckhart admonishes, "the more, that is to say, thou forgettest the creature, the nearer thou art" to the imageless truth: "where the creature stops, there God begins." *Meister Eckhart*, ed. Franz Pfeiffer (London, 1924), pp. 6, 49. See Joseph Collins, *Christian Mysticism in the Elizabethan Age* (Baltimore, 1940), esp. pp. 42–45; Plotinus, *Enneads* IV.7; Proclus *Metaphysical Elements*, trans. Thomas M. Johnson (Osceola, Missouri, 1909), proposition 129, pp. 97–98.

10. The movement in this direction parallels the rise of more sophisticated epistemological theories. Henry More, for example, is inclined to compromise with experiential theories of knowledge and to complicate traditional Neoplatonic epistemology with Cartesian implications. In his attempt to link spirit and matter, he finds that the mind has an inherent knowledge but that "outward" things cause it to run to a clearer and larger conception: "So the mind of man being jogg'd and awakened by the impulses of out-

The inner light of the Cambridge Platonists, which would seemingly anchor the soul in innate, universal verities, might in fact appear to have offered an adequate answer to both Calvinist and empiricist thought. The retreat inward would supposedly render the dialectic between self and scene unnecessary: if wisdom is shut out at one entrance,

> So much the rather thou Celestial light
> Shine inward, and the mind through all her powers
> Irradiate, there plant eyes, all mist from thence
> Purge and disperse, that I may see and tell
> Of things invisible to mortal sight.
> (*Paradise Lost*, III.51–55)

However, the confidence which Peter Sterry, Henry More, Benjamin Whichcote, and others among the Cambridge group place in the Candle of the Lord should probably not be taken quite at face value. The metaphor of the candle itself reveals a limited principle of immanence. In Locke the light will simply come from a "little" candle in a dark closet; it is put out in sleep and must be relighted daily from the senses.[11]

---

ward objects, is stirred up into a more full and clear conception of what was but imperfectly hinted to her from external occasions." *A Collection of Several Philosophical Writings* (London, 1662), I.5. The emphasis upon the soul's sensory experience is further revealed in his concept of the intensity with which the senses register, true and just engravings on the soul exciting it more and giving it greater "relish." The soul is thus firmly wedded to the world, though only at its own desire. We can see taking shape in More a psychologically founded epistemology and a Shaftesburian reliance on inward certitude and enthusiasm. See *Enchiridion Ethicum* (New York, 1930), facsimile of the English translation of 1690, published as *An Account of Virtue*, pp. 39, 41–42.

11. *An Essay concerning Human Understanding*, II.11. The transformation from a more dynamic inner illumination to this uncertain and spasmodic light can be seen, before the Cambridge group, in Jacob Böhme (1575–1624), the German shoemaker through whom much of the surviving medieval mystical tradition filters into the seventeenth century. Locke's predecessors in diminishing the function of the innate candle were primarily Aristotelians rather than Platonists, however. Cf. *sensus exterior* and

Whatever the importance of inner light to the Cambridge Platonists, Marvell (unlike Milton, Vaughan, and Traherne) says nothing of it. Given the prominence of the doctrine in the philosophical and religious thought of the time, it may seem a surprising omission. Though its "roundness" reflects the sphere from which it comes, the "soul" of "On a Drop of Dew" is totally isolated from its source while in the "humane flow'r." The Resolved Soul in "A Dialogue . . ." is celebrated by a semidivine chorus but demonstrates its integrity primarily through intellectual agility and wit rather than through claims to inner illumination. Self-definition is almost exclusively for Marvell a product of combat against exterior nature. Hence art rather than grace tends to become his chief mode of realizing the soul's self-sufficiency and of imposing order upon nature, which distinguishes him not only from religious poets such as Herbert and Crashaw but also from other poets in the "school" of Donne. The Resolved Soul counters the art of Created Pleasure with its own arts. "The Gallery" is a series of portraits designed to control the feminine (and therefore, for Marvell, naturalistic) savagery of Clora, "an Inhumane Murtheress" who needs civilizing: it is the gallery rather than divine illumination that resides in and protects the soul. In "Musicks Empire," nature is the domain of music, a "*Mosaique* of the air" supplementing if not replacing the prophetic Moses. The rejection of art in Damon the Mower is the prelude to self-destruction. In "An Horatian Ode" even Charles' beheading is converted into a "play," which makes it acceptable to the reticent poet. (I shall explore these themes in detail later.) As long as Marvell thinks in terms of a "nevertheless" calculus, art achieves its triumphs,

---

sensus interior in Pomponazzi, *Tractatus de Immortalitate Animae*, trans. William Henry Hay II (Haverford, Pa., 1938), p. 4; Andrew Halliday Douglas, *The Philosophy and Psychology of Pietro Pomponazzi* (Cambridge, 1910), pp. 67 ff; Ockham, *Philosophical Writings*, trans. Philotheus Boehner (London, 1957), pp. 18 ff.

controls the flux of nature, and limits the thrust of time; it enables the soul to emerge into the scene with some assurance. The use of art in Marvell is, in effect, the Augustan use—not pre-Keatsian or Wordsworthian so much as pre-Popian. Nature needs to be polished by art and purged of accidental qualities that conceal its universal truths; it can then be assimilated into polite society.

But the humanism that Pope secularizes and the nature that he finds essentially unerring, "still divinely bright / One clear, unchanged, and universal light"—in other words, a surrogate for God as "the source, and end, and test of art"—Marvell finds complicated by residual elements from another set of motives. The difficulty is that art and nature even at their best are not always compatible with the divine ground. The tension of his poetry is thus not simply a dualistic tension between art and nature, self and scene, but a triangular tension between art, nature, and grace.

The Divine Ground: Interplay of Grace and Nature

In lieu of an explicit theory of poetry from the period in terms of this triangular tension, perhaps the best commentary on it is again that of the Cambridge Platonists, for whom right reason and the inner light are in effect what art is to the poet. For they did not use the concept of the inner light as a basis for sealing off the life of the spirit from "history" (in the broad sense of all the institutions and arts of the temporal life). Consequently, with them, too, the secular arts—the modes of the soul's engagement and control of history—are in conflict with what they believed to be the clear ground of the soul in personal, divine immanence. After "retreat" and the discovery of inner light, what then? The answer of Neoplatonists in the tradition of Plotinus is a distinct *contemptus mundi*, but, as we have seen, this answer, though frequently associated with Marvell, would seem less appropriate both for him and for the Cambridge Platonists than commonly supposed. Since several of the Cambridge group were actively engaged in the Puritan revolution and none of them could escape its implications, they needed to translate the discoveries of the contemplative self into action without violating those discoveries. The need to do so is especially prominent in John Smith (1616–52) and Peter Sterry (1612–72), whose Puritan strain was stronger than that of More or Whichcote and whose attempts to answer the question "what then" are therefore more useful in exploring Marvell's.

Sterry was a Christian humanist of sorts, a lover of poetry well versed in the classics, though his approach to the problem of action was stated largely in metaphysical terms (in terms of the soul's "diversity and unity") and only secondarily in terms of moral program. He finds that "unity without distinction or variety is a barrenness, a melancholy, a solitude, a blackness or darkness"; but because continuity of self as well as stability in the cosmos requires that variety be no more than different facets of the same reality, diversity without unity he finds even more undesirable. It is doubtful that he would have prevented the proliferation of Puritan sects on this basis, since he felt the mystical union of souls strongly enough to forego the centralizing effect of a strong visible church. His monism, similar to that of his patron, Lord Brooke,[12] is an attempt to demonstrate

12. Lord Brooke rejected all theories of correspondence such as Lord Herbert's: "in spiritual beings and in these only, is true harmony, exact convenience, entire identity, perfect union, to be found": *The Nature of Truth* (London, 1640), preface. He was very likely influenced by Sterry, who also knew Sir Henry Vane and Milton and was possibly an assistant Latin secretary under Cromwell along with Marvell. He served as chaplain to Lord Brooke and to Cromwell. See Frederick J. Powicke, *The Cambridge Platonists* (London, 1926), p. 178; Rufus M. Jones, *Spiritual Reformers in the 16th and 17th Centuries* (Boston, 1914), p. 281; Vivian de Sola Pinto, *Peter Sterry, Platonist and Puritan* (Cambridge, 1934), pp. 4, 13, 33.

both the self-sufficiency of the soul, which owes its existence and unity to its divine source, and the value of the sensory world of flux. He did not find a coherent method of dealing with the dichotomy of the natural and the spiritual, however. His eclecticism lends itself to an inharmonious mélange rather than to a comprehensive synthesis. Though in the "natural heart" the "precious things of the sun, and the moon, of the invisible and visible image of the divine nature" come together in their most beautiful and concentric order, he finds that the heart of man is, notwithstanding, "triangular" and therefore cannot be filled "with the round world, but only with the Trinity."[13] The mystic illuminated by semi-apocalyptic visions, and the slightly awkward and sometimes foolish Puritan who stumbles over daily affairs, never quite become one man. The temporal world becomes for him a remarkable wilderness where black, white, and shadows, form and chaos, battle continually; he runs the risk of being torn to pieces in the struggle. Without doubt his Platonism is intensely experienced, but his attempt to encompass the paradox of unity and diversity has more emotional energy than rational direction. He is in the arena grappling with the mystery but we cannot be sure who is winning. For example:

Say thus to thy heart: my heart! canst thou tell a way to possess all things in one point, in a unity of Life? Hast thou looked on all things at once, and seen them in a harmony of beauty? Hast thou taken in the tunes and motions of all things created and uncreated in a concent of pleasures? Didst thou ever yet descry a glorious eternity in each winged moment of time; a bright infiniteness in the narrow points of every dark object? Then thou knowest what the Spirit means, that spire-top of things, whither all ascend harmoniously, where they meet, and sit together recollected, and concentred

13. *The Rise, Race, and Royalty of the Kingdom of God in the Soul of Man* (London, 1683), p. 194; cf. *The Appearance of God* (London, 1710), p. 89.

in an unfathom'd depth of glorious Life. From hence thou
lookest down, and seest all flesh, as a heap of single dusts;
dark, though falling from the midst of a bright flame; divided, though laid together.[14]

In his enthusiasm, he does not pause to ask what he wants to
emphasize in the paradox of things simultaneously centered in
the eternal spirit and yet lying divided below in time. (If "a
glorious eternity" exists in each "winged moment of time" the
implication is that time is redeemable. Sterry elsewhere asserts
that "everything is beautiful in time" and that the soul can
therefore rest easily, that "the time of everything is divinely
set, by a divine pattern, in a divine proportion, by a divine
power. Thus each thing is cloathed with a double beauty . . .
the divine harmony of the universal image in nature . . . and
an exact and ravishing harmony with the eternal image of the
supreme glories of God."[15]) When such meta-visions overpower
rational faculties, he exuberantly addresses the heart as the only
suitable audience. Impetuously piling up images and yoking
incompatible ideas together, he considers all things equally objects of wonder, equally difficult to articulate: we "descry" the
bright infinity, yet life is "unfathom'd"; depth and height contrast and yet are somehow the same; and creation and uncrea-
tion contribute equally to the "concent of pleasures." His concept of the self requires a darkness equal to the light, and yet
he must keep darkness "far below." He can, finally, only urge
that should his listeners likewise search themselves without
tarrying they might experience a similar erratic harmony.[16]

14. Ibid., p. 24.
15. Ibid., p. 185.
16. Cf. Cudworth (1617–88), who, though having a comparatively
well developed epistemological system, nevertheless falls into a similar un-
critical medley of mental processes in John Muirhead's opinion: *The Platonic Tradition in Anglo-Saxon Philosophy* (New York, 1931), p. 40;
Ralph Cudworth, *The True Intellectual System of the Universe* (London,
1839), I.222.

His Platonism is clearly something of a hobbyhorse, though a dynamic one.

Greater emphasis upon reason did not, however, guarantee a return to the earlier humanistic integration of reason, grace, and nature. In Benjamin Whichcote (1609–83) reliance on reason in itself became an extreme. A Socinian disregard for sacraments and the communal church, as his Puritan teacher Anthony Tuckney perceived, could result from severing personal convictions too decisively from dogma: the substitution of art for dogma in Augustan nature poetry is paralleled by the substitution of reason for dogma in the philosophy of the Enlightenment. In following the dictates of pure reason, Whichcote became aligned with such extreme latitudinarian positions as John Goodwin's[17] and received the dubious endorsement of the Earl of Shaftesbury as a defender of "natural goodness." For whether inward or scriptural, he writes, truth must satisfy reason: "Reason *discovers* what is natural; and reason *receives* what is supernatural."[18] And "if a man be once in a true state of religion, he cannot distinguish between religion and the reason of his mind; so that his religion *is* the reason of his mind, and the reason of his mind is his religion."[19]

Missing in both Whichcote and Sterry was the kind of sacramental or incarnational nature that would have converted the "scene" to a set of revelatory symbols more easily translatable to poetic symbolism. In one, the mode of discovery was beyond

17. See Ἀπολύτρωσις Ἀπολυτρώσεως, or *Redemption Redeemed* (London, 1651), IV.33, V.1; cf. William Haller's brief comments on this gadfly of the more orthodox brethren in *The Rise of Puritanism* (New York, 1957), p. 79, and Hershel Baker's estimates that the Latitudinarians ran the risk of a Godless nature to ensure a verifiable faith, realizing that if Christianity could not come to terms with the new experimental philosophy it must be destroyed by it—hence emphasis upon natural goodness and sufficient reason, *The Wars of Truth* (Cambridge, Mass., 1952), p. 128.

18. *Moral and Religious Aphorisms*, in E. T. Campagnac's edition, *The Cambridge Platonists* (Oxford, 1901), p. 67.

19. Ibid., p. 57, my italics.

reason (as in Traherne and Vaughan) and in the other, nature ceased being a revelation of an immediate divine presence. In neither case could the self discover its divine ground in transactions with nature, no matter how carefully it transformed and polished nature through art.

But here especially we need to guard against oversimplification; before we proceed to John Smith's approach to the polarity of nature and grace, a caveat might prove useful. The modern concern with locating a stable tradition of symbols has perhaps put excessive stress upon dogmatic aspects of "dissociation." It seems likely that theological currents paralleled general trends rather than channeling them. It may be, as Malcolm Ross writes, that the "Incarnation principle," which the medieval poet grasped more firmly than the renaissance poet (with exceptions), "makes possible, indeed demands, the sacramental vision of reality. The flesh, the world, things, are restored to dignity because they are made valid again. Existence becomes a drama which, no matter how painful it may be, is nevertheless meaningful."[20] But to believe in the "Real Objective Presence" in a religious rite seems not in itself enough to guarantee consciousness of meaning in all history,[21] or to ensure a fixed firmament of poetic symbols relating nature to grace. Likewise, of course, disbelief in the Eucharistic presence does not ensure the opposite—meaningless history, a chaos of symbols, and an absolute humanizing of man.

Though important changes occur more or less concurrently in dogma and poetry, we should not, then, emphasize too greatly the influence of a particular theological difference upon poetics. The pattern of withdrawal and emergence in Christian Platonism is undoubtedly the product of a widespread incapac-

20. *Poetry and Dogma* (Rutgers University Press, 1954), p. 11.
21. Cf. Vols. 1 and 2 of E. C. Messenger, *The Reformation, the Mass, and the Priesthood* (London, 1936–37); cf. Hooker, *Laws*, V.55.9, V. 67.12.

ity to see the world any longer as an emblematic structure; redemption becomes as much an act against nature as an outgrowth from it. But the change is too complex to be explained in dogmatic terms alone. Likewise, it is undeniable that writers such as Bacon or the Diggers tend to lose themselves in historical concretes, as Ross says, while Vaughan and Traherne tend to inhabit a "hidden garden locked forever against flesh and time," never emerging to engage history in dialectic: "For the garden of Vaughan and Traherne, unlike the Garden of Genesis, is a way out, not a way in. The child in Vaughan and Traherne is clad eternally in swaddling clothes. . . . He will never enter that darker garden of the sleepless agony. Though he is given the innocence of the dove, he cannot be intrusted with the wisdom of the serpent."[22]

But the causes again run too deeply to be redirected by a change of faith. (Marvell's own attraction to Catholicism at Trinity College was short-lived.) The danger of limiting the problems confronting the poet to dogmatic problems is that such varied and complex struggles to achieve order as Marvell's are hastily catalogued and poetic richness is lost in the shuffle.

Moreover, many Puritans and most Cambridge Platonists would have denied the sacrificial function of the Eucharistic rite, yet clearly believed in a theory of redeemable or providential history that made reform psychologically possible. If the word "providence" by itself tends to suggest special interruptions of history rather than continued atonement, Whichcote, Culverwel, Smith, Vane, and others nevertheless assert unequivocally at times that history as such can be redeemed: Christ is generally ὁ λογος who effects atonement through moral and reasonable means. They think of history as a kind of *progressive* incarnation, an incarnation of reason within and order without, rather than a divine presence effected through

22. *Poetry and Dogma*, p. 95.

ritual. At one extreme of the Puritan spectrum, Jonathan Edwards will later establish a rational lexicon of divine types in nature, adapting Locke's epistemology to a spiritual perception operating through sensation; he will make Newton the founder of a kind of typological physics,[23] so that withdrawal becomes less necessary in "taking over" the natural world—as, in the commercial spectrum, Sunday retreat becomes less important in sanctifying weekly business. Active life can *assume* the endorsement of spiritual life, even though the tendency among some sects is to lacerate enterprise even while covertly blessing it. At the other extreme, dogmatic conviction made nature more or less irrelevant.

The Platonists of the mid-century were not, of course, directly concerned with enterprise in the modern sense at all and had none of Edwards' speculative daring. But they did try to keep the active moral life integrated with religious mystery. Their emphasis upon the usefulness and residual goodness of nature went beyond that of early Neoplatonists, if not beyond the Florentine group, as Whichcote's statement concerning profane time reveals: "That time is lost that is not used; the virtue of it consists in the use of it. The true improvement of time is in the recovery of ourselves by reconciliation with God, our minds being renewed, our losses supplied, and our persons recommended."[24] They did not entirely separate philosophy from

23. See *Images or Shadows of Divine Things*, ed. Perry Miller (New Haven, 1948), p. 25. However, "That the knowable was confined to the perceptible did not mean for Edwards," Miller writes—whatever it may have meant for Locke—"merely that the mind was shut up within five meagre senses; it meant instead a new and exhilarating approach to reality" (p. 19).

24. *Works* (London, 1751), I.51–52 (discourse 3); cf. II.76 ff., "The Nature of Salvation by Christ" (discourses 30–33); II.204 ff. (discourse 39); II.286 (discourse 43). Cf. also Peter Sterry, *The Rise, Race and Royalty*, p. 59; Sir Henry Vane, *The Retired Mans Meditations, or the Mysterie and Powers of Godlines* (London, 1655), p. 145. See A. S. P. Woodhouse, *Puritanism and Liberty* (Chicago, 1951), p. 50.

dogma, or nature as a mirror of divine truths from nature as something confronted daily. Rather, they shifted the emphasis from sacramental dogma only far enough to imply that a moral and reasonable existence has as much to do with receiving grace as inexplicable mysteries and that "right reason" can extract the essences of things, the *vestigia dei*, from the record of history. Their benediction is meant to stimulate the soul's enterprise as the mastery of nature, their laceration to keep that enterprise relatively pure. The active life can at least lead to, if not directly incarnate, full and essential Existence—as Milton's Christ achieves knowledge of his divinity only after rejecting temptation and demonstrating patience. Enterprise is thus chiefly the agonistic return of the soul to its first principles; it is both aided and obstructed by nature.

It is on this point that John Smith is useful in formulating a seventeenth-century poetic. (Though much more Puritanical than Marvell, he is closely akin to him in some ways and was probably an influence on him.) It is true that if the relation of active moral life to divine grace was brought up under certain circumstances, Calvinistically inclined Puritans such as Smith insisted upon the impassable gulf between man's depraved nature and grace. But this insistence did not prevent secular enterprise, partly because if the active life had only marginal importance in determining one's ultimate spiritual health, it could be safely indulged daily. Enterprise was made free; the enterpriser could reach out with the hands while pushing away with the spirit. The chief requirement in Smith is that the active moral life be an emanation of divine and inner light, which is something more than reason and looks for something more in nature than rational order. (Reason by itself Smith finds too easily smothered by the "deep dye of men's filthy lusts," which threaten all "innate notions of divine truth."[25] Like Milton, he

25. *The True Way or Method of Attaining Divine Knowledge,* in *Selected Discourses,* ed. H. G. Williams (Cambridge, 1859), p. 6.

believes that truth and goodness grow from the same root and live in one another: "Such as men themselves are, such will God himself seem to be."[26]) But one can achieve temperance only through the tempering processes of the world.[27] The possibility of avoiding dissociation rests with the inner light *manifest* in action, in the moral will rather than in mere "notions."[28] The soul cannot behold God "unless it be Godlike" in moral performance; trial "by what is contrary" rather than sacramental mystery is its primary means of redemption. Dialogue between opponents rather than sacramental symbolism is its logical poetic mode.

In treatises such as *The Vanity of a Pharisaical Righteousness* and *Of Legal and Evangelical Righteousness,* Smith attempts to separate as completely as possible the outward vestments and laws of the organized church from "the spirit and vital influx" of the new law which can quicken men into a divine life, a "*vitalis scientia,* a living impression made upon the soul and spirit."[29] Like Whichcote, he anticipates the eighteenth century in distaste for unnecessary mysteries and dogma: "He that is most practical in divine things hath the purest and sincerest knowledge of them, and not he that is most dogmatical"—true religion, in fact, is nothing more than "a vigorous efflux and emanation" of God's first truth and primitive goodness upon "the spirits of men, and therefore, is called 'a participation of the Divine nature.' "[30] But unlike Whichcote, he makes it clear that the Tree of Knowledge bears evil fruit if not located next

26. Ibid., p. 5.

27. *Of the Immortality of the Soul,* ibid., pp. 119, 121.

28. See P. R. Anderson, *Science in Defense of Liberal Religion* (New York and London, 1933), pp. 38–39, 71; cf. Santayana, *Platonism and the Spiritual Life* (New York, 1934); Paul Henry, introduction to *Plotinus: The Enneads* (London, 1956), p. xxxviii.

29. *Of Legal and Evangelical Righteousness,* in *Selected Discourses,* p. 339.

30. *The Excellency and Nobleness of True Religion,* p. 390.

to the Tree of Life and watered with holiness, for "it is but a thin, airy knowledge that is bought by mere speculation."[31]

It is thus that he attempts to bring together the unpleasant existential facts about man's nature that trouble the Calvinist and the concepts of cosmic order and inner harmony that form an important part of any form of Platonism. Only if reason as a sergeant at arms can prevent sensuality from turning the soul into Pandemonium can the soul's main intuitional business be carried out: "All sin and wickedness is . . . a sedition stirred up . . . by the sensitive powers against reason."[32] The temperate and tempered man thus exists in a citadel stormed by brutish forces that can be kept out only by a vigorous containment of the self within the encircling wall of the moral will. If the *itinerarium mentis ad deum* suggests to Bonaventura a ladder of lower to higher created forms and certain methods of meditation, to Smith as to Milton and Marvell it suggests an allegory of warfare, or a pilgrimage among well-armed temptations, and a definition of the self which uses Created Pleasure as a negative indication of fortitude and chastity. Hence the new trinity of virtues so common among the renaissance Platonists,[33] faith, hope, and chastity: chastity as a containment of the soul's perimeters. The integral soul becomes known to itself through the tests it undergoes, intuiting a knowledge beyond the phantasms of sense and the "correction of science."[34]

The Puritan-Platonist alliance is not entirely defensive, however. The soul so armed with chastity, which is a kind of negative unity, issues from itself in a different kind of concern for the world in which "every created excellency is a beam descending from the Father of Lights" and in a new magnanimity:

31. *The True Way*, p. 2.

32. *The Excellency and Nobleness*, p. 398.

33. See Sears Jayne, "The Subject of Milton's Ludlow Mask," *PMLA*, 74 (1959), 533.

34. *Of the Immortality of the Soul*, p. 101.

"Religion begets the most heroic, free, and generous motions in the minds of good men." After choosing the narrow way of chastity, the soul finds in itself a universal "gallantry and puissance" which far excels that of those who are basically worldly.[35] Thus in the Platonist-Protestant sensibility, the soul at its highest moment, the same moment when it "annihilates all that's made," turns about to embrace the world, to wave in its plumes the various light.

This ambivalence felt toward nature in the Puritan-Platonist alliance helps explain the curious structure and mixed tone of poems like "The Coronet," the "Bermudas," "Clorinda and Damon," and the woodland sections of "Upon Appleton House," Marvell's principal religious poems. "Tuned" or "woven" by the poet's art, nature is discovered to be not totally purified, but on the other hand not valueless either. After carefully making the coronet, Marvell throws it at Christ's feet as a sacrifice, nature and art together becoming Christ's spoils. And it is the sacrifice itself that makes the poet worthy of grace. Action becomes a form of saving self-laceration, made possible by enterprise, where inaction would presumably leave one still in a state of ignorance about his true condition. The poet must weave the coronet before he can discover the serpent folded within it in "wreathes of Fame and Interest."

Art and the Transformation of History

Exactly what is to be embraced and what sacrificed, however, is often somewhat vague both in Marvell and in the Puritan Platonists and Milton. Puritan "enterprises" differ radically, of course, the only thing they have in common being their aggressive dialectic. As Perry Miller writes in the first volume of *The New England Mind*, the enthusiasm has perhaps more force than specific direction:

35. *The Excellency and Nobleness*, pp. 440 ff.

Perhaps the most highly paradoxical and ironic of the doc-
trines was that of total depravity, for it contained on the face
of it a view of life that seems to make all endeavor useless, yet
in effect it aroused Protestants to fervent action; it ought to
have inspired melancholy and humility, but it often gave rise
to Pharisaism and sanctimonious pride; . . . It ought to have
forced man to grovel in the dust, but instead one of its principal effects was a renewed emphasis upon the importance of
his rôle in the creation, a fresh vision of the boundless possibilities of his genius.[36]

These apparent contradictions are not merely signs of the un-
ease in Puritanism over whether to reject the world or remake
it, however; they are also part of a principle of spiritual (and
political) freedom that allows action within a generally hostile
scene. For the poet, that freedom took the form of release after
constriction, as the Lady in *Comus* joins the country merriment
of the Bridgewater estate after rejecting the merriment of the
forest. For Marvell, art as the outward manifestation of the
soul's unitive powers could remake the scene and thus make it
acceptable with some degree of safety. The pilgrims in the English boat in "Bermudas" keep time to their enterprise with "An
holy and a chearful Note" which is both a celebration of the
providence that has led them through the "watry Maze" and a
work chant. Damon converts Clorinda from temptress to fel-
low celebrator in Pan's choir; his oaten reed transforms nature
and "femininity," making them added voices in the swelling
chorus.

But the trial of the pilgrims and the temptations of Comus
and Clorinda are necessary preliminaries. When the negative process is less rigorous and nature appears to open more
easily to the unaided intellect, as in Nathaniel Culverwel,
for example, the sharpness of nature's ambivalence is lost. In

36. *The New England Mind,* Vol. 1: *The Seventeenth Century* (Cambridge, Harvard University Press, 1954), p. 181.

the soul's isolation from (and yet endorsement of) the macro-cosm lay much of the vitality of the Platonist-Puritan alliance. Platonists such as Culverwel and Whichcote tend to be less convincing in proportion to the ease with which reason and faith are discovered "twin lights."[37] They approach the philosophy of natural goodness at the expense of leaving the Platonist camp altogether.[38] (The confident assertion with which Culverwel begins and ends the *Discourse of the Light of Reason*, that reason and faith may kiss, indeed, in the course of his discussion, "*have* kissed each other," is not entirely warranted, though such union is the primary goal of his thought. The unity is a "mere dream image":[39] if reason and faith do in fact kiss,

37. Culverwel finds that faith and reason "sweetly conspire in the same end, the glory of that being from which they shine" so that to blaspheme reason is to reproach heaven itself (Campagnac, p. 213). And like Whichcote, he predicts some of the Deistic implications of natural reason: "God set up the world, as a fair, goodly clock, to strike in time, and to move in an orderly manner" (p. 225). The marriage of body and soul is a "most loving and conjugal union" (p. 273): "Many sparks, and appearances fly from variety of objects to the understanding; the mind . . . catches them all, and cherishes them, and blows them; and thus the Candle of Knowledge is lighted" (p. 286). Man's essence is a heavenly plant, an "*arbor inversa*, this enclosed being, the garden of God" (p. 256). Cf. the inverted tree image in "Upon Appleton House," stanza 71; *Timaeus* 90 A; Bishop Nemesius, *The Nature of Man*, trans. George Wither (London, 1636), III.3.

38. William R. Inge describes Culverwel as a "literal churchman" rather than a Platonist: *The Platonic Tradition in English Religious Thought* (London, 1926), p. 64. John Norris (1657–1711), perhaps in reaction against Culverwel and Burthogge, attempted to overthrow the compromise with natural goodness and made tentative efforts to construct an absolute idealism in its place. The influence of Malebranche's idealism, and such broad religious tolerance and stress upon the inner light that some Quakers considered him an ally, indicate his entrance into the evangelical and philosophical patterns of the eighteenth century. See Flora Isabel MacKinnon, *The Philosophy of John Norris of Bemerton* (Baltimore, 1910).

39. The phrase is Ernst Cassirer's in estimation of Pico and Ficino, *The Platonic Renaissance in England* (Austin, Texas, 1953), pp. 1 ff; cf. Paul Oskar Kristeller and John Herman Randall, Jr., "The Study of the Philoso-

it is a parting gesture. And with their separation, the possibility of seeing the self as a microcosm reflecting all nature disappears.) Marvell's optimism is seldom uncomplicated in this way; his claims for the transforming power of art are scaled down considerably from traditional Platonist poetics. His artists are generally limited persona figures without the magic of a Prospero or the prophetic ambitions of a Crashaw. (His opening comment on *Paradise Lost* is that, "misdoubting" Milton's intent, he feared that Milton "would ruin . . . The sacred Truths to Fable and old Song.") Though he glances at the esoteric tradition in which magic is a cure-all for nature, he is ironic and skeptical in its presence. Consequently, release from the tension between art, nature, and grace is only partial— where Paracelsus, for example, expected a good deal more from the arts: "All of us should know that art, science, and skill exist only to be conducive to joy, peace, unity, purity, respectibility . . . This is also true of music. It is the remedy of all who suffer from melancholy and fantasy. . . . An art is the most durable good, the best wealth. . . . Our life is founded not only in bread, but also in arts and words of wisdom that come from the mouth of God."[40]

Similar therapeutic power is reaffirmed by Spenser, Sidney, Milton, and Shakespeare at times; but for Marvell art is simply the limited power of the soul to engage the scene—to make little T. C.'s garden more pleasant, to control Clora or Clorinda. Moreover, its capacity for creating order is matched by its dangers as a snare: it is the chief weapon of the "fair singer" whose "fatal Harmony" entangles the soul and gains "both the Wind and Sun." The wise Resolved Soul is on guard against

phies of the Renaissance," *JHI*, 2 (1941), 492; Kristeller, "Ficino and Pomponazzi on the Place of Man in the Universe," *JHI*, 5 (1944), 220–26.

40. *Selected Writings*, ed. Jolande Jacobi (New York; Bollingen Series XXVIII, 1951), p. 205.

its "sweet Chordage," which is more enticing than Created Pleasure's other delights.

Marvell's diminished claims for the transformational power of art is accompanied by an uneasiness in suggesting analogues between contemporary history and cosmic order. If in treating history, seventeenth-century Platonists are forced to yield some ground to the orders of commerce and science, in treating political matters they are forced to yield to the logic of the revolution, which deposed a king because he was not sacred, not part of an inevitable divine order. If the people elect the monarch, kingship is a natural rather than a divine institution, or at most a combination of the two emphasizing the natural. And if the public order thus shares the ambiguity of nature, the Platonist is again apt to harbor the inner world in order to preserve its divine ground. The soul's encounter with politics is as risky as its temptation by Created Pleasure. Unquestionably the multiplicity of Puritan institutions and the consequent separation of church and state contributed to such a severance of private and public lives among the Platonists. The universal community of true believers in which the Puritan claimed citizenship necessarily became more invisible as the sects became more vociferous and local. Even in those committed to action, such as Cromwell and Thomas Fairfax (both of whom Marvell associates with the conflict between public duty and private fulfillment), the inner life and the life of action assumed an unusual dialectical relationship. Cromwell habitually preceded public action with prayer and followed it with meditation. Though it was not possible to separate the two lives entirely until church and state were much more completely divided than in the 1650s, neither could they be integrated in quite the same way as when the king himself was considered God's deputy. The emphasis upon the evangelical pulpit, political rhetoric, and poetic eulogy was perhaps a result of the lack of a commonly accepted political-religious institution. It was necessary to assert the connection between political motives and the divine ground *through* rhetoric. And even those who were willing to isolate religious experience from political affairs could not stand alone, as Luther had earlier discovered: "Satan tempts me. I need my brother's voice as the human instrument by which God assures me of his Grace. God appoints my neighbour to be representative. Through the voice of the brother, the preaching man, the power of the keys is exercised on my behalf, and I am assured of absolution and forgiveness."[41] Public opinion, then, as well as inner light and ritual absolution; and conversely, in political matters, verbal baptism before public celebration. In terms of political poetry, the poet of the 1650s begins to feel increasingly the need to transform political events into religious events before he commends them. (Once made an instrument of providence, for instance, Cromwell can be assimilated into Marvell's Horatian celebration, his violence in destroying the "work of time" becoming something like the sacrifice of the "spoils" in "The Coronet.")

The language problem for the political poet is thus much as Ross formulates for the seventeenth-century poet in general: once the habit of analogical or sacramental thought is broken by the causal method of empirical thought or by other forces, the poet cannot employ without some discomfort the standard tropes and symbols that were traditionally used to associate the temporal with the divine through "magical" means. Whereas a Tudor king was commonly assumed to have divine right both by inheritance and by the analogous structure of things (which made the body politic related to the king, as the cosmos, say, to the sun), Cromwell's claim to providential sanctions had only personal conviction behind it. Thus for the Platonist, the difficulty of linking him with the universal order is similar to the difficulty of redeeming nature. The poet is reluctant to abandon

41. J. S. Whale, *The Protestant Tradition*, p. 110. The quote is Whale's reconstruction of Luther's remarks.

the contemplative life for the active unless action has a higher sanction in the divine ground. The Platonist could look at temporal life in no other way, arguments derived from political expediency and pragmatism having very little cogency for him. Even if nature and politics are not sacramental, of course, the celebrational poet can conjure acceptance of them through rhetorical means, mixing the fragments of traditional symbolism with the rising techniques of image projection and salesmanship, as a means of convincing his audience. Calling the fish of a certain lord's estate a "finny tribe," for example, is a way of giving them "absolution and forgiveness" for being mere fish. And such eulogistic clichés, which confer divine right to the scene, are common by Marvell's time. But the arbitrariness with which the transaction is made is becoming more marked; Marvell resists reducing political commentary to modes of flattery. Though he insists that Cromwell is a delegate of providence whose destiny it is to redeem the times, he appears to do so with some conviction. The God-king-sun analogy of Elizabethan political rhetoric, for instance, still retains something of its original flavor; it has not become an automatic labeling device:

> *Cromwell* alone with greater Vigour runs,
> ('Sun-like) the Stages of succeeding Suns:
> And still the Day which he doth next restore,
> Is the just Wonder of the Day before.
> *Cromwell* alone doth with new Lustre spring,
> And shines the Jewel of the yearly Ring.
> 'Tis he the force of scatter'd Time contracts,
> And in one Year the work of Ages acts.
> . . . .
> . . . indefatigable *Cromwell* hyes,
> And cuts his way still nearer to the Skyes,
> Learning a Musique in the Region clear,
> To tune this lower to that higher Sphere.
> ("The First Anniversary," 7–14, 45–48)

Thus Cromwell's "art" is found to transform the lower sphere
—like any sacramental agent applying divine art to the current
civil disorder—transcending the works of time, not merely destroying them.

Despite this resistance to automatic political baptism, however, the ambiguities of Marvell's attitude toward nature in pastoral poems are compounded in the political poems in his attitude toward the active life and the arts of government. Even in
the passages quoted, Cromwell is praised primarily for *demonstrating* himself in action; his divine favor is not inherent—and
only he can contract the "force of scatter'd Time," no one else:
his is not a ritual redemption through which others are saved
by identifying themselves with him but a pragmatic redemption
demanding a political program. If in praising the good king,
the poet could consider himself part of a "consistent" humanism celebrating the order of the universe, in praising the ac-
complishments of a good politician, he remains an arm of the
state. Cromwell is half Machiavel, half saint, which is something different from a shrewd king. This may account for the
apparent fact that Marvell's own transfer of traditional symbols
and king-functions to Cromwell becomes less certain in the
sequence of poems on Cromwell; the identity between poet and
political scene, though more explicit, is less effective in "The
First Anniversary" and "A Poem upon the Death of O.C.,"
which move one step from ritual eulogy toward rationalization
and political realism. The realism is reinforced by the fragments of ritual and symbol but not fully incorporated into a
universal ground. Though they remain primarily eulogistic
poems, they reveal an irreparable severance of the immediate
political scene and the divine injunctions the resolved soul demands. In terms of poetic, the movement is from a symbolism
in which the historical fact is seen as an extension of religious
motives to a conscious use of transfer devices that assert that
extension as a tactic. (But the distinction between inflationary

salesmanship and genuine rhetorical strategy is admittedly difficult to make. Since it is largely a matter of tone and conviction, I shall postpone further speculation about it until the chapter on Marvell's political poems.)

That the relationship between poetry and politics shifted significantly during Marvell's lifetime seems clear, then. The Puritan revolution, with its emphasis upon the special intervention of providence in history, completed the destruction of the links between king and bishop, king and inherent divine prerogative begun much earlier and explored so thoroughly in Shakespeare's history plays and tragedies. It was followed not by a return to the old kingship, of course, but by an increasingly figurehead kingship in which, for the sake of appearances and national ritual, it was publicly assumed that the king was God's deputy as the government *worked* as local politics. The poet was still apt to cast political analysis in the cosmic-oriented language of the older system, but the transfer of universal language to local politics was more obviously a form of advertising, because, as we have seen, once the state was severed from the church as a parallel manifestation of universal order, cosmic rhetoric was deprived of its constituent grammar. And as modern politics have demonstrated, a state or party that becomes more local, by an unofficial law of rhetorical compensation tends to claim more forcefully that it is in fact universal. The official ode increases its orchestration; realism is left to satire and the novel, one the instrument of displaced Tories, the other a middle class instrument of unceremonial truth-saying. (While Gulliver discovers the distance between the laws of reason and human institutions, Robinson Crusoe amasses a fortune through minutely described daily affairs, under a watchful but impersonal banker-God.)

The shift from cosmic to local politics and the concurrent attempt in political eulogy to compensate for the shift—the social equivalent to Burke's shift from a consistent to a compensatory calculus—is perhaps more apparent in Dryden than in Marvell since Dryden feels less ambivalent about converting traditional symbols to new political uses, and more tellingly scores his opponents for doing the same. In *Absalom and Achitophel*, for instance, scriptural typology, traditionally one of the effective linguistic devices for associating kings with the King of kings, undergoes a definite modernization. In "To My Honor'd Friend Dr. Charleton," Dryden skillfully identifies the sacred religious rites of Stonehenge with the rites of Charles' coronation ("Stone-heng, once thought a *Temple*, You have found / A *Throne* where Kings, our Earthly Gods, were Crown'd"). He suggests in addition that the new science of Dr. Charleton shares the "restored" sanctity of both, so that science, the monarchy, and the ancient temple are all parallel aspects of "free Reason's claim" wherein "Th' *English* are not the least in Worth, or Fame." Though the triple identity is established on primarily rationalist rather than sacramental ground, the monarchy is no less "consistent" with God's purpose than with nature as the Royal Society sees it. These remnants of what Ross labels "sacramentalism" Dryden also exploits in "To His Sacred Majesty, a Panegyric on his Coronation" and "Annus Mirabilis." "Astraea Redux . . . On the Happy Restoration" gives Charles the same "Heav'nly parentage" Dryden so generously supplied Cromwell a few months preceding in "A Poem upon the Death of His Late Highness":

> O happy Prince whom Heav'n hath taught the way
> By paying Vows to have more Vows to pay!
> Oh Happy Age! Oh times like those alone,
> By Fate reserv'd for great *Augustus* throne!
> When the joint growth of Arms and Arts foreshew
> The world a Monarch, and that Monarch *You*.

In "Mac Flecknoe," however, Dryden plays typology against the tautology of Shadwell—which repeats, but not prophetically:

> Heywood and Shirley were but types of thee,
> Thou last great prophet of tautology.

The difference between tautology and typology is essentially the difference between the cliché and the common symbol. The diminished power of the types indicated by the wordplay—their inability to raise historical events out of temporal limits by associating them with a visionary pattern—points toward Pope's concept of the antilogos in the *Dunciad* and the conversion of types to the dunces' antitypes of repetitive, atomistic stupidity. Having lost its eulogistic function, typology could no longer stretch over the gulf between human words and the divine order, especially in the syntax of the dunces. Deprived of magic word power, the political poem ceases being *transformative*—as in Dryden's rhetorical strategy in linking temple, science, and king and thus transferring the best of each to the others—and becomes *reformative*, using the memory of an integrative humanistic order for satiric defense against the rising wave of writers from Grub Street, with their queen-goddess.

It is scarcely necessary to remind ourselves that the solutions which the Platonists proposed for these problems—the separation of history from concepts of cosmic and sacramental order, the concurrent change in the interplay of self and scene, and the relations of art and nature—were not found widely acceptable in their own times, and probably had little influence even among those who later might be expected to have learned from them, such as Blake and Keats. Together with Milton, Vaughan, Marvell, and a few others, the Cambridge group represents a last and in some ways desperate attempt to salvage an order beyond reclamation. The general movement is clearly toward Locke, the Royal Society, and Swift's incisive satire of microcosm and invested nature. Rochester's reaction is perhaps more representative of the large skeptical segment of Marvell's own time that delighted in puncturing philosophical *afflati*.

Disgusted with "mankind," Rochester declares that he would rather be "a Dog, a Monkey, or a Bear," or anything "but that vain *Animal*,"

> Who is so proud of being rational.
> The senses are too gross, and he'll contrive
> A Sixth, to contradict the other Five;
> And before certain instinct, will preferr
> *Reason,* which Fifty times for one does err.
> *Reason,* an *Ignis fatuus,* in the *Mind,*
> Which leaving light of Nature, sense behind;
> Pathless and dang'rous wandring ways it takes
> Through errors, Fenny-*Boggs,* and Thorny *Brakes;*
> Whilst the misguided follower, climbs with pain,
> *Mountains* of Whimseys, heap'd in his own *Brain:*
> Stumbling from thought to thought, falls head-long down,
> Into doubts boundless Sea, where like to drown,
> Books bear him up awhile, and makes him try,
> To swim with Bladders of *Philosophy;*
> In hopes still t'oretake th'escaping light,
> The *Vapour* dances in his dazled sight,
> Till spent, it leaves him to eternal Night.
> Then Old Age, and experience, hand in hand,
> Lead him to death, and make him understand,
> After a search so painful, and so long,
> That all his Life he has been in the wrong;
> Hudled in dirt, the reas'ning *Engine* lyes,
> Who was so proud, so witty, and so wise.

Some such disillusionment was likely to result from the optimistic and fragile premises of the Platonists. But Rochester was ignoring, of course, the pressures which caused them to fall victim frequently to mountains of whimsy, unfounded enthusiasm, and pride in the ignis fatuus reason. His own life dramatically illustrates what the Platonists felt to be the only alternative: consider the five senses sure instruments, throw over the sixth sense, sink the books and puncture the bladders of philosophy, and there would be nothing to maintain them in "doubts boundless Sea." Marvell, by combining the satiric capacity of Rochester (which he strongly admired, according to Aubrey) with an awareness of the seriousness of the Puritan-Platonist quest for unity, attempts to assimilate essence and existence, ideality and fact, into a comprehensive poetic order. The dissolution of an "o'er eaten faith" into fragments and relics is thus forestalled—at least until the "painter" places a canvas of Restoration Cressidas before an appreciative set of "scratching Courtiers" who have turned from "our *Lady State*."

Conclusions

Since the grouping of poems in succeeding chapters is based on Marvell's range of attitudes toward nature and the functions of art, it might be useful at this point to recapitulate some of the relations of art, nature, and grace that the poems and their background illustrate. Marvell's most obviously Platonist poems, such as "On a Drop of Dew" and "A Dialogue between the Resolved Soul and Created Pleasure," are essentially rejections of both nature and art on the basis of the soul's self-contained resistance and its reflection of the "clear Region where 'twas born." The method of that rejection is by no means simple, but the category itself is relatively distinct. More difficult to locate with respect to contemporary thought and internal structure is a group of poems which explore the possibilities of absorbing nature into the divine ground along with the self ("self" rather than "soul" because Marvell tends to use the latter term when emphasizing alienation from nature). In them, in various ways, the pattern of withdrawal and emergence and the pastoral tradition offer a way of engaging nature and controlling it through art. In some of them, nature is useful only as an adversary, as Jean Genet's playacting judge in *The Balcony* finds a genuine thief useful: "Look here: you've got to be a model thief if I'm to be a model judge. If you're a fake thief,

I become a fake judge. Is that clear?" As he later adds, "My being a judge is an *emanation* of your being a thief. . . . If I no longer had to divide Good from Evil, of what use would I be?" To the Puritan who defines good as the polar opposite of evil, the better the opponent the more convincing his victory. Marvell on occasion, like Milton habitually, imagines good as the overcoming of temptation and *thereafter* as the integration of nature and grace. He pursues the "negative way" of chastity and rejection to the discovery of the minimal essentials of the self and only then reaffirms confidence in the soul's strength. In "Clorinda and Damon" the rejection of nature precedes the song about it; in "The Garden" red and white passions and social commitments are sloughed off before the mind's creative power in the green shade is explored. Perhaps the most impressive aspect of these poems is their capacity to draw sustenance and self-knowledge from the conflict itself: even the Resolved Soul knows the workings of Pleasure from the inside, though it avoids committing itself to pleasure principles. The result is rejection, but rejection as sacrifice.

Insofar as the sacrifice is real and not merely a gesture, the poem tends to suggest Christian rather than Platonist views of nature, as "The Coronet" does, for example. ("A Dialogue between the Resolved Soul and Created Pleasure" is divided into two parts, one Platonist in orientation, the other Puritan.) The strict Platonist has no machinery for repentance or sacrifice, since he seeks order rather than mercy, intellectual clarification rather than spiritual purgation. He tends to think of "redemption" as the soul's process of freeing itself from the recalcitrant stuff of everyday life. But a Christian poem may presumably be not only an emanation of the world's being unpoetic in a certain way but also a purgation of the guilt the poet feels for loving it anyway, as "Lycidas" is elegiac and *Comus* restrictive because nature is both attractive and forbidden as an object of love in itself. The primary pattern of withdrawal and emergence in Marvell derives from this basic ambiguity of nature and the consequent antagonism between it and the self (or soul). Stated as a goal, the strategy is to reject the world in such a way that it may cooperate with the soul. Though the judge must have his thief, the Puritan sin, the Lady Comus, the Stoic passions, each may also feel some attraction toward his opposite, so that by sacrificing it he can demonstrate complete commitment to the divine ground. The structure of several of Marvell's poems is thus a process of meditative purgation in which the poet realizes, through agonistic trial, the cost of, and the way to, grace. Or he may discover that heaven and earth, art and nature are compatible enough to leave him free to enjoy the "garden" and hence to praise the active life. After willingness to make the sacrifice is indicated, the sacrificial object, like Abraham's son, may be reclaimed; or after one part of nature is "annihilated" (to use the severe and crucial word of "The Garden"), the remainder can be embraced as an extension of the divine ground (which is primarily a pastoral strategy: the controlled green world of the pastoral idyll is subsumed as copartner in self-definition). Marvell developed his own unique style of pastoral encompassing after annihilation, a style of ironic *sprezzatura* that accepts nature with detachment and humor. It may involve at times not so much contemplative retreat as recognition of a disappointing truth, which the poet accepts and makes the most of. If the coronet is not suitable to crown Christ's head, it might at least crown his feet, thus justifying a previous enterprise; if the poet lacks world enough and time, he might persuade a Coy Mistress to cooperate. In the Mower's case, nothing seems adequate in protecting the idyllic place from intrusions of reality or in converting it to some aspect of the divine ground; the self is destroyed in its dialectic with the scene.

Before proceeding to an analysis of these patterns as structural and textural elements of particular lyrics, I would like to look closely at one of Marvell's best achievements in the dialectical manner, "The Definition of Love," which is particularly useful to have before us first because it illustrates not only a poetic method but also a characteristic attitude. It is not cast in terms of the intellectual currents of the seventeenth century that I have categorized according to their manifestation of the art, nature, grace tension, but it may nevertheless be seen as a way of handling the mixture of "oppositional" and "consistent" humanisms that characterize Marvell. It arrives at an explicit compromise in the definition itself, which would seem to define (by implication) more than love: if we can assume that a "therefore" calculus is essentially medieval and a "nevertheless" calculus essentially modern, the poem lies squarely between the old order which believed that love moved the stars as well as the heart, and the new order that tends to find love a purely human (and star-crossed) affair. It is an important poem historically in another way as well. For it defines love neither as a romantic fusion of identities that compensates for the world's indifference (as in Arnold's "Dover Beach," say) nor as an isolated, temporary affair for the sophisticated man of the court. Rather, love both unites and divides. The tone is both serious and ironic. Whether human or divine (Marvell refuses to say which), love's conjunction is an affair of minds in a universe of opposed stars. If the "strange high object" is transcendent, it is still subject to the order of things; if it is human, it nevertheless joins with the lover's mind. Either way, the fusion-opposition is delicately balanced.

The terms of the definition itself are drawn in part from a tradition of love definitions stemming from Plato, but Marvell uses them with more critical analysis than reverence. Socratic irony is the mode of balancing conjunction and opposition. Like Rochester's satire "Upon Nothing," "The Definition" demonstrates a triumph of reason even while it undermines the capacity of the mind to have its way among recalcitrant circumstances. A disciplined and intense intellectual energy underlies the flat declaration of love's strangeness and elevation and the cryptic account of its begetting, which involves union in one sense but irrevocable disunion in another:

I

My Love is of a birth as rare
As 'tis for object strange and high:
It was begotten by despair
Upon Impossibility.

II

Magnanimous Despair alone
Could show me so divine a thing,
Where feeble Hope could ne'r have flown
But vainly flapt its Tinsel Wing.

Despite the apparent clarity, the "bright, hard precision" serves only to make vaguely felt the contours of an inexpressible, or at least of an unexpressed, emotion. Is the rarity of this kind of love, for example, a reflection upon a world which too seldom sees true love, or a special blessing? The basic paradox, of course, is clear enough: the very impossibility of achieving union has "begotten" love, the sexual metaphor reflecting ironically upon that impossibility. But we might expect despair to be more despairing. As a productive, even "magnanimous," creature (including the Latin sense of *magnus animus* or "great-souled"), Despair is more than a mere adjunct of love—it alone could reveal "so divine a thing" as the "strange and high" object, the implication being that unless there were a refractory "opposition of the stars" this kind of love could not exist. The impossibility is despairing, then, but Despair itself is magnanimous, and charitable to boot, because it prevents "feeble Hope" from arousing itself fruitlessly.

Despite the tautness of the dilemma, the discrepancy between what one desires and what the world gives is not treated solemnly. So portentous an event as Despair mating Impossibility and bringing forth Love, expressed in such bare and laconic terms, recoils upon itself. The poem combines metaphysical speculation with reflection upon the exaggerations common to the conventions of ordinary love poems. "Strange" and "object" at first glance seem merely curious; looking back at them from the end of a stanza or so, we grow apprehensive. Our momentary assumption that the object might be a Petrarchan mistress of some sort falls short of exhausting the possibilities but is never proved wrong. Whatever the object, lack of a name for it is scarcely an accident and not likely a trick. The word "Impossibility" also has curious effects. Filling nearly a line, it calls attention to itself as a word; it is part of a self-conscious "definition,"[42] an exercise in choosing the right words which dissolves suddenly into irony and yet refuses to dissolve completely. We cannot tell at this point whether to expect gaiety or seriousness; as we learn, either expectation by itself would be deficient.

The paradox and the irony are sharpened in the second stanza, which continues to reverse normal expectations, that is, expectations from run-of-the-mill poems on love: not only has Despair become great-souled and Hope a poor, tinsel bird, but satiric thrusts are made at love itself, or at least the kind practiced by ordinary hopeless lovers, those who feed their despair and starve their hope. In addition, there is a more than casual

42. Frank Kermode believes that Marvell is "not at all concerned to express *'la substance . . . et le naturel fond'* of love considered in abstract," but rather the "rarity, the unusual qualities, of his particular love." This seems to me a curious opinion, whether or not Marvell's poem belongs to the genre of abstract definitions cited by Miss Tuve and Davison; it would appear to be based on the assumption that general and particular matters are incompatible. See "Definitions of Love," *RES*, 7 (1956), 183–85; cf. Dennis Davison, "Marvell's 'The Definition of Love,'" *RES*, 6 (1955), 141–46; M. C. Bradbrook and M. G. Lloyd Thomas, *Andrew Marvell* (Cambridge, 1940), p. 45; Cleanth Brooks and Robert Penn Warren, *Understanding Poetry* (New York, 1952), pp. 293–97.

penetration into the common human dilemma in which a brief glimpse of Beatrice is nourished into divine aspiration, while love runs out of affairs that, not being star-crossed, are "fixed" by permanent union. But these satiric and ironic voices are muffled as though behind masks. The main statement continues to be perfectly straightforward and elusive. The focus upon personal despair and impossibility is broadened to a consideration of fate as the force behind disjunction:

III

And yet I quickly might arrive
Where my extended Soul is fixt,
But Fate does Iron wedges drive,
And alwaies crouds it self betwixt.

IV

For Fate with jealous Eye does see
Two perfect Loves; nor lets them close:
Their union would her ruine be,
And her Tyrannick pow'r depose.

Only now are we approaching something tangible in the way of definition. The union of "two perfect Loves" would be the ruin of Fate because Fate operates in the realm of becoming. When the soul is "fixt" where it is extended, it has in a sense achieved Being, having no desire for the unattainable, no mutability, hence no debt to Fate. But "extended" means "stretched out *to*," as well as "united *with*," the object, and both senses are involved. Fate can afford to be officious against love in its present state; it drives wedges between soul and object or, if the lover decides to send his soul on ahead, between the soul fixed in the object and the poor mortal it has left behind: either way, dissociation and Despair set in.

The personification of Fate completes the Petrarchan cast: despair, hope, and now the jealous lover. (The irony is continued in this and in a jauntiness of rhythm and sound, as in

47

the rhyming of "fixt" and "betwixt" and in the internal half-rhyming of "union" and "ruine.")

v

And therefore her Decrees of Steel
Us as the distant Poles have plac'd,
(Though Loves whole World on us doth wheel)
Not by themselves to be embrac'd.

That the whole world of love whirls on the axis of their separation, suspended between conjunction and opposition, is, of course, hyperbolic. But the cosmic imagery is introduced to define Love and to demonstrate that other lovers are in turn defined by this love, rather than simply to eulogize particular lovers or to deflate conventions through exaggeration. "The first in every genus is the cause of the whole genus," Ficino writes ("cause" in the sense of "essence"); "for example, if the sun is the first among the light-bearing things it does not lack any degree of light."[43] And so other lovers may be more successful, but none is more perfect. As divine love sustains and moves the real cosmos, this love, first in its genus, sustains and causes the world of love to be.

As the definition emerges, its reliance upon, but free manipulation of, Platonic doctrine becomes clearer. Like Socrates' attempt to define love in the *Symposium* and Ficino's commentary upon that attempt, it is concerned with the essential nature of love as well as the personal experience of the speaker, and it discovers both of these to be mixed blessings. For love, Socrates discovers, is of something desired but not possessed (200 A) or, in terms of the semi-humorous myth of Aristophanes, is a desire of the incomplete self for union with its other half

43. From the *Theologia Platonica*, quoted by Paul Oskar Kristeller, *The Philosophy of Marsilio Ficino*, trans. Virginia Connant (New York, 1943), p. 147. Marvell's use of Neoplatonist doctrine in other poems is discussed extensively by Ruth Wallerstein in *Studies in Seventeenth-Century Poetic* (Madison, University of Wisconsin Press, 1950), pp. 150 ff.

(189–91). Diotima of Mantineia, "a woman wise in these and many other kinds of knowledge," has demonstrated love to be neither foul nor fair, evil nor good: "He is a great spirit (δαίμων), and like all spirits he is intermediate between the divine and the mortal" (202 D).[44] And only he can bridge the chasm dividing mortal from immortal: "For God mingles not with man; but through Love all the intercourse and converse of God with man . . . is carried on" (203 A). Diotima's Love is born of plenty and poverty rather than of despair and impossibility, but, as her account of his activities shows, any set would have done equally well: ignorance and knowledge, mortality and immortality, beauty and ugliness. Only the beloved is truly beautiful; love itself can never be (204 A): the object may be high, but love is only a process of desiring it. As long as the soul desires the good and the beautiful, it seeks for what it does not, and cannot, have; actual possession of the good and the beautiful yields happiness, which is a static, or rather an ecstatic, condition, not a process as love is, seen in all its activities.[45]

The similarity of love's intermediate condition to that of the soul is noticed by Plotinus in his commentary upon Diotima's myth. The (All) Soul, directing its vision towards Kronos, the "Intellectual Principle," brings forth Eros, an outpouring of itself held firmly to itself, through which it looks toward Kronos. "Love, thus, is ever intent upon that other loveliness, and exists to be the medium between desire and that object of desire" (Enneads III.5.2), as the soul in the Middle Platonists is intermediate between the indivisible and the divisible realm of the body.[46] The soul, like love, upholds the world and makes

44. The Dialogues of Plato, trans. B. Jowett (New York, 1937).
45. Writing poetry, for example, is a passage of nonbeing into being, a creative "making" (205 B). In fact, Socrates concludes, "all desire of good" in any human activity "is only the great and subtle power of love."
46. See Philip Merlan, From Platonism to Neoplatonism (The Hague,

it possible. It subsists between the One and the many, is fixed firmly in both, and is partly defined by its position between them. And so Ficino and Pico declare that the soul "is all things together. . . . Therefore it may be rightly called the center of nature, the middle term of all things, the series of the world, the face of all, the bond and juncture of the universe"—the same definition Ficino had formerly given of love itself.[47] Because man's soul is a vital intermediary link in the great chain, it holds the world in line with God; because love is a conjunction of minds, it holds the lovers' world together.

Mounting a ladder from love of particulars, to love of universals, to love of "beauty absolute, separate, simple, and everlasting" is not, of course, what interests Marvell; rather, he is concerned with the dialectical interplay and tension between the poles Socrates describes, and concerned with these both as definition and as personal experience, as I have said, since the two are vitally related. Love is formed by the taut attraction of equal forces, between which man is suspended as between two exactly equal magnets. Total conjunction would involve the collapse of the universe into a dimensionless plane:

VI

Unless the giddy Heaven fall,
And Earth some new Convulsion tear;
And, us to joyn, the World should all
Be cramp'd into a *Planisphere*.

1953), p. 11. Plotinus is quoted from the translation of Stephen Mac-Kenna as revised by B. S. Page (London, 1917–30).

47. Marsilio Ficino, *In Convivium Platonis*, VI.2: "This is clearly the reason that Diotima . . . calls Love a spirit; just as spirits are intermediaries between celestial and earthly things, so Love is an intermediary between the beautiful and the unsightly." Cf. Kristeller, *Studies in Renaissance Thought and Letters* (Rome, 1956), p. 268; Pico, *Oration on the Dignity of Man*, trans. Elizabeth L. Forbes, in *The Renaissance Philosophy of Man*, ed. Ernst Cassirer, pp. 215 ff.; Plotinus, *Enneads* IV.8.7. See also Castiglione, *The Book of the Courtier*, trans. Charles S. Singleton (New York, 1959), p. 356 (IV.70).

Like Herbert's spiritual exercises, love gives "temper" by stretching one from here to the impossibly high. The cosmic demonstration is impressive from an imagistic standpoint, but the geometrical imagery has greater finality:

VII

As Lines so Loves *oblique* may well
Themselves in every Angle greet:
But ours so truly *Paralel,*
Though infinite can never meet.

The kind of love which allows lovers to meet at the corner gratifies the desire for union, but the implication is that, though loves not parallel have this minor advantage, they also soon part. Geometrical universals have their own irresistible laws, necessarily true at all times, and so love must have. The "bond and juncture" of love has in Fate, then, and in its own nature, a divisive obstacle which can prevent all union but that of minds. Like the Demiurge of the *Timaeus,* who has no luck persuading matter to be reasonable, the mind cannot conceive of any way to overcome recalcitrant stars, though, by the same token, the marriage of true minds admits no impediments. Thus both conjunction and disjunction: a true and irreconcilable parallelism.

Though in pursuing this line, Marvell would seem to have used Platonic doctrine only as a vantage point from which to explore the psychological and metaphysical implications of love, Ficino's definition may have further relevance. In the commentary on the *Symposium,* Ficino connects the intermediate condition of the soul and of love, which are exactly analogous, as we have seen, to the concept of man as the "third essence" or central link in a chain of essences. As the middle essence, man subsumes angelic and godlike, vegetative and animal, attributes, and thus holds the hierarchy together and apart. To fulfill love erotically after the manner of the Venus of desire, Aphrodite Pandemos,[48] is to destroy the stability of the chain by descending egoistically to a lower element, by abandoning the crucial middle state. But Marvell implies further that to achieve a complete union with the high object in the manner of Aphrodite Urania would also be to become something other than man. "Aspiring to be Gods, if Angels fell, / Aspiring to be Angels, men rebel," Pope will write: " 'tis plain / There must be, somewhere, such a rank as Man." Sliding off the sharp edge of the paradox implied by his own definition of man and by the Socratic definition of love, Ficino finds no very formidable barrier to the soul's reaching what it loves (VI.7); but in "The Definition of Love," Hope's angel-like flapping of unangelic tinsel wings is born of a full recognition of the special human dilemma. To achieve complete identity would be to turn the heavens "giddy" and to destroy the very structure of things. Hence only imperfect love, fostered by the spirits "intermediate between beauty and ugliness" (VI.5), is proper to man.[49] The paradoxical mystery of love is that, while it demands separation and by definition necessitates otherness and lack of identity, it also encompasses, as one circle may encompass another and remain unjoined.[50] For love to

48. *In Convivium Platonis*, VI.5.

49. Cf. *Phaedrus* 249 D: when the philosopher sees the beauty of earth, he "is transported with the recollection of the true beauty; he would like to fly away, but he cannot; he is like a bird fluttering and looking upward. . . . And I have shown this of all inspirations to be the noblest and highest . . . and that he who loves the beautiful is called a lover because he partakes of it." Cf. also 252 C.

50. The cosmic and geometric imagery read in the context of Ficino's definition of love suggests the possibility that circle imagery is involved. The Platonic chain of being with its fixed intervals and distances is a metaphor stressing the discreteness of individual essences, each of which has its own station. But the presence of the One in the many and of all things in "The Mind, that Ocean where each kind / Does streight its own resemblance find" requires another metaphor. Like Plotinus, Augustine, Dante, Castiglione, Donne, and others in the Platonic tradition, Ficino turns to the circle to express this identity-within-difference. And likewise, while

achieve pure identity, its perfection would have to be shattered, "cramp'd Into a *Planisphere."* Recognizing this more clearly, Marvell moves toward a wider and wider perspective, away from Fate as an interfering meddler toward Fate as part of a sustaining order, inexorable but detached and impersonal, the Fate of the stars.

The ambiguity of love is so carefully sustained up to the last stanza that it becomes a special mode of discipline and grace in itself. The loved object is both definite and intangible, something beyond grasp and yet precisely placed. ("Strange and high" suggests both transcendence and alienation.) This is not, I think, a game of words on Marvell's part, but an attempt to find the precise words to define the experience. The tension of the early part of the poem, however difficult to pin down, foretells the sharply defined contest between fate and the painfully human desire to destroy it, to cross lines and collapse spheres to achieve union (whether with a mistress or with something more transcending). The impulsive existence of the self is tempered only if one cleaves to the paradox of conjunction and opposition. Love cannot survive either the sacrifice or the indulgence of selfhood.

Perhaps with this preparation I can describe more fully Marvell's final attitude toward the paradox. Full concession has been made to love's undesirable family tree and to the human condition reflected in it. Yet the manifold moods which have had their moments in the poem—the lyric, the flatly declarative, and the satiric—give way to resignation in the last stanza:

Marvell's imagery of the poles suggests disjunction, love, of course, is also an "infinite" conjunction. I find the emphasis gradually shifting from an uncompleted, continuous yearning to a closed and defined experience. See Augustine, *De quantitate animae* in *Patrologiae Cursus Completus, Series Latina,* gen. ed. J. P. Migne, 32:1035 ff.; Ficino, *In Convivium Platonis,* II.3, VI.3; Castiglione, *The Book of the Courtier,* p. 342; Dante, *Vita nuova,* XII, and *Paradiso,* 27.106 ff., 28.41 ff., 33.115 ff.

VIII

Therefore the Love which us doth bind,
But Fate so enviously debarrs,
Is the Conjunction of the Mind,
And Opposition of the Stars.

The definition here arrives at a clarity and finality it has not had in previous stanzas. It is sealed as definition and as a logical proposition by "therefore" and by the exactly delineated *genus* (love = conjunction and opposition) and *differentia* (of the mind, of the stars).[51] Though founded upon union and opposition, love is one thing encompassing both. Because minds can be joined, Fate is still envious; but stars are not unworthy enemies of love. It is the recognition of this that brings resignation. But if the definition concludes in a static opposition, it is a dynamic stasis. Love becomes understandable through the dialectical process.[52]

Through analysis, satire, and irony, then, Marvell gives the definition classical precision and clarity; without sacrificing awareness of love's absurdities, he achieves oneness. Though all irony collapses a multiple awareness into one idea, Marvell's irony works vertically, reconciling things of different levels. Through it, Marvell purges the complexity of attitudes encompassed by the poem and adjusts to the order of things, an order

51. In his defense of John Howe (1678), Marvell writes that a definition "always consists, as being a dialectical animal, of a body, which is the genus, and a difference, which is the soul of the thing defined": *The Complete Works in Verse and Prose*, ed. A. B. Grosart (London, 1875), 4, 183; cf. Milton's *Art of Logic*: "For genus and form (which are as it were the body and mind of the definition) constitute the whole essence of the thing": *Works*, gen. ed. Frank Allen Patterson (Columbia University Press, 1935), *11*, 263.

52. Cf. John Wheatcroft, "Andrew Marvell and the Winged Chariot," *Bucknell Review*, 6 (1956), 42–43; Lawrence W. Hyman, "Ideas in Marvell's Lyric Poetry," *History of Ideas News Letter*, 2 (1956), 30; F. W. Bradbrook, "The Poetry of Andrew Marvell," in *From Donne to Marvell*, ed. Boris Ford, p. 198; Bradbrook and Thomas, p. 46.

embracing fate, love, minds, stars. Involved through love and detached through irony, he is resigned through their interworking.

The style of "The Definition" is second nature to Marvell; he will sometimes use it even without a comparable subject matter, sometimes in humorous contradiction to his serious poems. "Ametas and Thestylis Making Hay-Ropes," for example, progresses through a dialectical battle of wits solely for the sake of battle. Ametas believes that opposition must be entirely dissolved because "Love unpaid does soon disband: / Love binds Love as Hay binds Hay." But Thestylis realizes that parallel lines never meet:

> Think'st Thou that this Rope would twine
> If we both should turn one way?
> Where both parties so combine,
> Neither Love will twist nor Hay.

Which means that she will not agree, but neither will she disagree. Love must be taken, not merely consented to. And so they split the last stanza between them, combining and opposing simultaneously, agreeing and disagreeing, and ending, one supposes, kissing in twisted opposition *in* "the Hay." They can do so because their dialectic is a game and their love does not demand quite all their talents.

Marvell never totally forgets that such dialectical combat is a sport, an *agon* conducted according to definite rules. Ordinarily, of course, his dialectic and exploratory irony have a more serious duty to perform than in "Ametas and Thestylis." As in *The Rehearsal Transpros'd,* in which the court wit defends the plain nonconformist, they enable him to tread a narrow path between levity and seriousness and to hold together a head and heart which, as F. W. Bateson writes, tend to want different things.[53] Perhaps more important, they allow the

53. *English Poetry: A Critical Introduction* (London, 1950), pp. 99 ff.

Puritan-Platonist to explore his relation to nature without becoming too deeply entangled in it. The lyric medium, with its modulation of tone and mood and disciplined form, is ideally suited to handle the difficulties of Marvell's conjunctive-oppositional grammar; it is the rhetoric to match the grammar to match the historical situation.

2. Resolve against History

And Stars shew lovely in the Night
But as they seem the Tears of Light.
("Eyes and Tears")

ONE KIND OF idealist consigns everything obviously not right to nonexistence: good = being, evil = nonbeing. If life with its obstreperous evils appears to deny these categories, he can point out the powers of illusion, which make us mistake shadows for reality and see motion where, as Parmenides proved, there could logically be none; or he can think in terms of a cycle of descent and return set in motion he knows not how but ending in the apotheosis of the soul. A second kind of idealist uses the cycle to avoid Manichean dualism and explains cosmic indiscretions as the result of an archetypal fall. Only a redemption equal in magnitude to the original mistake can restore universal harmony, which means that nearly any degree of worldliness or otherworldliness and several gradations between optimism and despair are possible, depending on how deep the original cosmic fault is believed to have penetrated. To Pope in the *Essay on Man* it is a matter of perspective: from one point of view the Dunces appear to be smothering the world in unreason; from another, more inclusive perspective, everything balances out, like Jack Sprat and his wife: "Respecting man, whatever wrong we call, / May, must be right, as relative to all."

Marvell's idealism is not like either of these, though it adopts elements of each. As a poet, Marvell ordinarily focuses upon the internal world and sees the cosmic-mythic encounters of the soul reflected there, as the androgynous Adam is reflected in the garden wanderer, for example. The Resolved Soul rejects Created Pleasure, as Damon rejects Clorinda's proposal, without the indignation of the Lady repulsing Comus, or Samson Dalila, or Christ Satan. A soul with immortal longings is disappointed by external reality but not necessarily offended by it; it is clear to it that what is offered, though it may be a good deal, is not enough. Nor does it tantalize its desires in order to have the pleasure of squelching them, though Marvell finds a measure of Stoicism useful to counterbalance a measure of Epicureanism. The more pervasive pattern is to create and expand in withdrawal rather than to destroy and constrict. If the Stoic's idealism centers upon a belief in the self as an integral armed camp, Marvell's idealism in one form emphasizes the soul's ultimate transcendance and the momentary open dialectic between it and the surrounding world; in another form, as we have seen, the mind contains "each kind" as its epitome and mirror and "creates, transcending these, / Far other Worlds and other Seas." His vacillation between endorsing and rejecting nature is probably as great as that of other Platonists whose inconsistencies in this regard Arthur Lovejoy has chronicled in *The Great Chain of Being;* but what appear to be extreme rejections he often makes with full awareness of the implications, that is to say, with irony (as the affirmation of such poems as "The Garden" and "To His Coy Mistress" is qualified in context).

The poems considered in this chapter reveal the flexibility and subtlety of Marvell's modes of rejection and withdrawal.

If we read them expecting a single kind of commitment we are apt to miss the ironist's indirection. The commitment itself, of course, is generally clear enough, but the dialectic it fosters is as much stylized dance as deadly combat.[1] In dialogue and temptation poems, the structure of the poem and the strategy of the debate are obviously inseparable, since the manner of posing a temptation predetermines to some extent the reaction to it. A diametrical opposition will cause emphasis to fall upon total withdrawal or total victory; but if the temptress is in the main friendly, as Damon finds Clorinda to be, some chance of reconciliation may be possible. The dramatic modes of Marvell's temptation poems are thus an extension of his attitude toward history. Through them, Marvel explores the nature of the soul and its relation to time.

The Soul in "A Dialogue between the Resolved Soul and Created Pleasure," for example, is a timeless "thing Divine" in a world of time seeking in its relation to Pleasure a key to its own mode of being. The poem is Horatian in wit and in polished urbanity but metaphysical in complication. And so the solution to the Soul's dilemma is more than a simple declaration of idealistic faith: it grows out of the progressive, exploratory drama itself. For even while rejecting nature, the Soul can be defined by and proved in temptation.[2] Though this may sug-

---

1. Cf. F. W. Bradbrook: "though there is an atmosphere of siege" in "A Dialogue between the Resolved Soul and Created Pleasure," the attitude "of the poet towards his subject is ironical. The almost jaunty rhythm emphasizes the playfulness with which the theme is to be treated. . . . Behind the antithesis there lies harmony. The replies of the soul are gentle and genial. There is a suggestion of the dance as well as of the debate." *From Donne to Marvell*, ed. Boris Ford (Penguin Books, 1956), p. 194. Cf. also Louis Martz, *The Poetry of Meditation* (New Haven, Yale University Press, 1954), p. 131.

2. Louis Martz quite appropriately considers the poem with other examples of meditations in which the poet seeks self-knowledge through spiritual combat: *The Poetry of Meditation*, pp. 130–31.

gest the stock warfare metaphor of the Puritans, the spirit in which the Soul enters the contest is not so much militant as expectant. The last-minute battle instructions with which the poem begins come from the apprehensive and encouraging voice of the poet:

> Courage my Soul, now learn to wield
> The weight of thine immortal Shield.
> Close on thy Head thy Helmet bright.
> Ballance thy Sword against the Fight.
> See where an Army, strong as fair,
> With silken Banners spreads the air.
> Now, if thou bee'st that thing Divine,
> In this day's Combat let it shine:
> And shew that Nature wants an Art
> To conquer one resolved Heart.

The unusual number of first-foot inversions and the jaunty rhythms reinforce the spirit of exhortation: since the enemy is impressive as well as fair, delight in the sheer spectacle of the battle qualifies the anxiety. The Soul is only now learning to wield its immortality, which is ironically "weighty." The weight, of course, presents the main problem, which is the incarnation of its immortality. The Soul must not allow its armor to become its grave. Marvell as poet has another problem, however. Since a poetic meditation is committed to imagery in a way not involved in less pleasurable forms of debate, how can he create without inconsistency a pleasant poem on the Soul's unqualified rejection of Created Pleasure? The answer is found in the sophisticated and multiple ironies peculiar to Marvell. Without these the poem would run the risk of being delightful in the wrong way. Milton avoids a similar problem in *Comus* by granting a wide range of legitimate pleasures to the Lady and by momentarily presenting the tempter himself without disguise, as a stage villain, so that his pleasures will not be confused with those subsumed by grace:

I under fair pretense of friendly ends
And well-plac't words of glozIng courtesy,
Baited with reasons not unplausible,
Wind me into the easy-hearted man,
And hug him into snares. (161–65)

The stylistic problem, like Shelley's in "Adonais," is to assert in imagery the reality of the imageless Truth. Paradoxically, the contest can be taken seriously only because conceived ironically and executed with wit; it is through irony that the Resolved Soul engages Pleasure's images without endorsing them.

The apparently simple preliminary address is thus burdened with complexities with which the Soul must deal in order to prove its autonomy and discover its essential self.[3] These complexities are manifest in the play on "nature" and "art," as they will be later in music's "sweet Chordage," the best battery the opposing army has. The function of the temptation is to prove that nature indeed "wants an Art," a sensuous art, to conquer the Soul, and that the Soul has an extra-natural art with which to conquer nature. If nature is thus found lacking in art, the immortality of the Soul will have been demonstrated and the processes of time shown to have no part in it. In a sense, then, the *manner* of the poem demonstrates the Soul's immortality, which will "shine" in its own light rather than in the light of nature's metaphors only if the Soul is truly "that thing Divine," if its dialectic is not governed by Pleasure's language. Of the several ways the Soul has of escaping Pleasure's terms, the pun is perhaps the most striking. Ambiguity can serve the duplicity of Pleasure's world, but it also reveals the shadowy stuff that makes up nature, which the Soul penetrates in discovering its

3. Cf. Geoffrey Walton's statement concerning the dialogue: "whereas Herbert's main theme is the spiritual life and man's relation to God, Marvell sorts out worldly experience in the light of the spiritual and is concerned to compare and evaluate the doings of the human world." *Metaphysical to Augustan* (London, 1955), p. 128.

divine ground. Perhaps more important, the incongruity of certain key words creates the exact tone, the combination of levity and seriousness, that the urbane Puritan-Platonist wanted.

Thus partly through its very manipulation of language, the Soul tries to prove itself a self-contained unity with "resolve" as its only attribute, resolve in two senses, both "staunch" or "courageous" and ultimately, as the Soul wins a more complete knowledge of itself from the struggle, "explained" or "discovered." We might include both of these in the paradoxical grammar of a withdrawal that is finally transcendent rather than polemic: the Soul must be "loose and easie hence to go," in the phrasing of "On a Drop of Dew," "congeal'd on Earth," but ready to *dis*solve and run "Into the Glories of th' Almighty Sun," an unreserved giving of itself. It transcends the negative way of its dialectical agon, which carries it just so far in self-definition; being "resolved" leads to dissolution, the problem solved once and for all by absorption into the divine source, a melting of the self in absolute, uncreated pleasure.

Marvell sets the stage carefully. Nature begins not only with a pompous and attractive demonstration of silken banners but with a definite craft. One way to disarm the Soul is to invite it as a friend to a banquet of pleasures and to flatter it as "Lord of Earth, and Heavens Heir" (line 12). The very word "guest" goes more than halfway toward conceding the Soul's independence of creation. But Pleasure is not a Cartesian dualist allowing each element of man's component self to go its own way. The Soul, Pleasure says, can profit from its mortality: fruits and flowers, too, have souls and can "heighten" the Soul, should it so bid; they stand entirely at its command, as the stone which Satan presents to Christ stands ready to become bread for the divine body (*Paradise Regained*, I.343). However, as Christ replies, "Man lives not by bread only, but each word / Proceeding from the mouth of God"; and so the Soul likewise cannot afford to be dualistic:

I sup above, and cannot stay
To bait so long upon the way.

It picks off Pleasure's dining metaphor, strips it of its art, and, exposing the bait, hurls it back.

One piece of art having failed, Pleasure turns to another, an Epicurean gambit behind a Stoic mask. It pretends to offer only such contact with nature that the Immortal Side need not be dislocated:

On these downy Pillows lye,
Whose soft Plumes will thither fly:
On these Roses strow'd so plain
Lest one Leaf thy Side should strain.

The plainness is refuted by the language itself, which is wrapped in luxurious metaphors. Pleasure makes plumes seem lightweight, soul-like objects flying "thither"—to the place above, where the Soul would sup. Nature is a Bowre of Bliss offered as a House of Alma where the warrior Soul can rest. The Soul's answer is as effective as it is genuinely plain:

My gentler Rest is on a Thought,
Conscious of doing what I ought.

The complexity of the dialectic and the ironic undertones save the answer from priggishness. Since Pleasure has returned the irony of the Soul's play on "bait" with the double implication of "plain" (that is, both flat and unadorned, not intruding either physically or metaphorically upon the soul) and "strain" (the Soul will not find the leaves dissolving into it), the Soul must recognize the two dimensions even while rejecting one: it rests "gentler," with no "strain," no lumps at all, on moral thought. It will concede only as much contact with beds as it has to in order to account for its moral will and for having to undertake its present trial. Thought's hard bed of resolve is indeed sustaining it above the rose-strewn trap.

The third temptation reverses tactics with a specious offer of quick transcendence. If Pleasure hides behind the mask of a perfect host in the first temptation and behind the mask of spiritual physician in the second, in the third it is disguised as a priest, unfortunately a pagan priest who allows the perfumes of the service to dominate the worship:

> If thou bee'st with Perfumes pleas'd,
> Such as oft the God appeas'd,
> Thou in fragrant Clouds shalt show
> Like another God below.

Concealed behind all of Pleasure's arts to this point is a very simple progression through the highest luxuries the five senses can offer, which are all Pleasure has, first taste and touch, now smell, and, coming, sight and sound. As expected, the Soul penetrates the "fragrant Clouds" and separates the physically based pseudo-spiritual from the truly spiritual:

> A Soul that knowes not to presume
> Is Heaven's and its own perfume.

Ironically rhyming Pleasure's perfume with the sin it involves, the Soul shows that expecting even to *show* like a god is sheer presumption—souls that know not to presume are self-contained rewards. And only one "God" has lived below who is able to appease the God above. In repeating the poet's original phrase "if thou bee'st . . .," Pleasure has substituted "with Perfumes pleas'd" for "that thing Divine," which, of course, is a step downward toward concreteness and toward the senses.

Since sight is normally taken to be the highest of the senses, Pleasure appropriately gives it a high pseudo-spiritual function. To see is to perceive; but to Pleasure "seeing" means to observe the "face" rather than essential being, which is the object of the search:

> Every thing does seem to vie
> Which should first attract thine Eye:
> But since none deserves that grace,
> In this Crystal view *thy* face.

If only the narcissistic reflection of one's own form is revealed in the dark mirror of nature, Pleasure surely errs in introducing the word "grace," which can only serve to suggest a more enlightened self-interest than this. The danger is primarily that in valuing nature in itself too highly, the Soul will look away from its source, where its full being is reflected. As Peter Sterry writes of the "shadowy figure" of matter that "we call this world and the body,"

> the soul often looking upon this, like Narcissus upon his own face in the fountain, forgets it to be itself, forgets that itself is the face, the shadow, and the fountain [that is, of "all forms of things in their original, eternal, glorious truths and substances"], so it falls into a fond love of itself in its own shadowy figure of itself. So it languisheth and dies, becoming only a shadow of itself, in which itself with all its superior and true glories lies buried.[4]

The Soul's answer is again iconoclastic, and scornful of mirror theories of nature:

> When the Creator's skill is priz'd,
> The rest is all but Earth disguis'd.

Marvell reverses the normal order of sight and sound because "Musick" is the highest temptation for the artist who has a definite stake in the temptation-by-metaphor. Pleasure speaks directly to the Soul's poetic instincts when it says,

> Heark how Musick then prepares
> For thy Stay these charming Aires;

---

4. *Peter Sterry: Platonist and Puritan*, ed. V. de S. Pinto (Cambridge, Cambridge University Press, 1934), pp. 161–62.

Which the posting Winds recall,
And suspend the Rivers Fall.

Like the temptation of the spiritual perfume that offers a false
way to become a god, control of nature through art offers a
specious transcendence. The Soul's reply shows that the reverse
of Pleasure's assumption is in fact the case: if art obtains a firm
hold on the soul, so will nature. To condescend even to *re*create
Pleasure is to end by being ruled by it. The trap is especially
subtle because to argue either for natural law or for Orphic
power over it would be to commit the Soul to this world. But
the Soul again turns Pleasure's tactical errors against it: recalling the posting winds and suspending the river's fall would be
not to create but to uncreate, to set one's own sense of power
against whatever nature has in its own right.

Had I but any time to lose,
On this I would it all dispose.
Cease Tempter. None can chain a mind
Whom this sweet Chordage cannot bind.

Ambiguity and irony are especially essential to poetic success
here. While the Soul, as it said in the first exchange, is in a
hurry to get where it is going, it is paradoxically timeless, having no time at all, to lose or to keep. It exists in a medium of
time and proves itself in time, but has none. To lose time even
if it could do so, however, would only be to destroy the laws
of nature, whose "posting" winds have to get somewhere in
time. The implication is that Pleasure's concept of art contra-
dicts its own pure naturalism, which is only thinly veiled in
talk of fruit and vegetable souls, flying plumes, and transcendent perfume. The apparent dilemma and its answer might be
put in this way. Pleasure proposes: "If you are unsatisfied with
nature's motion and the processes of time, as you seem to be,
you can enjoy them in art, which can stop the river's fall and
freeze motion altogether in its permanence. If satisfied, your at-

titude is inconsistent." The Soul answers, in effect: "Were I a creature of time, art, if anything, would tempt me; and if art did tempt me, I would be a creature of time. But neither is the case; far from being dissatisfied with nature and time, I have no vital connection with them at all, even in their 'permanent' form in art." Thus the attempt to entangle the Soul only succeeds in showing it more fully the nature of its freedom. So identical, it discovers, are sweet poetry and human bondage that the word "chordage" (in itself a sensuous metaphor) encompasses both of them. The trap is again exposed even as the image is used.[5]

We have heard three voices up to this point, each representing parts of a potentially divided self attempting to prove that it is not divided. Marvell now shifts the responsibility for voicing created beauty to a chorus with higher authority for poetic license:

> Earth cannot shew so brave a Sight
> As when a single Soul does fence
> The Batteries of alluring Sense,
> And Heaven views it with delight.
>   Then persevere: for still new Charges sound:
>   And if thou overcom'st thou shalt be crown'd.

The Chorus, too, in giving the Soul credit for fencing the "batteries of alluring sense," demonstrates a marked agility in playing ironically with metaphor. Earth cannot show a "sight" *as such* to equal resolved bravery ("brave" also means brightly

5. The Soul may be rejecting the Pythagorean-Platonic notion that the world is in part redeemed by its 'harmony.' Leo Spitzer conjectures in another connection that the spelling "chord" represents a "fusion of *accord, concord* with *cord* (*chorda*), 'string,'" just as *acc(h)ordare* is itself bicephalic, a coalescence of the *cor-* and *chorda-* family in which moral and sensual music come together: "ears hear well-tempered sounds while, at the same time . . . hearts sense the well-tempered order of the world." "Classical and Christian Ideas of World Harmony," *Traditio*, 3 (1945), 324–25.

attired) and the Soul can win singlehandedly against the multiple senses because it is in fact a "single" entity.

But the condition "if thou overcom'st" still holds. It might seem that, having rebuffed these progressively more difficult temptations with an ironic counterattack consisting of punning, directness, and indirectness, metaphor and scorn for metaphor, Marvell might rest the case for immortality. The brilliant display of rational capacity and dialectical skill would appear to have refuted Pleasure's claim for an inseparable body and soul: the strong, fair army has been soundly defeated and scattered. But Marvell is a Puritan as well as a Neoplatonist. Heaven itself is enjoying the rout; why not carry it on? To resolve its problems and to win the war as well as the battles, the Soul must be not only intellectually brilliant but also morally "persevering." It must now demonstrate how to deal with women, gold, political power, and, finally, knowledge itself. Pleasure drops metaphysical subtleties momentarily and the temptations become simply, almost blatantly, what they seem. It begins strongly, however, by putting three senses together into one surpassing creation (if Margoliouth's emendation of "cost" to "soft" is correct, as it would seem to be):

> All this fair, and soft, and sweet,
>   Which scatteringly doth shine,
> Shall within one Beauty meet,
>   And she be only thine.

Human beauty sums up all miscellaneous pleasures in the kind of unity the Soul might be expected to like. And woman can also pledge loyalty, being "only thine," and thus avoid distracting the Soul's attention from essential pleasures.

The Resolved Soul's answers are likewise comparatively blunt; it does not attempt to return the metaphors because it has already proved that the language of pleasure has no inherent value:

> If things of Sight such Heavens be,
> What Heavens are those we cannot see?

The replies are now those of an assured and confident opponent on top of the argument who, like heaven, enjoys the battle. The Soul's challenging questions are ignored by Pleasure, which needed to do better in the first skirmish in order to claim that things are other than the Soul asserts. Though Pleasure's arguments have had a clear progression and order, now that the Soul is pressing, it begins to lose coherence; it offers bigger and better things, going from lust to greed for money, political power, and universal knowledge and getting further and further from its proper domain of created pleasures, into abstract speculation. Ironically, the tempter pulling down is dragged up with the Soul's ascent. As in Satan's desperation in *Paradise Regained*, it is most dangerous when cornered, but also like Satan, or more exactly like Mammon, it helps to bring forth good from evil. And like Mammon, its economics is faulty:

Pleasure.

> Where so e're thy Foot shall go
> The minted Gold shall lie;
> Till thou purchase all below,
> And want new Worlds to buy.

Soul.

> Wer't not a price who'ld value Gold?
> And that's worth nought that can be sold.

The Soul extracts the word "price" with some joy from Pleasure's inflationary minting of self-interests. True sights cannot be seen; things of true value cannot be bought and sold (even if the Soul had a "Foot" to put down on the golden street). The Puritan can handle practical affairs as deftly as the Neoplatonist handles metaphysical ones, though, as the next reply shows, the two are interdependent:

69

> What Friends, if to my self untrue?
> What Slaves, unless I captive you?

The rejection of glory and power requires both self-knowledge and the ability formerly demonstrated to "fence" Pleasure: the macrocosm is easily controlled only if the microcosm is in order.

Like the first set of temptations, which has had its practical moral side (as in "Conscious of doing what I ought"), the temptation of knowledge combines the practical and the theoretical, which are distinguishable but not entirely separate. The Soul is thus tested from two sides and its unity doubly assured: "For it is not by running hither and thither outside of itself that the Soul understands morality and right conduct," Plotinus writes; "it learns them of its own nature, in its contact with itself, seeing deeply impressed upon it the images of its primal state" (*Enneads* IV.7.10). The difficulty is that Pleasure has learned rapidly and makes knowledge the highest pleasure of all:

> Thou shalt know each hidden Cause;
> And see the future Time:
> Try what depth the Centre draws;
> And then to Heaven climb.

Being able to pry into nature's inmost secrets and to penetrate beyond the useful sciences would indeed be flattering to the Soul's intellectual power. To make the depths of the symbolic circle yield their secret would be to earn heaven by self-creation, to "climb" there without the aid of grace. (Pleasure follows Plotinus in using the circle to express the symbolic relation of the soul, with or without humility, to the center to which all radii run: "Within our nature is such a centre by which we grasp and are linked and held; and those of us are firmly in the Supreme whose collective tendency is 'There.' "[6])

6. Cf. Castiglione, *The Book of the Courtier*, trans. Thomas Hoby (London, 1928), p. 308.

Pleasure's last trick is thus to make the Soul's own unity and self-containment a snare. The Soul is encouraged to forget the paradox of its mortal-immortal state, which is both the central paradox of "The Definition of Love" (except that here it can be "resolved" ultimately) and the paradox that Dorinda finds beyond solution in "Thrysis and Dorinda, where inside and outside, here and there, are somehow the same: both meet in the "Center of the Soul" and have their real life "there."

> Do not sigh (fair Nimph) for fire
> Hath no wings, yet doth aspire
> Till it hit, against the pole,
> Heaven's the Center of the Soul.

The Resolved Soul rejects the proposition on a purely moral basis, or rather on principles previously established that enable it to know what not to know. The Christian framework prevails over Neoplatonist elements:

> None thither mounts by the degree
> Of Knowledge, but Humility.

Cause and future exist only in time and cannot be steps or degrees to the timeless. They are revealed only to those possessing humility, who do not overlook the last goal of resolve—to dissolve and run "Into the Glories of th' Almighty Sun." All virtue, in fact, depends on humility, which is discoverable, as Bernard of Clairvaux had written, only through just such a process of self-discovery as the Soul has undergone. Humility is "the virtue which enables a man to see himself in his true colours," which depend on grace and are therefore no cause for self-love; and so only when humility is achieved does the "recognition of truth begin."[7] In the midst of a tour de force of

7. *The Twelve Degrees of Humility and Pride*, trans. Barton R. V. Mills (London, 1929), pp. 10–11; cf. Martz, p. 131.

intellectual maneuvering and in an exulting victory over the routed army, it is humility that gains heaven.

Chorus.

> Triumph, triumph, victorious Soul;
> The World has not one Pleasure more:
> The rest does lie beyond the Pole,
> And is thine everlasting Store.

"Here" and "there" are not identical, but the Soul's behavior, especially its final submergence of the self in transcendent not-self, gains a measure of communication with the hereafter. That it is "that thing Divine" is fully acknowledged, as the Chorus plays upon the contrasting economics of heaven and earth and promises an everlasting "Store" as a "rest" for the hardworking Soul. It perhaps implies also that the world has in fact afforded a legitimate pleasure in giving the Soul opportunity to prove itself: the world enables the Soul to "shine" in combat, to find its immortality in mortal action.

Though "On a Drop of Dew" is not explicitly a temptation or dialogue poem, its idealism is in some ways similar to that of "A Dialogue," which it follows in the 1681 edition. And like "The Definition of Love," its tone is more complex than it first appears. Though it works toward an absolute separation of body and soul, its emotional lines do not fall precisely in accord with that dualism; an exercise in precise intellectual scrutiny is again the preliminary to emotional clarity and "resolve":

> See how the Orient Dew,
> Shed from the Bosom of the Morn
>   Into the blowing Roses,
> Yet careless of its Mansion new;
> For the clear Region where 'twas born
>   Round in its self incloses:
> And in its little Globes Extent,

Frames as it can its native Element.
How it the purple flow'r does slight,
Scarce touching where it lyes,
But gazing back upon the Skies,
Shines with a mournful Light;
Like its own Tear,
Because so long divided from the Sphear.
Restless it roules and unsecure,
Trembling lest it grow impure:
Till the warm Sun pitty it's Pain,
And to the Skies exhale it back again.

The emphasis of the first eighteen lines is upon the insecurity of
the soul-dewdrop, which resists the "purple flow'r" but is at
a disadvantage, shifting "as it can" in the "Mansion new." The
soul mourns the separation from its proper sphere (a separation which may or may not have been of its own doing—"shed"
may be reflexive, but the elliptical construction is obscure).
The process of descent into, and progress through, time is one
of restlessness and longing, and the return has very little triumph about it: uncomfortable and trembling in pain and fear,
the soul is passively "exhaled" back by the pitying sun. The
dewdrop metaphor suggests a "tear" as well as the soul—the
soul may reflect the Light, but light on earth is "mournful."

At the central pivot of the poem, as in "A Dialogue," the
metaphysical aspects of the soul's life have apparently been ac-
counted for, but the soul has not revealed its "puissance," its
power to emerge. If it does indeed move "but on a point below," disdaining what is beneath and loving what is above, it
should react with more fervor toward the processes of time.
Hence, along with the shift in focus from "vehicle" to "tenor,"
from dewdrop to the soul itself, comes a shift in mood. The
soul is no longer passive in framing "as it can" its native element, but "shuns," "disdains," "loves," and finally "runs." In
remembering its former height, it re-collects itself, memory
being both the means and the act of re-establishing its integrity.

In discovering its own inner powers it attains to "pure and circling thought" and expresses (presses out) the greater heaven it has in memory in the "Heaven less" which is its present life:

> So the Soul, that Drop, that Ray
> Of the clear Fountain of Eternal Day,
> Could it within the humane flow'r be seen,
>   Remembering still its former height,
>   Shuns the sweat leaves and blossoms green;
>   And, recollecting its own Light,
> Does, in its pure and circling thoughts, express
> The greater Heaven in an Heaven less.
>   In how coy a Figure wound,
>   Every way it turns away:
>   So the World excluding round,
>   Yet receiving in the Day.
>   Dark beneath, but bright above:
>   Here disdaining, there in Love,
>   How loose and easie hence to go:
>   How girt and ready to ascend.
>   Moving but on a point below,
>   It all about does upwards bend.

As the mood shifts, the antithesis is more tightly drawn and circularity becomes a positive achievement of the soul, which arms for battle against a well-defined opposition. The chant-like repetition and the wit suggest gaiety and spiritual power; the rhythm and rhyme scheme have a more pronounced order. Whereas suspended and poignant lines such as "Like its own Tear" and constricted movements as in "restless it roules" entangle the rhythm of the first half, the energy of the second half is less nervous; it is channeled into purposeful, disciplined exuberance: the dance is indeed "Moving but on a point below." In the metrical rapidity, the soul trains in meditative quickness; the "upward bend" brings into play all of its spiritual muscles and it ascends partly through its own power:

Such did the Manna's sacred Dew destil;
White, and intire, though congeal'd and chill.
Congeal'd on Earth: but does, dissolving, run
Into the Glories of th' Almighty Sun.

If the second eighteen lines act as the emotional antithesis
of the first eighteen, the last four synthesize the two aspects of
the descent and return, the chaste *fear* and the *power* of the
soul. The "chill" is subordinate, however: "White, and intire,
though congeal'd"; and "Congeal'd *on Earth*" but dissolving
and running into the glories of the sun. Though chill is necessary for "intirety" on earth, the soul is now clearly celestial
dew belonging to "th' Almighty Sun"; dissolving in the presence of the sun is self-fulfilling. The tightly woven couplets,
in expressing the distilled essence of the poem and recapitu-
lating the attitude toward time, are conclusive in both statement and feeling.

Despite the obvious technical skill of "On a Drop of Dew"
—its structural balance, its answerable rhythmic effects, and its
precisely articulated and extended imagery—its effectiveness is
difficult to account for. It is without the irony of "A Dialogue"
and yet avoids the slackness of many poems devoted to otherworldly yearning, such as Traherne's "The Instruction":

Spew out thy Filth, thy Flesh abjure,
Let not Contingents thee defile;
For Transients only are impure,
And empty Things thy Soul beguile.

On the other hand, though it has a disciplined joy, it lacks the
personal *feeling* of spiritual power that characterizes the soul
in Traherne:

Then was my Soul my only All to me,
A living endless Ey,
Scarce bounded with the Sky,

Whose Power, and Act, and Essence was to see:
  I was an inward Sphere of Light,
Or an interminable Orb of Sight,
  Exceeding that which makes the Days,
A *vital* Sun that shed abroad his Rays:
  All Life, all Sense,
A naked, simple, pure Intelligence.

Its effect is partly due, I think, to its peculiar combination of
emotion and controlled form. The question would seem to be
how this combination strikes us as being *witty*. One answer is
simply that the extension of the central figure, like the comparison of lovers to a compass, draws attention to technique
and to the image as such. But another, more intangible answer
occurs to me as possibly more important in explaining the
poem's compression, intensity, and control. The strategy is in
a sense to invert the *carpe diem* tradition while borrowing its
customary feelings and even its customary structure. Linguis-
tically, it is a matter of applying the rhetorical flavor of one
kind of motive to a totally different kind. From previous experience with literary flowers and dewdrops, we expect them
to be symbols of ephemeral life, about which the elegiac poet
moralizes as he directs our attention to the object and argues
for consolation. The elegy is thus normally a literary form that
offers consolation for our having to lose contact with nature.
Marvell simply distills the elegy's mode of consolation, freeing
it from its implication in nature and making it seem the logical
product of a *contemptus mundi* motive. In terms of imagery,
he exploits the vehicle while denying its importance, just as
the Resolved Soul uses Pleasure's images while avoiding entanglement in them. Life is too long rather than too short; the
theme is *memento vitae* rather than *memento mori*.

   This strategic inversion enables the idealist to arouse a comparatively well-defined emotion for the soul's descent from a
native sphere about which we have no firsthand knowledge.

He ex-presses the heaven above in the object below and then discards the object. "The high order of the poetic insight that the final insight must elude us," Allen Tate writes, "is dramatic in the sense that its fullest image is an action in the shapes of this world: it does not reject, it includes; it sees not only with but through the natural world, to what may lie beyond it. . . . It never begins at the top; it carries the bottom along with it."[8] Marvell thus carries the object to which he has drawn attention, loaded with its traditional emotion, to the linguistic "top" where it becomes "the Manna's sacred Dew"; he then dissolves it and converts the elegiac mood to eulogistic celebration. The final movement is toward transcendence: the soul's life begins where the temporal life and the metaphor "melt."

"On a Drop of Dew" is perhaps Marvell's most explicit handling of the soul's experience of time, but other poems dealing with similar themes are similarly poised and sharp in focus. "A Dialogue between the Soul and Body," for example, like "On a Drop of Dew," is clearly conceived within the dualistic metaphysic of Platonism, but unlike other poems in that framework its poise is that of suspended and uncommitted judgment. Though setting the two equal antagonists against each other without editorial comment may appear to suggest that their conjunction was a grim mistake, it does not imply an outright rejection of nature. For Marvell has them condemn each other without anger; in fact, the wit of the poem would again seem incompatible with the otherworldliness of the unironic Platonist.

Though we would normally expect Marvell's sympathies to lie with the Soul, then, it gains no decisive victory. Partly because of this, Miss Tuve finds the poem ambiguous, especially

8. "The Symbolic Imagination," in *The Man of Letters in the Modern World: Selected Essays, 1928–1955* (New York, Meridian Books, 1955), p. 112.

in the concluding figure.[9] The difficulties actually begin before
that, in the Soul's first monologue:

> O who shall, from this Dungeon, raise
> A Soul inslav'd so many wayes?
> With bolts of Bones, that fetter'd stands
> In Feet; and manacled in Hands.
> Here blinded with an Eye; and there
> Deaf with the drumming of an Ear.
> A Soul hung up, as 'twere, in Chains
> Of Nerves, and Arteries, and Veins.
> Tortur'd, besides each other part,
> In a vain Head, and double Heart.

Three interpretations of this appear possible: (1) with Marvell's approval, the Soul speaks straightforwardly against an
exacerbating human condition; (2) as Miss Tuve believes, the
Soul is *excessively* critical and Marvell does not entirely agree
with its "diminishings" of the Body, thus exposing the Soul to
an ironic criticism; (3) the Soul itself is ironic and therefore
not so singlemindedly opposed to the Body as it pretends to be
(and vice versa). The first of these we can dismiss, as I have
suggested, as out of keeping with Marvell's customary proce-
dure and attitude and incompatible with the artful *staging* of
each protest. The second would make it necessary to distinguish
between poet and persona by superimposing one irony on another, which seems unnecessary. In choosing the third, which
makes the Soul and Body aware of their own theatrics (and
thus the initiators of the irony rather than its unconscious vic-
tims), we are relieved of having to determine Marvell's side:
in acknowledging even grudgingly each other's special prov-
ince, the combatants make an unqualified commitment unnecessary. Nor is it necessary to concede that Marvell rests "dans
une suspension toute pyrrhoniene," as Legouis writes, or that he

9. *Elizabethan and Metaphysical Imagery* (Chicago, 1947), pp. 207–
08.

could not "descendre . . . profondement dans le mystère de la double nature de l'homme"[10]; the poem presents the experience of that mystery without being a treatise about it. Its chief value lies in the wit with which each side handles the other— again in complexity of vision and attitude rather than in the commitment or the solution proposed.

That the wit is the Soul's and Body's own is suggested by the exaggerated paradoxes, the blatantly excessive poetic techniques, and the ceremonial dance and song-like movement of their acts. Like a character in pre-Elizabethan drama making a first entrance, each begins with a formal introduction. The Soul points up its antitheses with alliteration: a *s*oul in*s*laved, *b*olts of *b*ones, *f*eet that *f*etter, and "*D*eaf with the *d*rumming of an Ear." It plays with etymologies in order to compound its paradoxes and confuse the Body, pointing out, for example, that the very terms for imprisonment derive from bodily parts, as in fettering feet and *mana*cling hands. It is complacently and self-consciously coy in the "as 'twere" parenthesis in the midst of its brilliant figure of the "Chains" of nerves and arteries. And its final name-calling is direct and subtly indirect at the same time. Since the Soul is nonmaterial, the head is empty ("vain") and is, in addition, entirely useless to a self-contained Soul that can only be blinded by bodily sight. The heart, in simple anatomical fact, is double, but it is also treacherous.

The Body's answer is fittingly less witty but has ironies of its own:

> O who shall me deliver whole
> From bonds of this Tyrannic Soul?
> Which, stretcht upright, impales me so,
> That mine own Precipice I go;
> And warms and moves this needless Frame:
> (A Fever could but do the same.)

10. Pierre Legouis, *André Marvell: poète, puritain, patriote, 1621–1678* (Paris, 1928), pp. 79 f.

And, wanting where its spight to try,
Has made me live to let me dye.
A Body that could never rest,
Since this ill Spirit it possest.

While the Soul desires to be raised, the Body has a declination for rest, coldness, and nothingness. It knows that it has some freedom even now and that it will be delivered by dissolution, but who can deliver it in one piece? By "impaling" it in an upright position, giving it form and stature, the Soul only makes it a "Precipice," ready to tumble down and disintegrate at death, even as the Soul has made itself "ill." The humor is perhaps grim, but characteristic of the Body's Calibanish sensibility. To the Body, Soul and fever are the same: a temporary warmth leading to ultimate decay; and the frame itself is "needless" to what would prefer to be a nonintelligent collection of healthy atoms.

The Soul's answer picks up this concern for physical well-being:

What Magick could me thus confine
Within anothers Grief to pine?
Where whatsoever it complain,
I feel, that cannot feel, the pain.
And all my Care its self employes
That to preserve, which me destroys:
Constrain'd not only to indure
Diseases, but, what's worse, the Cure:
And ready oft the Port to gain,
Am Shipwrackt into Health again.

The Body may grieve, but the Soul, having come to "feel" through it, grieves beyond the Body's grief. The paradox turns on the distinction between the Soul in itself and the Soul incarnated, held by magic and ship-racked by health. Are they the same, or has the union altered both Soul and Body in essence? Their *débat* explores both of these possibilities and discovers the conjunction to be binding to the extent that all missiles aimed at the opponent strike oneself. The Soul's intellect and wit are in the service of the very clay which complains against it. The irony is thicker here, and the argument tends to become a meditative soliloquy rather than a public performance; but wit makes the death-yearning taut—neither death nor life is sentimentalized—and the irony is still the Soul's own and still directed against the Body's hypochondria.

The Body, unconvinced that its physical grievances are trivial, continues with its own wit, turning all the Soul's lower functions to causes of diseases; and by implication, the pain from these illnesses, too, rebounds upon the Soul, which becomes the victim of its own mortification of the Body:

> But Physick yet could never reach
> The Maladies Thou me dost teach;
> Whom first the Cramp of Hope does Tear:
> And then the Palsie Shakes of Fear.
> The Pestilence of Love does heat:
> Or Hatred's hidden Ulcer eat.
> Joy's chearful Madness does perplex:
> Or Sorrow's other Madness vex.
> Which Knowledge forces me to know;
> And Memory will not foregoe.
> What but a Soul could have the wit
> To build me up for Sin so fit?
> So Architects do square and hew,
> Green Trees that in the Forest grew.

While the Soul attempts to understand the "magic" which binds it to the Body, the Body ponders the "physick" that might cure itself, each approaching the mystery of their union from its own direction and tacitly admitting that it is not sufficient by itself to account for the subtle knot that makes them man. Each depends on the other and is afflicted by that dependence. The passionate Soul's Hope, Fear, Love, Hatred, Joy, and Sorrow have corresponding bodily diseases in Cramps, Palsie, Pestilence, Ulcers, and Madness, or is it that the diseases have corresponding passions? The fusion forces each upon the other until even a body preferring oblivion "knows" and cannot forget.

Miss Tuve finds the concluding figure troublesome: are we to read it as a Rousseauistic notion showing Marvell's rebellious preference for the natural and the unspoiled, or, with heavy irony, emphasizing the inappropriateness of the Body's analogy, which suggests unreasonably that an architect is responsible for sins occurring under the roof he has built?[11] Considering the poem as a dramatistic contest between antagonists who need each other, we can safely pass the problem by. Either the Body or the Soul must have the final word, which by the nature of their fusion cannot be very final; the Body's argument is not conclusive. If it is natural for green trees to grow wild in the forest, it is also natural for architects to "square and hew" them into some form. The misfortune lies in the inevitability of their being what they are and in their coming together through no desire of their own. The Body is built up for sin whether or not the Soul desires to be tyrannical. Encroaching upon the realm of ethics, which properly belongs to the Soul, the Body scores an important point: souls, rather than bodies, sin. But it is a moral point that it could not have made without borrowing the Soul's wit. Nothing is less sinful than a tree, but it is equally true that souls without bodies would not sin either; and bodies without souls would not care.

The Body's final exaggerations are typical of the poem as a whole and strictly within the bounds of its own irony. The contest ends, as it begins, suggesting not so much a serious debate as a poised and purposefully hyperbolic agon. If history is rejected, it is with a minimum of bitterness and a hint, on both sides, of recognition and humor.

11. *Elizabethan and Metaphysical Imagery*, p. 208.

Before leaving Marvell's otherworldly idealism, I want to consider one other example, "Eyes and Tears," which deserves consideration in itself and is useful besides in distinguishing Marvell from other metaphysical poets, both in quality of wit and in attitudes toward nature. Most seventeenth-century poets turn sooner or later to the imagery of eyes and tears, and how they handle it is some indication of their sense of decorum and form. Because eyes may serve both as mirrors and as instruments of seeing, they suggest to Donne an interchange and revelation of identities, an ecstasy or "going out" in love without sacrificing the self. Being round, tears may be found to add to this a suggestion of pregnant growth:

> Let me powre forth
> My teares before thy face, whil'st I stay here,
> For thy face coines them, and thy stampe they beare,
> And by this Mintage they are something worth,
> For thus they bee
> Pregnant of thee;
> Fruits of much griefe they are, emblemes of more,
> When a teare falls, that thou falls which it bore,
> So thou and I are nothing then, when on a divers shore.

Because "thou and I" are created in the confrontation, when parting (as when a tear shatters upon a divers shore) "we" become "nothing."

Thus seeing and weeping readily lend themselves to a kind of metaphysical speculation that might be expected to appeal to Marvell. The contrast between sight and in-sight may reveal the gulf between divine and human, spiritual and physical values, as in the soul which finds itself "blinded with an Eye," or as in the poignant dilemma of Herbert's "Sacrifice":

> *Oh all ye,* who passe by, whose eyes and minde
> To worldly things are sharp, but to me blind;
> To me, who took eyes that I might you finde:
> Was ever grief like mine?

But the imagery of eyes and tears also runs a greater than ordinary danger of losing contact with reality or of becoming immersed in the fact of weeping and thus detracting from what must be a delicately handled artifact: a poem of eyes and tears must be formulary or it will appear sentimental, but more than that or it will become precious and meaningless. If Donne and Herbert find safe passage between the sentimental and the precious, Crashaw, Carew, Henry King, Traherne, Quarles, and others rebound from one to the other.[12]

Marvell's "Eyes and Tears" is a "tissue of success and failure," as George Williamson writes,[13] having both the skill of Donne and Herbert and the faults of their imitators. It is a connoisseur performance in wit in some respects, a mere curiosity barely avoiding decadence in others, and yet remarkable in its own way. Like many of its predecessors, it is highly stylized, an exercise in imagistic control and fine articulation in which the weeping itself counts for little (though, as Legouis writes, embarrassment over it is not an unnatural response: "nous ne sommes plus assez chrétiens pour contempler ce spectacle sans quelque ironie ou quelque gêne"[14]). More to our purposes, however, is the fact that the imagery is made responsible to a rigorously pursued and significant theme: the price of joy, the value of nature, and the process of distillation by which the soul in time reduces everything to an essence of tears (a withdrawal process) before returning to the "all-seeing Sun" (an emergence process).

Though the structure of the poem is loose, each stanza con-

---

12. See, e.g., Quarles' *Emblems Divine and Moral;* Hugo's *Pia Desideria,* trans. Edmund Arwaker (London, 1690), 2, v; Crashaw's "The Teare," "The Weeper"; King, "The Exequy"; Carew, "Lips and Eyes," "Parting, Celia Weepes"; Traherne, "An Infant-Eye," "Sight," and others; Knevet, "Remorse." Cf. Martz on Southwell and the "literature of tears," pp. 199 ff.

13. *The Donne Tradition* (Cambridge, Mass., 1930), p. 154.

14. Legouis, p. 79; cf. 149–52.

tributes something to the thematic and emotional movement, which culminates in a hortatory colloquy of poet and eyes and in a final definition of the central symbols. In terms of the imagery, the movement might be described as a muscular effort to bend straight lines into curves, to prevent the soul from emerging in the wrong direction:[15]

> And, since the Self-deluding Sight,
> In a false Angle takes each hight;
> These Tears which better measure all,
> Like wat'ry Lines and Plummets fall.

The simple opposition of vain upward sight and downward tearful humility must be resolved so that seeing and weeping together define the human plight:

> Thus let your Streams o'reflow your Springs,
> Till Eyes and Tears be the same things:
> And each the other's difference bears;
> These weeping Eyes, those seeing Tears.

The blurring doubleness of desiring what is seen and then weeping in repentance is thus overcome: the "waves" of tears drench the straightforward "sparkling Glance that shoots Desire" and in the process quench the "Thund'rer's" unbending lightning and deaden his thunder to a hiss. The plummet fall of tears, as in Crashaw's weeper, turns upward and "Heavens bosome drinks the gentle streame."

Though much of this is implied as early as the first stanza, Marvell explores the paradox extensively before endorsing it with enthusiasm. The early stanzas weigh the price of joys with perhaps too much calculation. Sorrow at first is willing to pay

15. Cf. Marjorie Nicolson's statement that the circle of perfection, read into Nature by God, is a clue to Marvell's ethics and aesthetics, to both of which limitation, restraint, proportion were basic. *The Breaking of the Circle* (Evanston, Ill., 1950), p. 57.

only two tears for joy, while full repentance calls for a profusion of tears in which, first, clouds dissolve, then fountains trickle, and finally floods "o'return and drown." Not till eyes are swimming in tears are there weeping eyes and seeing tears, humble seeing and informed humility. The necessary storm clouds are gathering during the trip through the garden; by stanza nine the eyes have enough tears to float a greater cargo than that in "full sailes hasting loaden home." And as the tears swell, the ambivalence Marvell feels toward nature dissolves and he fulfills the demands of humility and repentance with greater singleness. Even the "Incense" of church services has only negative value:

> The Incense was to Heaven dear,
> Not as a Perfume, but a Tear.

And stars are serviceable only as emblems of grief: "And Stars shew lovely in the Night, / But as they seem the Tears of Light." The image is a fitting climax to the preparation for the colloquy. Though we might expect stars to be far enough above to serve as an image of pure beauty giving "light upon the earth," that expectation only gives the sacrifice more purchase: if only seeing tears ("Tears of Light") are genuinely "lovely in the Night," even stars must join the universal lamentation. The image fuses the double power of seeing and weeping, desire for beauty with sorrow over it when perceived: insight and upward sight become identical. The constriction and the self-laceration ritually complete, the poet can then turn to action: "Ope then mine Eyes your double Sluice . . ."

That tears must not be the product of a vague and general weltschmerz but something informed of light, a product of weltansicht, is not Marvell's invention, of course. Peter Sterry writes, for example, that as Christ's blood would have been of no value if it had not been the blood of a God, "in like manner your tears cannot be heavenly and divine if they be not the tears of the heavenly and divine principle in you."[16] But the ingenious manner and the extended manipulation of the symbols are peculiarly Marvellian in their mixture of absurdity, wit, and self-awareness. History has only one paradoxical value: according to the wise decree of nature that made "the same Eyes to weep and see," it reveals its own lack of value. However, as the wit and the dialectical powers reveal, Marvell withholds part of himself from that commitment; what he rejects has a potential value that might assert itself in less constrictive, less severely masochistic moments. Unlike Traherne, Marvell never quite precludes seeing the whole problem from another viewpoint, shifting the emphasis from an ironic resolve against to an ironic acceptance of history. It is not surprising, therefore, to find in the bulk of his poems that the same wit and dialectical capacities can serve another cause.

16. *The Rise, Race, and Royalty,* pp. 176–77.

3. Pastoral and Reconciliation with History

He hangs in shades the Orange bright,
Like golden Lamps in a green Night.

("Bermudas")

BECAUSE PASTORAL often involves opposition between an idealized concept of nature and actual existence, and conflict between the search for simplicity and a complex, pressing society, it is not surprising that Marvell found it a hospitable medium. Overwhelmed by the existent, the pastoral poet frequently retreats from the "red and white" into the "green" world. In poems of pastoral success (as I shall call them—without implying a value judgment), he often consolidates gains, becomes reoriented toward the world, and finally reenters society. The general pattern varies from poet to poet and from poem to poem, but is remarkably persistent. Of all Marvell's poems, "The Garden" perhaps most obviously falls into it. Though the poet does not emerge from the *hortus conclusus* where fair Quiet and Innocence dwell, he nevertheless endorses the processes of time that have threatened the contemplative life: "How could such sweet and wholsome Hours / Be reckon'd but with herbs and flow'rs!" "Upon Appleton House," too, works within the same general framework, with the threat greater and the withdrawal more enigmatic. Whatever he learns from the grove, the poet leaves its contemplative sanctuary having gained a new capacity to deal with the active world. The order and harmony of the forest is suffused through art and the moral life: the scorching sun in the warlike meadow is metamorphosed into the "*tuned* Fires" of the birds and only the "equal Flames" of the stock-doves "burn." Hence, after leaving the protective shades, Marvell finds the world to be no longer "a rude heap together hurl'd," a "putrid Earth," but a cosmos "vitrifi'd" by a "flame" tried in heaven. The forest sanctuary is in a sense an instrument of immanence brought into action by the symbols the poet finds there, symbols which enable art to reorder, "tune," and "straighten" nature.

This pattern of retreat, discovery of creative capacity, and resurgent control over nature, then, we discover in much pastoral poetry as in seventeenth-century Puritan-Platonism. Distraction, motion, and diversity are frozen, and in a quiet moment of meditation or song, the shepherd relocates himself. In so doing, he may re-examine the function of poetry itself, that is to say, relate self-creation to artistic creation. The soul-artist in "The Garden," singing and waving in its plumes the various light, fuses the creative power of the mind with the body's vegetative functions. It reflects physical nature but transforms, *idea*lizes it. When the antagonism between the self and what exists, or between art and nature, is found to be resolvable like this, the effect is usually one of release—the prophetic poet goes off to "fresh woods and pastures new" or simply enjoys in a kind of primitive, spontaneous way the "fruits and flow'rs."

Thus successful pastoral ordinarily discovers an elementary link "of man with all beings as beings, vague as to its special content, but far-embracing and generalising"[1]—elementary

1. Werner Brock, to Martin Heidegger's *Existence and Being* (London, 1949), introduction, p. 174.

because the diurnal course of rocks, stones, and trees is part of pastoral, but also because what is necessary to well-being tends to be estimated differently in rustic surroundings. Freedom from constricting forms, social torments, and perhaps psychic distortions results in simplified manners and decorum. To be sure, a great deal may be excluded which might tend to destroy the links with "all beings as beings." (Keats' "Ode to Psyche" is an extreme case. Only "some untrodden region" of the mind will serve for the "rosy sanctuary" of the imagination—in the heart of "the wild-ridged mountains steep by steep" the working brain secludes itself, and only at night and only through a small casement lets "the warm love in.") But we can usually expect at least a symbolic recognition of the real world of passion, death, and poverty.

In contrast to this discovery of elemental being, anti-pastoral poems, or poems of pastoral failure, to give them a convenient name, describe an inability to stay inside the protected world where "letting things be" is possible. Keats' nightingale is eventually "buried deep / In the next valley-glades," leaving the poet in a state of bewilderment, alone in the unsatisfactory company of his "sole self." Juliana causes the Mower himself to lose himself, never to find his "home." A corrupted idea of art undermines nature and turns the Mower himself into a destroyer, a "Mower *against* Gardens." The "wanton Troopers" violate the sanctified shelter of the nymph. The mowers of "Upon Appleton House" needlessly slaughter the quail. In addition, the artist's difficulty in transforming landscape to symbol may be involved. If the link with nature is broken, hopes of achieving order and meaning fail, or, in the special jargon of the pastoral, the "greenness of the Grass" is destroyed, as Juliana destroys the Mower, the keeper of the meadow: "She / What I do to the grass, does to my Thoughts and me." Instead of achieving rapport with nature, the Mower acknowledges the descent of chaos—"And Flow'rs, and Grass, and I and all /

Will in one common Ruine fall"—just as Spenser's Colin falls
in ruin as lover, religious reformer, and artist in the December
eclogue. And so in "A Dialogue between Thrysis and Dorinda," Elysium lies only in "yonder Skie" where all shepherds
are equal; in this world, shepherds are "sick and fain would
dye." The artist's instruments are of no avail here; and in
heaven, where "thine Ears / May feast with Musick of the
Spheres" without the help of artists, they have no use.

Both patterns—the successful reintegration and the severance of the ideal and the real—are prominent, of course, not
only in Marvell but in classical and modern writers as well.
Rilke's "Eingang," for example, is a modern variation of the
reintegration pattern:

> Whoever you are, go out into the evening,
> leaving your room, of which you know each bit;
> your house is the last before the infinite,
> whoever you are.
> Then with your eyes that wearily
> scarce lift themselves from the worn-out door-stone
> slowly you raise a shadowy black tree
> and fix it on the sky: slender, alone.
> And you have made the world (and it shall grow
> and ripen as a word, unspoken, still).
> When you have grasped its meaning with your will,
> then tenderly your eyes will let it go. . . .[2]

If Pan is the dread opener of mysterious doors for Keats, the
"shadowy black tree" performs the same function for Rilke:
the release of a journey from a town where everything is known
to a country on the edge of the infinite is telescoped in the act
of crossing the threshold of the room and observing the tree, a
locus amoenus of sorts.[3] One "makes" the world in that act,

2. *Selected Poems*, trans. C. F. MacIntyre (Berkeley, University of California Press, 1958), p. 21.
3. See Ernst Robert Curtius, *European Literature and the Latin Middle
Ages*, trans. Willard R. Trask (New York, 1953), pp. 195 ff.

which is also an act of the imagination analogous to a word rising in the consciousness—"und sie ist gross / und wie ein Wort,
das noch in Schweigen reist." When the imagination has done
its work, the will may incorporate its vision; then tenderly the
landscape may be released: the opposition between a stale and
limited environment and an imaginative and infinite one is resolved. "Whoever" the reader may be, he can perform the ceremony and then return to the well-known room.

Traditionally, art and the tree are intimately connected in
this way. The protection of the "green shade" where the famil-
iar world can be both shut out and let in under control is essential to "green thought." Shepherds meet in the shade to resolve
their troubles or at least express them in dialogue and in singing contests. They forsake the world of labor and common
sense in order to seek an uncommon harmony. Despite these
mythic and romantic aspects of the form, however, the successful pastoral figures in Marvell do not ordinarily sustain themselves in thought alone, even green thought. Marvell discovers
sensuous, concrete links with elemental life—grass, melons,
curious peaches, and so on—and through them seeks a strategy
for dealing with history. Neither the success nor the failure pattern is fully explicable in terms of otherworldly motives. Marvell generally balances the ideal and the real carefully instead
of absorbing one into the other, though their reconciliation is
not quite as equals: if Adonis is dead and bleeding, "the blood
and tears become flowers upon the ground," as Bion's "Lament
for Adonis" puts it; "of the blood comes the rose, and of the
tears the windflower." However, the green world is violently
disturbed at times. The contemplative life is pursued within
a context of struggle, as in the civil wars and military achievements of Fairfax in "Appleton House," the love chase of "The
Garden," the shattered frame of "The Coronet," the slaying of
the fawn in "A Nymph," and the benevolent but potentially
dangerous tyranny of little T. C. The context of disturbance is

traditional in pastoral also, but suffering in traditional love lyrics and even in the elegy are typically more stylized than the violence of Marvell's retreats. Nature in Marvell is not "Unerring Nature, still divinely bright, / One clear, unchanged, and universal light" which art need only imitate. Rather, nature stimulates ambiguously the impulse to maim, and the impulse to be absorbed into it and to absorb it in return.

Though Marvell's primitivism has little in common with romantic primitivism of the eighteenth and early nineteenth centuries, in thus emphasizing the *threats* to pastoral ceremony he looks forward to Blake, Keats, and one strain of post-Darwinian pastoral. For the "Song of the Happy Shepherd" in later times, of course, is not to be, ordinarily, a happy song at all:

> The woods of Arcady are dead,
> And over is their antique joy;
> Of old the world on dreaming fed;
> Grey truth is now her painted toy.[4]

As in T. S. Eliot's "Burnt Norton," the pastoral ideal serves primarily as a reminder of what might have been:

> Footfalls echo in the memory
> Down the passage which we did not take
> Towards the door we never opened
> Into the rose-garden.

When Yeats heard a voice from the past, it was a

voice of lamentation out of the Golden Age. It told me that we are imperfect, incomplete, and no more like a beautiful woven web, but like a bundle of cords knotted together and flung into a corner. It said that the world was once all perfect and kindly, and that still the kindly and perfect world existed, but buried like a mass of roses under many spadefuls of earth. The faeries and the more innocent of the spirits dwelt within it, and lamented over our fallen world in the lamentation of

4. W. B. Yeats, *Collected Poems* (New York, Macmillan, 1954), p. 7.

the wind-tossed reeds, in the song of the birds, in the moan
of the waves, and in the sweet cry of the fiddle. It said that
. . . the best of our moments are marred by a little vulgarity,
or by a needle-prick out of sad recollection, and that the fiddle must ever lament it all. It said that if only they who live in
the Golden Age could die we might be happy, for the sad
voices would be still; but they must sing and we must weep
until the eternal gates swing open.[5]

Modern pastoral, in Edwin Muir's phrase, thus has but "one
foot in Eden." The old theme by and large has been inverted:
"even in the land of death, I, Arcadia, dwell."[6] Or the poet may
discover that Eden is lost altogether. The Darwinian-minded
speaker of Rupert Brooke's "Town and Country," for example,
discovers the city to be a protection against a ruthless and indifferent cosmos, a far more formidable enemy than traditional
frigid nymphs: "We've found love in little hidden places," he
says, "Under great shades, between the mist and mire," but in
nature

Our unwalled loves thin out on vacuous air,

And suddenly there's no meaning in our kiss,
And your lit upward face grows, where we lie,
Lonelier and dreadfuller than sunlight is,
And dumb and mad and eyeless like the sky.

5. *The Celtic Twilight*, in *Mythologies* (London, Macmillan, 1959),
pp. 104–05.
6. See Erwin Panofsky's essay on this theme in the Renaissance and
later, "*Et in Arcadia ego:* On the Conception of Transience in Poussin and
Watteau," in *Philosophy and History, Essays Presented to Ernst Cassirer*,
eds. R. Klibansky and H. J. Paton (Oxford, 1936), pp. 223–54; also in
Meaning in the Visual Arts (New York, 1957), pp. 295–320. For other
useful commentaries on pastoral see Calvin Truesdale's unpublished dissertation "English Pastoral Verse from Spenser to Marvell," University of
Washington (1956); Walter W. Greg's standard work, *Pastoral Poetry
and Pastoral Drama;* and William Empson, *Some Versions of Pastoral*
(London, 1950).

He has an obvious kinship with the man with the double axe in Frost's "New Hampshire" who

> . . . went alone against a grove of trees;
> But his heart failing him, he dropped the axe
> And ran for shelter quoting Matthew Arnold:
> 'Nature is cruel, man is sick of blood; . . .'
> He had a special terror of the flux
> That showed itself in dendrophobia.

Marvell's forests and gardens reflect a "terror of the flux" also; Marvell did not share the dendro-eudaemonia of a later poet who held that "One impulse from a vernal wood / May teach you more of man, / Of moral evil and of good, / Than all the sages can." Unlike Frost's New York alec, however, he found nature meaningful as well as threatening. In the poems I shall examine in this chapter, he either discovers a principle of compromise between art and nature, the active and contemplative lives, and thus an integration of nature and the supernatural, or he examines obstacles to such integration. The chief patterns are (1) withdrawal, to purgative, masochistic pain or perhaps pleasure, to enlightenment, and finally to symbolic or actual emergence and (2) withdrawal, to constriction, to symbolic self-annihilation.

In "The Coronet," once the kind of pastoral that looks for atonement in the beauty and innocence of nature is rejected, the poet finds a valid use for another kind. If the coronet is spoiled as a crown for the head of "the king of Glory," it may still crown his feet—in fact, the act of writing the poem, symbolized in the gathering and weaving of the flowers, shows the natural man to be compatible with the religious man. The pastoral garland, violently shattered at Christ's feet, thus becomes the spoils of victory as well as a spoiled wreath. The poem is a forceful and unique version of the traditional pastoral reconciliation of art, nature, and the supernatural:

> When for the Thorns with which I long, too long,
>   With many a piercing wound,
>   My Saviours head have crown'd,
> I seek with Garlands to redress that Wrong:
>   Through every Garden, every Mead,
> I gather flow'rs (my fruits are only flow'rs)
>   Dismantling all the fragrant Towers
> That once adorn'd my Shepherdesses head.
> And now when I have summ'd up all my store,
>   Thinking (so I my self deceive)
>   So rich a Chaplet thence to weave
> As never yet the king of Glory wore:
>   Alas I find the Serpent old
>   That, twining in his speckled breast,
>   About the flow'rs disguis'd does fold,
>   With wreaths of Fame and Interest.
> Ah, foolish Man, that would'st debase with them,
> And mortal Glory, Heavens Diadem!
> But thou who only could'st the Serpent tame,
> Either his slipp'ry knots at once untie,
> And disintangle all his winding Snare:
> Or shatter too with him my curious frame:
> And let these wither, so that he may die,
> Though set with Skill and chosen out with Care.
> That they, while Thou on both their Spoils dost tread,
> May crown thy Feet, that could not crown thy Head.

The final lines, in which the offering, ruined by Satan, becomes the spoils of the second Adam's feet, may refer to the phophecy of Genesis 3:15: "I will put enmity between thee and the woman and between thy seed and her seed; it shall bruise thy head and thou shalt bruise his heel."[7] St. Gregory had found the mystery of the Incarnation symbolized by Christ's feet, by

7. Quoted by Walafred Strabo, *Glossa ordinaria* in Migne, 113:95; cf. John Diodati, *Pious Annotations* (London, 1648), p. 4; Sir Henry Vane, *The Retired Man's Meditations* (London, 1655), p. 402.

which divinity touched earth.[8] And so the coronet of flowers, like May in Vaughan's "St. Mary Magdalen," finds its place at that point where the natural and supernatural meet:

> Why art thou humbled thus, and low
> As earth, thy lovely head dost bow?
> Dear Soul! thou knew'st, flowers here on earth
> At their Lords foot-stool have their birth;
> Therefore thy wither'd self in haste
> Beneath his blest feet thou didst cast,
> That at the root of this green tree
> Thy great decays restor'd might be.

The flowers of the gardens and meads are thus not entirely useless. If they cannot be salvaged in any other way, they may at least serve a sacrificial function, like the slain shepherd of the pastoral elegy, whose death results in renewed ceremonies and new life. The impulse to create something of value out of nature is neither pure nor impure, the coronet neither complete gain nor complete loss. But only after gathering and weaving the flowers, "set with Skill and chosen out with Care," can one arrive at self-recognition and awareness of the gulf that separates nature and grace. Fame and interest shatter the pastoral daydream, but the pastoral artist discovers a valid use for his art.

For this reason lavishing skill and care on a poem offered for destruction is no contradiction. As part of the poem's strategy, Marvell weaves the curious frame as tightly as he can. The opening quatrains, equivalent to the composition of place in a three-part meditation, present the problem and the poet's reaction to it. One couplet completes the self-recognition hinted

---

8. "Potest quoque per pedes ipsum mysterium in carnationis eius intelligi, quo divinitas terrum tetigit, quia carnem sumpsit," *Homiliarum in evangelia*, lib. II, Migne, 76:1242. On the concept of sacrifice, see Ernst Cassirer, *The Philosophy of Symbolic Forms* (New Haven, 1955), 2, 226–30.

earlier and turns the artist in the right direction ("Ah, foolish Man . . ."), followed by a colloquy with a more complex interweaving of rhyme (klmklm) but with regularized, pentameter lines, as the poet sees his involvement in the winding snare in the light of Christ's relationship with nature. "Though set with Skill . . ." thus concludes a six-line section of intricate interweaving on a curiously ambivalent and lamenting note. Marvell places the qualifying clause in a climactic position and calls attention to it as a parting gesture before throwing the "curious frame" at Christ's feet. The sacrifice, he indicates, is as intricate as one might expect from a previous maker of "Towers" for shepherdesses' heads; it is the tribute of a fabricator whose lavish expenditure only makes for greater "spoils." The poem ends, in the circular manner of a coronet, with the original idea of crowning, but the difference between the final sacrifice, with its mixture of reluctance, wit, and resignation, and the original industry only points up the contrast between naive hopes for nature and art and the Christian poet's recognition of their sacrificial use.

However, though "The Coronet" (like "Lycidas") progresses from innocent ceremony to realization of corruption to a kind of release through sacrifice, its peculiar integration of nature, art, and grace does not leave the poet free to seek new ceremonies in "fresh woods." If it were the only poem on the subject among Marvell's lyrics, its proper place would be at the end, as a kind of palinode: making other frames only to have them shattered would be fruitless. (The suggestion that Christ disentangled the serpent without destroying the garland is not made very hopefully.) In "Clorinda and Damon," on the other hand, though Damon begins by thinking of nature strictly as a temptation comprising a banquet of pleasure like that rejected by the Resolved Soul, the poem eventually finds the fountain's liquid bell to be in harmony with the song of great Pan (Christ). Only by comparison with that song do natural things appear to Damon to be spoiled by sensuality, the cave of love to be a cave of iniquity.[9]

It first appears, however, that the sun from which the pastoral retreat is meant to offer protection, "Heaven's Eye" (*sol justitiae*), exposes the sheltered darkness to hostile scrutiny. No retreat is quite safe. Nor is the pagan fountain baptismal, a place where the soul might bathe and "slake its Drought." The opening lines suggest that the process of reading clearly and purely the signs on the grassy "Scutcheon" was lost when the flock went astray, when, in shepherd dialogue, Adam's golden world lost its integrity. It is this fall from innocence that has made nature dangerous and taught Damon to expect death in Arcadia:

> C. I have a grassy Scutcheon spy'd,
>   Where *Flora* blazons all her pride.
>   The Grass I aim to feast thy Sheep:
>   The Flow'rs I for thy Temples keep.
> D. Grass withers; and the Flow'rs too fade.

The flowers are thus undermined by the fall, and their beauty, though having splendor as Clorinda sees them, will not satisfy the Christian shepherd. Reading nature in the way the divine *allegoria* of the Canticles was read, however, offers a way to sublimate one's attraction to nature. The limitations inherent in the signs on nature's "Scutcheon" (about which "poor Shepherds" sing) are overcome by the transcending song of Pan:

> C. What did great *Pan* say?
> D. Words that transcend poor Shepherds skill,
>   But He ere since my Songs does fill:
>   And his Name swells my slender Oate.

9. John D. Rosenberg's perceptive article "Marvell and the Christian Idiom," *Boston University Studies in English*, 4 (1960), 152–61, approaches "Clorinda and Damon" from approximately the same direction.

The "Name" supersedes the design of Flora's "Scutcheon," but an enlightened shepherd like Damon may incorporate nature in his song, which is composed of harmonic parts and precisely those images from nature just rejected:

> *Chorus.*
> Of *Pan* the flowry Pastures sing,
> Caves eccho, and the Fountains ring.
> Sing then while he doth us inspire;
> For all the World is our *Pan's* Quire.

Nature's various forms as divine *vestigia*, then, are allowed a function;[10] though they "swell" the shepherd's pagan "Oate," they do not make it an altogether different instrument. The world becomes "Our Pan's Quire" by means of its echoing capacity. A Miltonic hierarchy reclaims all forms of life from lowest to highest: Damon is for Pan, Clorinda for Pan through Damon ("Sweet must *Pan* sound in *Damons* Note"), and the rest of creation for Pan through their combined song. No withdrawal is possible, but none is necessary if the temptress herself is rendered harmless. Guilt and rejection are transformed to divine eros and eulogy.

This manner of bringing together pagan and Hebraic pastoral and thus healing the broad fissure of nature and grace, though seldom so succinctly expressed, is not uncommon in renaissance pastoral. For example, Herman Hugo, in a popularized version of a commentary by Honorius on the Canticles, suggests that a tree's protective shadow "is the traveller's covert from heat, his protection from the storm," because it is "The Tree of Life, to wit, the Apple Tree." It is "the holy cross, its

10. Cf. St. Bonaventura, *The Mind's Road to God*, trans. George Boas (New York, 1953), pp. 8–11; Etienne Gilson, *The Philosophy of St. Bonaventure* (New York, 1938), p. 230; Ruth Wallerstein, *Studies in Seventeenth-Century Poetic* (Madison, 1950), p. 194; Bellarmine, *The Mind's Ascent to God* (1615), trans. Monialis (Oxford, 1925), pp. 36, 110, 117.

fruit is Christ, its shadow the refreshment and defense of mankind."[11] This is to say simply that the shadow cast by the Incarnation sanctifies the forest. The crucifixion "tree" blesses the fruit and makes spiritually beneficial the trees in actual groves encountered by the pilgrim on his simultaneously horizontal journey through time and his vertical *itinerarium mentis in deum*.[12]

Marvell returns to this theme on several occasions, most explicitly in "Bermudas," which in the compact precision of his best style suggests that the two journeys can be made to coincide, that a classical concern with nature-as-such and the Christian book of emblems are not entirely incompatible. Captain John Smith's account of the Summer Isles in *The Generall History of Virginia* (1624) and the experiences of John Oxenbridge may have provided suggestions for the compromise, but more important would seem to be the fact that the Bermudas could be considered mythic without contradicting geography. The myth of the eternal return was not entirely myth:[13] in the climate of the Bermudas was a hint of what had been before the fall, an embodiment of what history, redeemed by providence, could be at any time, and the promise of a future Eden. The remote past and the future are thus brought together in a natural shrine whose message is a "gospel" transmitted to the listening winds. The impulse to retreat is transformed to an exploratory motive and purged of its masochism and symbolic annihilation.

Even so, the poem has its own kind of intensity. The pil-

11. *Pia Desideria*, trans. E. Arwaker (London, 1690), p. 149. On the traditional associations of cross and tree see C. G. Jung, *Symbols of Transformation*, trans. R. F. C. Hull (New York, 1956), pp. 271 ff.

12. Cf. Bernard Clairvaux, *Vita et res gestae*, I, 4 (Migne, 185:240) and *Tractatus Ascetici* (Migne, 184:251 ff.); cf. Boethius, *Consolations of Philosophy* VII, 8.

13. See Mircea Eliade, *The Myth of the Eternal Return*, trans. Willard Trask (New York, 1954).

grims in their small boat hover on the edge between their old, unstable world and this "far kinder" one. The "watry Maze" leads back to a place now "long unknown" that they find rising above the storms of their journey:

> What should we do but sing his Praise
> That led us through the watry Maze,
> Unto an Isle so long unknown,
> And yet far kinder than our own?
> Where he the huge Sea-Monsters wracks,
> That lift the Deep upon their Backs.
> He lands us on a grassy Stage;
> Safe from the Storms, and Prelat's rage.
> He gave us this eternal Spring,
> Which here enamells every thing;

By racking sea monsters, pruning nature, and regulating time, providential art resolves a tension between tameness and wildness, nature as a threat and nature as a harbor and shrine. Even while things change and grow, spring is eternal and enameled (that is, surpassing in adornment). The islands are a "grassy Stage" combining the fullest potential of art and nature. Fowl visit daily in harmony with cosmic purposes, while providence itself

> . . . hangs in shades the Orange bright,
> Like golden Lamps in a green Night.

The fruit hangs for both beauty and guidance, set like divine light brilliantly against a threatening background. From their side of the line, rowing simply "along" in their small boat and singing, the pilgrims given thanks for this presence of grace in nature: God "in these Rocks for us did frame / A Temple, where to sound his Name." The song from their Protestant English craft may not pierce directly to Spanish and Catholic "Mexique Bay," but if they sing loudly enough it may perhaps get there rebounded from "Heavens Vault."[14] Meanwhile, the temporal task of rowing the small boat is perfectly synchronized with, and regulated by, their religious "chime." The song is "An holy and a chearful Note" because of that divine-human congruity that gets their boat to its goal. Its holiness is natural, its naturalness holy; essence and existence, art and nature, are perfectly fused.

The mower poems, taken as a group, are concerned with the loss of that congruity. Man's fall occasions nature's, and so the integrity of the self and the integrity of garden and meadow are lost together.[15] Love, along with death the shepherd's traditional spoiler, causes the Mower to turn the instrument of his trade against himself and to bring chaos to the meadow. In the Mower's accident, the fall is re-enacted, bringing death once again to Arcadia:

> Only for him no Cure is found
> Whom Julianas Eyes do wound.
> Tis death alone that this must do:
> For death thou art a Mower too.

Death as mower will thus ransack nature where the Mower has kept order, and the Mower who has mowed himself awaits it as cure for the wound heterosexual love has given him.

14. Cf. Rosalie L. Colie, "Marvell's 'Bermudas' and the Puritan Paradise," *Renaissance News*, 10 (1957), 75–79.

15. See Lawrence Hyman on the androgynous Adam theme, "Marvell's 'Garden,'" *ELH*, 25 (1958), 13–22 and Maren-Sofie Røstvig, "Andrew Marvell's 'The Garden,' a Hermetic Poem," *English Studies*, 40 (1959), 65–76. For useful commentaries on nature in the mower poems and in the renaissance in general see Joseph Summers, "Marvell's Nature," *ELH*, 20 (1953), 121–35; Truesdale, "English Pastoral Verse," pp. 223–24; Jim Corder, "Marvell and Nature," *N&Q*, 6 (1959), 58–61; Harold S. Wilson, "Meaning of 'Nature' in Renaissance Literature," *JHI*, 2 (1941), 430–48.

It is impossible to say whether or not the mower poems were meant to be taken as a series, but in the original folio order (retained by Margoliouth) the progress in the Mower's dilemma up to this point of self-destruction is unmistakable and, I think, especially meaningful when considered in relation to the general pastoral pattern I have examined. The Mower's loss of identity and his alienation from nature are seen in the context of the ideal harmony of mind and landscape, nature and art, that pastoral idea and form traditionally embody.

In the first poem, the Mower is sharply critical of society's sins but has no perception of his own fallibility. His attitude leads to a clear-cut opposition between art and nature—he is simply nature's mower against society's gardens. As John D. Rosenberg writes, he surprises by the fine excess of his vituperation. His is a single but strong voice calling from the wilderness to a false civilization,[16] though to him, of course, no real wilderness exists, only a "wild and fragrant Innocence" on the one hand and total corruption on the other: imposing form on nature makes the living air a "dead and standing pool." If his voice is angry, however, it is also subtly modified. He is an articulate and lyrical Diogenes striking out against the arts of horticulture, which represent all sophistication and artful complexity:

> Luxurious Man, to bring his Vice in use,
> Did after him the World seduce:
> And from the fields the Flow'rs and Plants allure,
> Where Nature was most plain and pure.

Having already fallen, man tries to get "use" out of vice; playing Satan to nature, he forces voluptuousness upon it and causes it to become fragmented like himself: "The Pink grew then as double as his Mind; / The nutriment did change the kind." Man's natural condition is to think green thought in green

16. "Marvell and the Christian Idiom," pp. 159–60.

shade; his greatest sin is tampering with the natural forms until nature becomes a conglomeration of "forbidden mixtures," a false *hortus conclusus* locked against innocence. And in this poisonous air, the ordinary pastoral situation in which the controlled, artfully shaped green world reduces motion and flux to the benefit of the shepherd is totally inverted. Though little T. C. tells the untamed flowers what smell becomes them, the Mower can only lament such presumption:

> With strange perfumes he did the Roses taint.
> And Flow'rs themselves were taught to paint.
> The Tulip, white, did for complexion seek;
> And learn'd to interline its cheek:

The difficulty with the Mower's position is that the normal machinery for effecting a compromise between nature and art is destroyed. Because he believes any degree of civilization to be suffocating, he becomes uncritically involved in what he believes to be unfallen meadows and "sweet Fields." Whatever the polish of formal garden statues, real "Fauns and Faryes" live only in the meadow; and they far transcend artistic reproductions: "Howso'ere the Figures do excel, / The *Gods* themselves with us do dwell." The creative art of the shepherd no longer imposes order upon a potentially chaotic nature. For the Mower, "Fauns and Faryes" simply exist; they do not till the meadows, which have no need of cultivation, though Candide might sensibly warn, "cela est bien dit, mais il faut cultiver le jardin."[17]

The extent to which Marvell endorses this position is not entirely clear. The plural voicing of the conclusion, the obvious moral fervor, and the tone of personal conviction lead Rosenberg to believe that the Mower and Marvell speak more or less together, which is a justifiable conclusion but one which re-

17. Quoted from Basil Willey, *The Religion of Nature* (London, 1957), p. 15.

quires separating the poem from the rest of the series. It would seem more likely that if the Mower's point of view has Marvell's sympathy, it is a momentary and limited sympathy, overstated in order to reinforce the satire of "Luxurious Man." The succeeding poems show that a state of innocence, however desirable it may be, cannot endure and that nature is not always "plain and pure."

In "Damon the Mower," having been stung with love of Juliana, the Mower discovers a number of correspondences between his fair enemy, his own fallen state, and nature. Fair eyes and fair day, scorching sun and "am'rous care," sharp "Sythe" and "Sorrow," withered hopes and grass, all reveal a new side to man's relation to nature:

I

Heark how the Mower *Damon* Sung,
With love of *Juliana* stung!
While ev'ry thing did seem to paint
The Scene more fit for his complaint.
Like her fair Eyes the day was fair;
But scorching like his am'rous Care.
Sharp like his Sythe his Sorrow was,
And wither'd like his Hopes the Grass.

The pathetic fallacy shows the correspondences between man and nature to be something different from what the Mower first assumed. Under the influence of Juliana, nature turns quickly into a wasteland, and the Mower's identification with it on the assumption of both its innocence and his own becomes more and more a disheartening entanglement. Meadows formerly filled with Fauns are now seared with heat:

II

Oh what unusual Heats are here,
Which thus our Sun-burn'd Meadows sear!
The Grass-hopper its pipe gives ore;

And hamstring'd Frogs can dance no more.
But In the brook the green Frog wades,
And Grass-hoppers seek out the shades.
Only the Snake, that kept within,
Now glitters in its second skin.

The same scorching sun quite often causes shepherds to retreat
to the noon shade, but the Mower, taken by surprise and too
suddenly conscious of realistic animal and astronomical facts,
finds no solace there. The grasshoppers leave their singing and
the limping movement of hamstrung frogs replaces the innocent dance of the Fauns. But these creatures, at least, have
their retreats, as the snake has a second skin; the Mower's
"heat" is inner and hence beyond retreat or rebirth.

His alliance with innocence not only fails to protect him but
also fails, apparently, to impress the fair shepherdess, who is
indifferent to the breed of snakes "Disarmed of its teeth and
sting" and the "Oak leaves tipt with hony due" that he brings
her. His country achievements, related with naive braggadocio,
leave her unmoved:

VI

I am the Mower *Damon,* known
Through all the Meadows I have mown.
On me the Morn her dew distills
Before her darling Daffadils.
And, if at Noon my toil me heat,
The Sun himself licks off my Sweat.
While, going home, the Ev'ning sweet
In cowslip-water bathes my feet.

Damon's rusticity and crudeness should not, however, weaken
our response to his discovery of himself. He has a natural poetry which gradually takes on dimensions lacking in his first
expression of innocence and satiric fervor. Though his crudeness offers an ironic means for Marvell to show that rusticity

is not the same as simplicity, he is no less ingratiating for his tattered clothes. He is totally absorbed in his task, mirrored in his scythe "as in a crescent Moon the Sun" (an especially revealing simile because he gives the mirror whatever light it has). The Mower and his work define each other reciprocally, and if he were indeed "fragrant," more dear to the morning than the daffadils are and encircled always by the ring of "deathless Fairyes," his scythe would not turn against him. But the quasi-ritualistic dance of the Mower and his scythe now belongs to the past (despite the present tense):

> The deathless Fairyes take me oft
> To lead them in their Danses soft;
> And, when I tune my self to sing,
> About me they contract their Ring.

The unfortunate part of the Mower's condition, then, is not his country crudeness but his growing alienation from true simplicity. The disruption which Juliana brings distracts his mind from its true nourishment. Song and dance are given over and the protective circle is broken, as innocence ceases to be an immediate reality and becomes, like the distant reminiscence of Arcadia in much late Victorian and Georgian pastoral, an intangible property of memory. "How happy might I still have mow'd," Damon laments, "Had not Love here his Thistles sow'd!"

> But now I all the day complain,
> Joyning my Labour to my Pain;
> And with my Sythe cut down the Grass,
> Yet still my Grief is where it was:
> But, when the Iron blunter grows,
> Sighing I whet my Sythe and Woes.

Undoubtedly the Mower's self-understanding is limited here, but it is impressive in particularly Marvellian ways. The very clumsiness and the half-conscious adroitness with which he characterizes himself are dramatically functional: this is the state of one who began in innocence, fell into confusion, and does not as yet know quite what to do with himself. Like the drunken dizziness of Milton's Adam after eating the apple, the ineffectual swinging of the scythe, the "joyning" of simple labor to complex "Pain," is the first staggering movement of the *totentanz*. Woes are whetted with the scythe, grief grows where the grass falls, and eventually the fall itself comes:

> The edged Stele by careless chance
> Did into his own Ankle glance;
> And there among the Grass fell down,
> By his own Sythe, the Mower mown.

So sharp a satire could easily have upset the balance between comic absurdity and pastoral simplicity, but the Mower's awkwardness only prepares for a final (and I think generally sympathetic) irony in the recognition of death as mower, an irony leading beyond the Mower's limited vision (the poem begins and ends in the poet's own voicing). The Mower looks to death as a cure for his love wound, against which the crude folk-cures, the "Shepherds-purse, and Clowns-all-heal," will be of no use; but a more complete identity of the two mowers is implied. Damon and Death work side by side in the once innocent meadow; the unqualified quest for innocence leads to a quest for death, to the Mower mowing himself.

In going from "The Mower against Gardens" to "Damon the Mower" we discover the ambiguity of nature; in "The Mower to the Glo-Worms" nature still serves as a reminder of innocence: the Mower simply has increasing difficulty in identifying himself with it. The poem falls somewhere between idyllic and wasteland versions of pastoral. The Mower is outside a paradise irretrievably lost, and yet the myth of a perfect Eden is in some ways as real as the fact of disillusionment: the disruption of the mind's wholeness (its feeling of being "home") is the central fact of the Mower's experience, but the concept of an ideal and unfallen nature is a defining framework.

I

Ye living Lamps, by whose dear light
The Nightingale does sit so late,
And studying all the Summer-night
Her matchless Songs does meditate;

II

Ye Country Comets, that portend
No War, nor Princes funeral,
Shining unto no higher end
Then to presage the Grasses fall;

III

Ye Glo-worms, whose officious Flame
To wandring Mowers shows the way,
That in the Night have lost their aim,
And after foolish Fires do stray;

IV

Your courteous Lights in vain you wast,
Since *Juliana* here is come,
For She my Mind hath so displac'd
That I shall never find my home.

The Mower's intimate address to the "living Lamps" reveals his sense of alienation: he is lost and needs light, and the light therefore becomes "dear." The existence of an ideal world of mutual cooperation and moral order is taken for granted, but the Mower sees it from an ambiguous and confused perspective. He exists in two worlds, an innocent one of harmless comets which he now sees as an outsider and a world of experience where comets augur the fall of princes. Having addressed the glow-worms as lamps and comets, in the third apostrophe he grows more directly involved. The glow-worms, guides through the "selva oscura," the dark wood where the "straight way is lost," seem the more necessary in getting moral bearings as their service is the more helpless.

The final poem of the Mower group, "The Mower's Song," is a Song of Experience that deals with displacement in still another stage. Mowing the grass now becomes a hostile act turning the disrupted meadow itself into a "selva selvaggia" where the mind, once "the true survey / Of all these Medows fresh and gay," finds nothing but hatred and enmity. Mower and nature, like Adam and his garden, in "one common Ruine" will fall; grass will no longer serve as a companion but as "heraldry" for the Mower's tomb. Juliana thus succeeds in dividing the Mower not only from the green meadow (which continues to grow luxuriantly despite his own blight) but also from his own thoughts. In distinguishing between what he is and what he thinks, the Mower turns against himself and exhibits the very "double mind" he has cursed in "The Mower against Gardens."

Perhaps because his self-division is more severe, he is now presented less sympathetically. His attack on the meadow is apparently without self-awareness, as the half-awkward, half-witty refrain is without irony, at least of his making:

III

Unthankful Medows, could you so
A fellowship so true forego,
And in your gawdy May-games meet,
While I lay trodden under feet?
When *Juliana* came, and She
What I do to the Grass, does to my Thoughts and Me.

Marvell's detachment is revealed in the humor with which the Mower is portrayed; but at the same time, the dilemma is intensely serious. The puritanical temperament evident in "The Mower against Gardens" becomes much more prominent in the Mower's verbal laceration of the meadows. Psychological

disintegration is combined with moral aimlessness in his pledge
of common destruction:

IV

> But what you in Compassion ought,
> Shall now by my Revenge be wrought:
> And Flow'rs, and Grass, and I and all,
> Will in one common Ruine fall. . . .

V

> And thus, ye Meadows, which have been
> Companions of my thoughts more green,
> Shall now the Heraldry become
> With which I shall adorn my Tomb;
> For *Juliana* comes, and She
> What I do to the Grass, does to my Thoughts and Me.

It is appropriate that the adornment on the tomb be dead
grass—a sign both of thoughts once "more green" that Juliana
has now mown and of the flesh. After his song is finished, ar-
ranging the heraldic grass will be the Mower's last work of
art: the successful shepherd's mastery of nature through art,
mastery especially of love and death, is thus fully inverted. The
Mower's reasons for laying waste the meadows are succinctly
put, despite his limited awareness, and as accurate as they
would be for Milton's Adam: when Juliana comes, she annihilates both green shade and green thought.

The Mower's final view of himself is the product of an un-
resolved conflict between what is and what might have been,
rather than a reconciliation of what is and what ought to be.
He does not see his dilemma in sharply focused moral terms;
he simply finds his condition too real to be tolerated in the context of meadow May-games. The failure to arrive at some sort
of compromise is that of a limited persona, however, and not
necessarily an indication of Marvell's own despair of nature,

though the fear of heterosexual love is characteristic. Like "A Dialogue between the Soul and Body," the Mower poems are dramatic rather than lyric. In "Upon Appleton House," on the other hand, the mask figure, clearly a projection of the poet himself, is much more sophisticated and hence capable of discovering meaning and purpose in the "annihilation" that takes place in the forest. The process of withdrawal has several levels and ironic and symbolic resources that would have been out of place in the Mower; it is political as well as personal and involves the Fairfax family history as well as the poet's own retreat into the forest.

The personal and political elements are so strangely assorted that many critics of "Upon Appleton House" are not convinced that it succeeds in encompassing all of them. Lawrence Hyman finds in the excursion into the forest an escape from the demands of an active life—an escape the divided mind of the poet cannot sanction, which causes unrest and an intense passivity evocative of the crucifixion (stanza 87).[18] M. C. Bradbrook, while describing Marvell in Wordsworthian terms as one who extols the pleasures of the countryside and merges with it—"the whole scene takes on for him a mystic unity"—leaves other scenes essentially isolated.[19] Ruth Wallerstein, like Douglas Bush, has an inclination to read the "light Mosaic" symbolically, which would offer a way to subsume various sections of the poem within it; but she believes that religious intent should not be drawn into sections not explicitly religious: "for Marvell these scenes . . . are to be read quite simply as they appear on the surface."[20] And "on the surface" they remain largely unconnected. D. C. Allen, in attempting to inter-

18. "Politics and Poetry in Andrew Marvell," *PMLA*, 73 (1958), 475–79; cf. Empson's comments on Marvell's "acceptance of nature more masochist than passive," in *Some Versions of Pastoral*, p. 123.

19. "Marvell and the Poetry of Rural Solitude," *RES*, 17 (1941), 37–46.

20. *Studies in Seventeenth-Century Poetic*, p. 315.

pret the poem as a whole, reads the enigmatic passages more closely, with an eye to the political and literary setting. He finds the poem to be "a sequence of dramatic poems, skillfully divided, that celebrates the 'house' in several ways. It is about the actual house, the actual gardens, fields, meadows, streams, and wood. It is about the house of Fairfax in past, present, and future. It is also about the house of flesh, the body and mind of man."[21] Still, a sequence of separate dramatic poems, even linked as tightly in thematic matters as this, is not the same thing as a single, organic poem.

It would seem that, while reflecting the complex problems of the times from the civil wars to individual moral struggles, "Appleton House" manages to bring them together in a relatively unified emotional movement and to propose a common solution for them. It does so primarily through the intensity of the woodland scene, which despite the structural looseness of the poem offers Marvell an inherent symbolic view of and control over the historical disorder described earlier. The difficulty is that the woodland passage itself gives the impression of saying more in private than in public, of having secrets that might provide necessary connecting links and reveal a greater coherence in nature—and thus in the poem—than either appears to have. The explicit statement of stanza 73, however, that nature's signs, like those of books, can be read, and that the reading is a particularly happy experience, indicates that it is precisely because they have a "touch of the old symbolic and religious concept of nature as the art of God"[22] that Marvell can find them of special value in reconciling man to nature and thus to history.

21. *Image and Meaning: Metaphoric Traditions in Renaissance Poetry* (Baltimore, Johns Hopkins University Press, 1960), p. 117.

22. Douglas Bush, *English Literature in the Earlier Seventeenth Century 1600–1660* (Oxford, 1945), p. 160; cf. R. G. Cox, "A Survey of Literature from Donne to Marvell," in *From Donne to Marvell*, ed. Boris Ford (1956), pp. 62–66.

The tradition of the "book," then, is probably intended to be somewhat riddling: the lines "Thrice happy he who, not mistook, / Hath read in Natures mystick Book" sound like a private message intended perhaps for the Fairfax family whose "one History" (Marvell has been saying) has indeed taken "all the Plumes." (The body of Hermetic material with which Fairfax and Marvell were preoccupied may be involved in the riddle.[23]) But at least some relationships between the woodland and other sections of the poem are less secretive. Before Marvell reaches the woodland stage of the mystical experience, for example, he discovers signs among the creatures of the Fairfax garden that serve as preface to the book of natural signs he is about to read. An atmosphere of moral watchfulness is evident in the fort of five bastions "aiming one for ev'ry Sense" (stanza 36). In the stanzas on the garden (37 ff.), the *paysage moralisé* is vigilant against a hostile outer world; its watchful innocence, as "when Gardens only had their Towrs," reveals by contrast the unnaturalness of the fallen English garden.[24] The patrol of stars keeps guard around the pole, and the bee as sentinel is inclosed in a flower, "And sleeps so too: but, if once stir'd, / She runs you through, or askes *the Word*" (stanza 41). This description indicates the order that nature is capable of in an ideal state, and in the bee especially is a hint of what is to follow when the full lesson of nature is learned. Aristotle, Pliny, Solinus, Manuel Phile, and other early naturalists had commented upon its alert defense[25] and later Christian encyclopedists turned their remarks into tropological interpreta-

---

23. See Røstvig, "Andrew Marvell's 'The Garden,' a Hermetic Poem," p. 68.

24. Cf. Røstvig, *The Happy Man* (Oslo, 1954), 1, 55; Allen, pp. 128–29.

25. Respectively: *Historia animalium* I.9; *Natural History*, ed. Loeb, 3, 438–75; *Collectanea rerum memorabilium* (Berolini, 1864), pp. 158–59; "Versus de animalium proprietate," in *Poetae bucolici et didactici* (Paris, 1862), p. 14.

tions, keeping in mind the sting Eros received while ravaging a rose in which a bee was sleeping.[26] Francis Quarles had popularized for the seventeenth century the idea that each drop of "petty-petty sweet" was accompanied by a thousand stings.[27]

But the garden world to which the bee belongs is surrounded with dangers for the "luckless race" that has tasted the mortal apple (stanza 41). The effects of this unnatural condition are evident in an anti-pastoral regimentation that removes "tender Plants" and in their place sows "Ord'nance" and "Powder" (stanza 43), in the plundering of the wounded quail in the meadow on its perimeter, and in the spoils of the "massacred grass." History is an unfathomable "abyss" into which the poet passes, wondering how one who dives in can "rise alive." The chance deaths, the untimely funerals of the birds (stanza 52), and the monstrous elevation of grasshoppers with "squeking Laugh" destroy the fragile security of the garden, whose only troops are those "of the Tulips pinke and Rose" (stanza 39). The "parliamentary mowers," the vexing "Sun's" providential instruments (stanza 49), and Thestylis-Cromwell (as Allen calls them in *Image and Meaning*), are nearly as grotesque and even more threatening than the abyss of grass they mow: "Death-Trumpets creak in such a Note, / And 'tis the *Sourdine* in their Throat." In place of the hay harvest, the meadow lies "quilted ore with Bodies slain"; for the dance of the May is a victory dance around the bodies; and for the dance of the "deathless Fairyes" around the Mower are the victors' amazon "Females" treading "in Faery Circles"—clearly more dangerous

26. See Hugh of St. Victor, *De bestiis* 3:38 (Migne, 177:99); E. P. Evans, *Animal Symbolism in Ecclesiastical Architecture* (New York, 1896), pp. 1 ff.; Mario Praz (the transformation of the innocent world of Theocritus into that of sacred love in Otho Vaenius' emblems), *Studies in Seventeenth-Century Imagery* (London, 1947), 1, 122–23; Max Goldstaub and Richard Wendriner, *Ein tosco-venezianischer Bestiarium Herausgegeben und Erläutert*, 1892), p. 270.

27. *Emblems Divine and Moral* (London, 1858), p. 11.

in their aggressive heterosexuality than the subtle nuns who tempt the "Virgin Thwates." The scene is one of nightmarish discord, of pastoral idealism distorted by violence.

But as the Fairfax garden has suggested, reconciliation with history is possible by returning to nature, not by taking refuge in an innocent pastoralism, but by discovering in nature a way to embrace historical fact and control it at the same time. The problems of history, art, and nature, of action and contemplation are so inextricably bound up with each other that only the encompassing symbolic mode of the "mystick Book" can subsume them; and only by passing into the remote woodland can Marvell find the mythic nature he requires.

In the forest, he notices that some trees have been cut for the war but the rest "to Heaven shooting are"; he is to follow their direction, looking upward, even becoming an "inverted tree" with roots in heaven.[28] And the music that this "great Prelate of the Grove" finds in his green temple indicates further the direction that he must take:

> But I have for my Musick found
> A Sadder, yet more pleasing Sound:
> The *Stock-doves*, whose fair necks are grac'd
> With Nuptial Rings their Ensigns chast;
> Yet always, for some Cause unknown,
> Sad pair unto the Elms they moan.
> O why should such a Couple mourn,
> That in so equal Flames do burn!
> (stanza 66)

The elm tree and the doves are undoubtedly suggested by the actual Fairfax estate that Marvell ostensibly describes, but the gardens of literature are fused with the actual scene. The basis

28. See note 37, Chapter 1 on the inverted tree image; cf. A. B. Chambers, " 'I was But an Inverted Tree': Notes toward the History of an Idea," *Studies in the Renaissance*, 8 (1961), 291–99. Chapman's *Biron's Tragedy*, III.1.1, gives a political turn to the image.

for the dove's emblematic qualities, as in those of the bee, lay in the early naturalists and in the amplifications of various bestiaries which connected it to "our Savior."[29] Commenting upon the Canticles ("vox turturis audita est in terra nostra"), Hugh of St. Victor finds that by the voice of the dove is meant the sorrow of the weary mind devoted to God.[30] The dove-soul comes to the garden and builds its nest of "deliverance and safety" in the branches of the scriptural tree. When it sings its mournful song, the perceptive ear recognizes Christ's laments upon the cross and the soul's own sorrow when remembering the mystery of the crucifixion. Hugh's forest, like Marvell's, thus becomes a scriptural milieu with the tree-cross at its center and a mystic lesson to be read in its leafage.

The doves also suggest to Herman Hugo the marriage of the chaste soul to Christ. In *Pia Desideria* (II.14), which presents the scriptural forest in emblem form, a penitent sinner kneels before an apple tree in which Christ is crucified, apples and leaves hanging about so as nearly to absorb him into the tree. The prayer he utters is a mixture of Christian and classical pastoral tropes:

> Oh! who will shade me from this scorching heat?
> See on my head how the fierce Sun-beams beat!
>
> . . . .
>
> Then you I praise, dear Groves, and shady Bowers,
> Blest with cool Springs, and sweet refreshing Flow'rs,

29. *Physiologus latinus versio y*, ed. Francis J. Carmody, *University of California Publications in Classical Philology*, 12 (1933–34), 131.

30. See Migne, 177:25; cf. comments by Pliny, X:52; Phile I:24–29; St. Gregory, *Moralium*, 19:1 (Migne, 76:97); Quarles IV, xii; Crashaw, "To the Name of Jesus: A Hymn," "On a Prayer Book sent to Mrs. M.R.," "On the Assumption," and "On a Treatise of Charity"; Vaughan, "H. Scriptures"; Bede's commentary on Matt. 13:31 in Migne, 92:173–74; and other versions of the scriptural forest in Vaughan's "Jesus Weeping," "Retirement," and "The Revived"; J. Mason Neale and B. Webb, *Du Symbolisme dans les églises du moyen age* (Bourasse, 1847), p. 12.

> Then with th' expanded Poplar wou'd o'erspread,
> Or leavy Apple shade my weary head.

And Christ answers:

> Implore refreshment from the Apple's shade ...
> Beneath my shadow ease your weary grief.
> Behold my Arms strech'd on the fatal Tree!
> With these extended boughs I'll cover thee:
> Behold my bleeding feet, my gaping side!
> In these free Coverts thou thy self maist hide.
> This shade will grant thee thy desir'd repose,
> This Tree alone for that kind purpose grows.

There, pensive, the speaker continues, "I'll bewail my wretched State, / Like a sad Turtle widow'd of her Mate"; his tears will flow like Christ's blood as he embraces the fatal tree and writes this "sad inscription": "Two Lovers see, who their own Deaths conspire! / She drowns in Tears, while He consumes in Fire."

The mixture of secular and divine Eros and of world-weariness and religious hope is more explicit here than in Marvell. And in an emblem, unlike a regular poem, the fusion of Christ and forest can be made graphic. That Marvell intends something similar, however, seems very likely to be the purpose of the biblical-erotic language in the description of the grove and the explicit guidance offered by stanza 73. The paradoxical song—the "Sadder, yet more pleasing Sound"—of the doves replaces the song of the nightingale, the poet's bird (in Herbert's "Jordan, 1" and Vaughan's "Idle Verse," the bird of nonreligious poets). The doves have more endurance and more contact with the world of thorns than the nightingale, for whom "The Thorn, lest it should hurt her, draws / Within the Skin its shrunken claws" (stanza 65). Like Hugo's repentant sinner, they are consumed by the fire of celestial love but at the same time "drowned in the tears" of that love's imperfection

in its historical form: "O why should such a Couple mourn, /
That in so equal flames do burn!" Like Damon in "Clorinda
and Damon" Marvell is a kind of voyeur-participant in a divine Eros that transcends both the autoeroticism of the reclusive
life and the violent heterosexuality of the amazons and Julianas
that inevitably destroy the pastoral haven.

In contrast, the "Suttle Nunns" have attempted to draw the
virgin Thwates into a seclusion designed to avoid altogether
the conflicts of the *conditio humanitatis,* making "tears" those
only of celibate pleasure:

> 'Within this holy leisure we
> 'Live innocently as you see.
> 'These Walls restrain the World without
> . . . .
> 'Not Tears of Grief; but such as those
> 'With which calm Pleasure overflows;
> (stanzas 13, 15)

Though heavenly innocence and sheltered virtue cannot be
properties of an active life, the "wooden Saints" would have
the family ancestor believe that she is even now angelic:

> 'I see the Angels in a Crown
> 'On you the Lillies show'ring down:
> 'And round about you Glory breaks,
> 'That something more than humane speaks.
> 'All Beauty, when at such a height,
> 'Is so already consecrate.
> (stanzas 18, 19)

She will become the mediary between them and heaven until
sanctity grows so fast that "miracles it works at last" (stanza
21). By the end of the poem Marvell will give a lesson in pay-
ing compliments; at this stage we see only that the nunnery
cannot properly be a "Religious House" (stanza 35) until the
masculine vigor of Fairfax destroys it and establishes the family

line, the fort of five bastions, and the regimentation of an active, Protestant moral sense. Even at the risk of violence, the homoerotic principle of sheltered Beauty and sisters "consecrate" must give way to the heterosexual principle of the active life, though the subtle nuns ask of Fairfax,

> '. . . can he such a *Rival* seem
> 'For whom you *Heav'n* should disesteem?
> 'Ah, no! and 'twould more Honour prove
> 'He your *Devoto* were, then *Love*.
>
> (stanza 19)

That virtue is actively committed to history, then, would seem to be the lesson Marvell has learned from both the family history and his experience in the meadow by the time he enters the forest. Though he has lamented the fall from Edenic innocence that places holders of real muskets where there had been only the sweet militia of flowers, the Fairfax family weeds ambition and restores the sensitive plant of conscience. The loss of innocence is the gain of "Flowrs eternal, and divine, / That in the Crowns of Saints do shine" (stanza 45). It is necessary, however, to transmute the struggle into the scriptural symbolism of the grove in order to overcome its dangers and purge it of reclusive, Catholic connotations. Thus the poet retires "from the Flood" and takes "Sanctuary" in the forest (stanza 61) as in an ark.[31] Darkness gives way and the grove opens to discovery,

> And in as loose an order grows,
> As the *Corinthean Porticoes*.
> The arching Boughs unite between
> The Columnes of the Temple green;
> And underneath the winged Quires
> Echo about their tuned Fires.
>
> (stanza 64)

31. The ark as sanctuary and temple is a common figure.

The forest is "loose" but stable, with boughs arched and united and trees forming supporting columns. The birds contribute a harmony noticeably absent in the creaking death note of the meadow fowl (stanza 52), and the threat of eroticism is removed by amorous trees that block all the darts Beauty aims at the heart. Although it is now difficult to obtain a clear index to the meaning of many of the creatures from the brief description, the caterpillars, strawberries, serpent, crocodile, woodpecker, and so on are presented as though their importance extended beyond their physical presence in the woodland. Bestiaries and other books of creatures overlook none of these, but Marvell gives special emphasis only to the woodpecker. Like Hugh's woodpecker,[32] Marvell's "hewel" has an uncommon ability to divine the soundness of his future home and steadfastly to root out whatever he finds unsuitable, felling even the tallest royal oak because it is tainted within. Its battle with the "worm" (whatever the "tree" may be), when connected with the "luckless Apple," suggests that what is required before state affairs can be straightened out is a strong moral sense. Because it "examines well / Which fit to stand and which to fell," it is one of those creatures the "easie Philosopher" finds it especially profitable to "confer" with. The oak, perhaps like Charles I, would not have been felled had it not fed

> A *Traitor-worm*, within it bred.
> (As first our Flesh corrupt within
> Tempts impotent and bashful Sin.[)]
>   (stanza 70)

Hence the erotic-religious terms in which Marvell addresses the woodbines should come as no surprise:

> Bind me ye *Woodbines* in your 'twines,
> Curle me about ye gadding *Vines*,
> And Oh so close your Circles lace,

32. *De bestiis*, III, 32, 95–96; cf. Allen, pp. 144–45.

That I may never leave this Place:
But, lest your Fetters prove too weak,
Ere I your Silken Bondage break,
Do you, *O Brambles,* chain me too,
And courteous *Briars* nail me through.

(stanza 77)

When we have seen the grove as a *paysage moralisé* whose spiritual authority is clinched by brambles and briars, this will perhaps seem less an eccentric and unmotivated outbreak of masochism and dendro-eroticism than a logical outgrowth of the harsher, "sadder" truth, symbolized by the doves, that alone is able to cope with a world so disordered. Unlike the "sweet Chordage" of "A Dialogue" or the "winding Snare" of "The Coronet," nature's bondage must not be broken; it must bind tighter, until the thorns are felt. (A commonplace observation of Jonathan Edwards suggests why Marvell thinks of the nails in the context of the brambles: roses grow on briars to signify that "pure happiness, the crown of glory, is to be come at no other way than by bearing Christ's cross, by a life of mortification."[33])

This passionate apostrophe, like the rest of the woodland experience, is projected in a semi-humorous mood, as though reading in this increasingly outmoded book of nature required taking refuge behind a shield of irony. The commitment to the "mystic Book" seems vital enough, however. The "sensuous self-identification," the "sense of unity," and the "masochistic passivity" that critics have found in the passage depend upon the validity of the symbols. Marvell knows the "play" to be an imaginative and childlike gesture, as he indicates in stanza 74, but he is nevertheless taken by the "actors" that present the divine pageant. Although his awareness of the stage as stage is greater than Vaughan's or Traherne's in comparable forest scenes, he is no less serious.

33. *Images or Shadows of Divine Things,* p. 43.

It may be that we find the experience more convincing, certainly more encompassing, *because* of the tonal complexity. We do not expect to find a poet as modern as Marvell absorbing tradition without some awareness of his distance from it. The impulse is still with us to want nature to be like that, but an intimate and complex relation of poet to symbol is no longer possible in the same way.

> Time and the bell have buried the day,
> The black cloud carries the sun away.
> Will the sunflower turn to us, will the clematis
> Stray down, bend to us; tendril and spray
> Clutch and cling?

These plants, from Eliot's "Burnt Norton," though they follow the sun and are thus regulated by an order "above," are obviously not personal messengers of providence. The mood is meditative and interrogative, the relation of poet to object impersonal except, perhaps, for an underlying fear they have in common of the "black cloud" carrying the sun away. "Will the sunflower and clematis, having no sun, now cling to us, who have none either?"

The identity of nature and man which occurs even in late renaissance poetics results in a different kind of pastoral, however. The lesson of Herrick's "Marygolds," for example, depends on a certain erotic-botanical transcendence:

> Give way, and be ye ravisht by the Sun
> (And hang the head when as the Act is done)
> Spread as He spreads, wax less as He do's wane;
> And as He shuts, close up to Maids again.

The marigolds, being helio-tropes, take their significance from the sun; but the vegetative fact derives its metaphoric value from its parallels in man's relation to God. A second statement, "be open to God and to nothing else," is thus suggested by the

marigolds themselves in dialogue with the voyeur (as Whichcote makes more explicit in his statement, "the soul of man
to God is as the flower to the sun; it opens at its approach and
shuts when it withdraws"[34]). Because the world is an emblematic rose garden, only failure to see the temporal object clearly,
and not an inevitable "black cloud," can carry the symbolic
meaning away. Nature "lovers" with their strange variety of
eroticism are not necessarily existence-haters, though the masochistic violence of Marvell's woodlands may suggest an un-
recognized, compensatory laceration.

Although Marvell's self-conscious irony in the woodland
seems on the verge of modernity, then, the forest as avatar reflects enough of the old analogical pattern to make his involvement, his symbolic crucifixion, enough of an annihilation to
clear the air. When he leaves the forest, he does not close the
book of nature entirely, but his experience lacks the intensity
it has had. By incorporating the particular times into a vision
transcending history, the forest experience has enabled him to
prophesy the future and consume "all the Plumes" of the past
("What Rome, Greece, Palestine, ere said / I in this light Mo-
saick read"). Mythic, providential time filters into human
time like light screened through "these scatter'd *Sibyls* Leaves"
out of which the fancy "weaves" its prophecies. After this, the
final section, which returns more directly to the Fairfax family,
is somewhat anticlimactic, though it has an important contribution to make in completing the emergence pattern and fulfilling the antic mood of the "easie Philosopher."

As Miss Røstvig writes, Mary Fairfax is an important element in the structure of the poem: "The garden at Nun Appleton derives its ordered beauty from her; she is the only image

---

34. *Aphorisms*, no. 26; cf. V. de S. Pinto, *Peter Sterry*, p. 127; Donne,
Candlemas Day Sermon, *LXXX Sermons*, 9; Vaughan, "And man is such
a Marygold, these fled, / That shuts, and hangs the head" (in "Sure, there's
a tye").

of Paradise, while the outside world is 'but a rude heap together hurl'd; / All negligently overthrown.' "[35] Though there seems to be less imaginative conviction in her symbolic value than in that of the grove, her capacity to order chaos is not unrelated to the lesson of the woodland. In the presence of her "that already is the *Law* / Of all her *Sex,* her *Ages Aw,*" and who sums up all that has been loosely lying about, Marvell puts aside the "toys" with which he has amused himself in the role of voyeur-boy:

> See how loose Nature, in respect
> To her, it self doth recollect;
> And everything so whisht and fine,
> Starts forth with to its *Bonne Mine.*
>
> (stanza 83)

Mary Fairfax is thus made an active prototype of the virtue previously contained in the fort of five bastions and present finally in a purified nature: "by her Flames, in Heaven try'd, / Nature is wholly vitrifi'd."[36] That is, by this flame, as by the tuned fires of the grove and to a lesser extent by the "equal Fires" of the garden, nature's opaque materiality is rendered transparent like crystal; one can see through it and beyond. This comes about through her imitation of an archetypal pattern that gives order to all creatures:

> 'Tis *She* that to these Gardens gave
> That wondrous Beauty which they have;
> *She* streightness on the Woods bestows;
> To *Her* the Meadow sweetness owes;
>
> (stanza 87)

She replaces the homoeroticism of the sisters and the threat of

---

35. *The Happy Man,* p. 255.

36. Cf. *OED:* " 'Surely, that grand Universal-fire . . . at the day of judgment may by its violent ardor vitrifie and turn to one lump of Crystal, the whole Body of the Earth' (Howell, Lett. I, 1. xxix)."

the amazons with goddess-femininity, which, because it is goddess-like, is far enough above the poet to preserve his role as passive onlooker and eulogist. As the poet had begun to call in the language of the birds (stanza 72), so Mary, raised to higher beauties (not alone by learning classical languages from her tutor),

> Disdains to be for lesser prais'd.
> *She* counts her Beauty to converse
> In all the Languages as *hers;* . . .
> Nor yet that *Wisdome* would affect,
> But as 'tis *Heavens Dialect.*
>
> (stanza 89)

The struggle described in the earlier sections of the poem, having been transmuted into the terms of the forest, thus devolves upon her. She is a modest halcyon flying "twixt Day and Night" calming the "horrors" and easily winning the wars of love which threaten her (stanza 90). But the Fairfax line must be preserved; and so "for some universal good, / The *Priest* shall cut the sacred Bud," not as a crude act of lust and violence but as a ceremony that further sanctifies the "family tree," the "Fairfacian Oak" (stanza 93), and enables it to endure in history. The metaphoric identity of family and forest (stanza 62, 93) reinforces the final reconciliation with destiny: ". . . her *glad Parents* must rejoice, / And make their *Destiny* their *Choice,*" as the poet has conceded the heterosexual requirements of the world of action. Mary's "heaven" is "domestic" (stanza 91) but much more than that. In a sense, as Marvell's pun brings out, celestial, active "Goodness" is as much an impregnating principle as the "Suttle Nunns" have found "the great *Bridegroom*" to be:

> And *Goodness* doth it self intail
> On *Females,* if there want a *Male.*
>
> (stanza 91)

As he apotheosizes the fair maiden, however, Marvell cannot resist incantation against the dark Ladies. He casts off the remaining feminine demons under the combined aegis of knowledge and virtue, the alliance of Neoplatonist and Protestant qualities that uphold the Resolved Soul and sustain Cromwell in "An Horatian Ode." For it is knowledge and virtue that "till" the furrows and set nature straight (stanza 92). Even the meadows, formerly the scene of the civil war allegory, are now "fresher dy'd" a deeper green (stanza 79) as nature is reborn after the struggle and new grass springs up where the hay was "fal'n and dry'd." The now quiet stream is the meadow's only "Snake," a harmless thread "Betwixt two Labyrinths":[37]

> See in what wanton harmless folds
> It ev'ry where the Meadow holds;
> And its yet muddy back doth lick,
> Till as a *Chrystal Mirrour* slick;
> Where all things gaze themselves, and doubt
> If they be in it or without.
> And for his shade which therein shines,
> *Narcissus* like, the *Sun* too pines.
>
> (stanza 80)

Unlike former historical gardens, more luxuriant perhaps, but also more wanton (stanza 95), and unlike Created Pleasure's "Crystal," vitrified nature on the Fairfax estate is a perfect mirror of the "Sun" that gazes into it. Marvell can vegetate on the river bank, staked down safely where the "Floods did lately drown," temples crowned "with heavy sedge," because it is indeed true that now

> 'Tis not, what once it was, the *World;*
> But a rude heap together hurl'd;
> All negligently overthrown,

37. The Nile (stanza 79) is sometimes a symbol for national health and sovereignty, as in the chorus of Daniel's *Cleopatra* beginning "And canst, O Nilus, thou . . ."

> Gulfes, Deserts, Precipices, Stone.[38]
> Your lesser *World* contains the same.
> But in more decent Order tame;
> *You Heaven's Center, Nature's Lap.*
> *And Paradice's only Map.*
>
> (stanza 96)

In the presence of such protections, if the poet speaks the
"learned original" of the mystic book—and has a patron like
Thomas Fairfax—the "dark *Hemisphere*" is not threatening.
It becomes comfortably like salmon fishermen with canoes on
their heads (stanza 97), or like rational turtles carrying their
means of withdrawal and emergence, their own Appleton
Houses, with them.[39]

"The Nymph Complaining for the Death of Her Faun," like
"Upon Appleton House," has seemed to critics especially enigmatic. Whether or not or to what extent it is a religious allegory, for example, and whether its allusions are directly rele-
vant or indirectly enriching have become questions of some
nicety.[40] Its abundant store of literary allusions compounds
critical problems because even if we assume at the outset that
an allegory to which a key can be supplied is not the primary

38. This stanza means, I think, that the world is now changed for the
better (no longer being "but" a rude heap) through incorporation into
Mary's world, which is better still (cf. stanza 87: "*She* yet more Pure,
Sweet, Streight, and Fair, / Then Gardens, Woods, Meads, Rivers are");
it probably does not mean, as Margoliouth, Allen, and Røstvig take it, that
by comparison to her world, the larger world is not as it was but instead a
rude heap. Cooke, Thompson, and Grosart place a comma after "world"
which makes the former reading clearer, but as the next line shows, a semi-
colon could also be used to separate appositional modifiers.

39. T. S. Eliot finds "misshapen bodies" still evident in the imagery of
the final stanza: see "Andrew Marvell," in *Selected Essays*, p. 256; cf.
George Williamson, *The Donne Tradition*, pp. 154, 174.

40. See D. C. Allen, "Marvell's 'Nymph,'" *ELH*, 23 (1956), 93–111
(also in *Image and Meaning*, pp. 93–114); Leo Spitzer, "Marvell's
'Nymph . . .': Sources versus Meaning," *MLQ*, 19 (1958), 231–43.

mode of the poem, the temptation to get beyond or underneath the surface is strong. Ruel E. Foster, for instance, appropriately suggests that the poem is a stylized piece in which "the nymph, fawn and garden are prototypal figures of the pastoral," figures whose primitivism is set against civilization (the troopers) and who emerge "superior to the world which destroys them."[41] Like most pastorals resembling Empson's "versions," it works a "subtle reversal of values." Thus the fawn is a "form of the pure human soul slain by the world" complicated and enriched by allusions to saints and Christ. Foster concludes this suggestive reading of the poem, however, by stating that "for the critic who evaluates poetry solely in terms of craftsmanship, as well as for the average reader who asks only of poetry that it give him a few moments 'out of space, out of time,' this is a profoundly satisfying poem," which takes away as much with one hand as it gives with the other.

A charming story, even of an unfortunate nymph, does not necessarily, of course, lack significance, nor must it achieve its significance through allegory.[42] Rather, it may have its own meaning and parabolic extensions; it may be mythic in a manner that combines the simplicity of the fable and the complex, involuted fabric of allusive technique. Such would seem to be the case with "The Nymph," the simple lyric grace and pathos of which are apt to make us overlook the serious dilemma it explores. Despite the fragility of the nymph's protection in the secluded corner of the forest, Marvell does not present her monologue in a simple mood of lamentation. The decorum is that of the "complaint," but the nymph is not in fact easily

41. "A Tonal Study: Marvell, 'A Nymph . . . ,'" *University of Kansas City Review*, 22 (1955), 74.
42. See Karina Williamson, "Marvell's 'The Nymph . . .,' a Reply," *MP*, 51 (1953-54), 268-71; Edward Le Comte, "Marvell's 'The Nymph . . .,'" *MP*, 50 (1952-53), 97-101; Emerson, "Andrew Marvell's *The Nymph* . . .," *Études Anglaises*, 8 (1955), 105-10; Legouis, "Réponse à E. A. Emerson," ibid., 111-12.

destroyed, thanks largely to her own remarkable powers of transformation. She has been quite satisfied, for example, in exchanging a false lover for the fawn, which she converts into a kind of virgin saint associated with holy "Frankincense" and the "brotherless Heliades." When everything else fails, she finds consolation in tragic mechanisms, with their ceremonies and weeping marble statues. Most centrally, however, the virginal sense of deprivation and unfulfillment over which the nymph has brooded has led her, as D. C. Allen writes, to enlarge "the token of love into a life symbol"[43] a symbol reaching backward into the mythic time of saints' lives, the lives of blessed creatures, and even the life of Christ—though the poet and his readers are more aware of these particular implications than the nymph. For if the implications are manifold, her monologue itself seems on the surface very simple, with the simplicity of primitive myth:

> The wanton Troopers riding by
> Have shot my Faun and it will dye.
> Ungentle men! They cannot thrive
> To kill thee. Thou neer didst alive
> Them any harm: alas nor cou'd
> Thy death yet do them any good.
> I'me sure I never wisht them ill;
> Nor do I for all this; nor will:
> But, if my simple Pray'rs may yet
> Prevail with Heaven to forget
> Thy murder, I will Joyn my Tears
> Rather then fail.

The Ancient Mariner's slaying of the albatross, as Foster suggests, is parallel in some ways. The troopers, like the Mariner, have deranged "the primal order of nature, so nature will turn on them and destroy them,"[44] or, more accurately, God may.

43. *Image and Meaning*, p. 94.
44. "A Tonal Study," p. 75.

It is the "wantonness" of the original sin that makes it inexplicable and causes the nymph to interrupt her narrative with impassioned apostrophes to the fawn and the troopers. Because the troopers had nothing to gain, her attempts to rationalize the slaying are fruitless.

The killing is especially disturbing to one whose impulses are gentle and whose basic mercy demands that she intercede with heaven on behalf of the troopers. On the other hand, however, the gentleness runs counter to her personal "fears"; and in the clash between the impulse to embrace, to create mythic beauty and ritual, and even art, out of murder and the impulse of fear, Marvell explores the difficulty of maintaining kind-hearted innocence in a "wanton" forest. The fact that the fawn will die, stated with such apparent resignation at first, becomes increasingly unbelievable to the nymph as she reflects upon what she supposes to be a just world:

> But, O my fears!
> It cannot dye so. Heavens King
> Keeps register of every thing:
> And nothing may we use in vain.
> Ev'n Beasts must be with justice slain;
> Else Men are made their *Deodands*.
> Though they should wash their guilty hands
> In this warm life-blood, which doth part
> From thine, and wound me to the Heart,
> Yet could they not be clean: their Stain
> Is dy'd in such a Purple Grain.
> There is not such another in
> The World, to offer for their Sin.

Mercy is based on selflessness but justice on the rights of the self, and even beasts have their rights. How then can mercy and justice be reconciled? If "Heavens King" keeps an accurate register, all wantonness and guilt will be requited and no prayer can "Prevail with Heaven to forget." And if no blood-letting ritual will atone for this sin, violence must be answered with violence rather than with gentleness:[45] men must be made sacrifices ("Deodands") to divine wrath. The contrast between ineffectual handwashing and the Atonement (the first definite religious allusion) enters the fable as an inclusive dimension rather than as an allegorical identity defining the fawn itself: because there is not "such another in / The World, to offer for their Sin," the history of Christ-fawns has only negative application, the focus on the nymph and the fawn as such becoming all the sharper through it. The nymph's dilemma forces us to recognize that to examine the slaying solely in terms of nature and natural atonement is insufficient —the stain, as the nymph realizes, goes too deep to be set straight in terms of what is "in / The World." The warm life-blood of the fawn, then, wounds her "to the heart," because it will not cleanse the murderers' hands. Put in these terms, the problem refuses to be mythologized.

The difficulties are compounded by the fact that the nymph sees in the fawn the constancy, tameness, and virginal purity she prescribes for herself. Because innocence fosters identification rather than dialectic, part of herself has been slain with the fawn. In effect, she has come to deify what cannot serve as deity and to take upon herself an intercessional office she cannot perform. The history of how she came to do this occupies the bulk of the poem. In the light of her desire for gentleness and virginal inviolability and the tradition of pastoral nymphs rejecting lovers, Sylvio's inconstancy and sudden turn to wildness become understandable, if not excusable. He, too, understands something of nature's "primal simplicity." She recalls but probably does not clearly understand his small joke when presenting the fawn to her:

45. Legouis correctly reads 'this warm life-blood which departs from thine (heart) and wounds me to (my) heart' (lines 19–20). See Legouis, "Marvell's 'Nymph . . .': A *Mise au Point,*" *MLQ,* 21 (1960), 31, and Spitzer, p. 234.

Said He, look how your Huntsman here
Hath taught a Faun to hunt his *Dear*.

Underneath the joke, of course, lay the sharp laws of the love
hunt in which gifts are designed to lead the hunter to his prey.
But one need not become an *advocatus Sylvii* to see that to take
the nymph's view of this harshness for Marvell's would be to
oversimplify things. The difficulty is that both the nymph's
impulse to tame things and Sylvio's wildness are equally natural, or at least equally part of the world the nymph has to
confront. Sylvio is the forest, she the maker of secluded gardens; the fawn lives in each world in turn and through its
attractiveness draws her emotionally into the forest (as Sylvio
thought it would, but in another way), the existence of which
cannot be ignored even in the protected corner. And the gifts
of the forest the forest can reclaim. Virginal love depends upon
a sanctity which the world does not freely offer, and human
love, which is a mixed affair somewhere between wildness and
gentleness, art and nature, is nearly as antagonistic to the
nymph as the murder itself. The garden and the forest, like
mercy and justice, stand opposed. Marvell presents both the
beauty of her innocence and her inability to reconcile innocence and the struggle of the forest.

In reconstructing the nymph's psychological biography,
critics have tended to omit the latter aspect, making her own
predicted death a result simply of the hunters' and Sylvio's
cruelty. (Spitzer, for example, takes Sylvio's words to be a ruthless mixture of huntsman's frivolity and heartlessness, and ab-
solves the nymph herself of all blame.[46]) She is obviously too

46. The nymph's simple words and syntax "carry a sense of convincing-
ness and sincerity. What is more, the repetitious phrasing seems to imply
that the maiden, even now, must make an effort not to wince at the hurting
quality which those words still contain" (Spitzer, pp. 234–35). In like
manner, the nymph's description of the fawn's metamorphosis is taken to
argue solely for innocence and simplicity. Eliot's original definition of wit

good a poet, however, to be killed by the fawn's death. It is she rather than Marvell who converts the fawn's tears into an offering at Diana's shrine and desires that the statue be erected lacking both the red of guilt and (as Allen points out) the red of sentient life. Likewise, her reaction to the first disappointment, the substitution of a tame creature for a wild one, despite its ingratiating simplicity and beauty, is not without its drawbacks:

> Thenceforth I set my self to play
> My solitary time away,
> With this: and very well content,
> Could so mine idle Life have spent.
> For it was full of sport; and light
> Of foot, and heart; and did invite,
> Me to its game: it seem'd to bless
> Its self in me. How could I less
> Than love it? O I cannot be
> Unkind, t' a Beast that loveth me.

The fawn seems more attractive than Sylvio partly because she can identify with it and assimilate it more easily into the world of "sweetest milk, and sugar." Though it may prove false, its "Love was far more better then / The Love of false and cruel men," who remain enigmas to her. The ceremonies and games of innocence thus gradually repair one sorrow only to increase the likelihood of a greater one. Because Sylvio has abandoned the garden and the "beast" has apparently abandoned the forest, it momentarily seems possible for each world successfully to exclude the other. The nymph, the fawn walking al-

---

as something involving "a recognition, implicit in the expression of every experience, of the other experiences which are possible" would seem more appropriate to the poem. This does not mean, of course, that the poet gratuitously adds details to an experience but that he looks upon it in a complex frame of mind. Wit "is not cynicism, though it has a kind of toughness which may be confused with cynicism by the tender-minded. . . . It is confused with cynicism because it implies a constant inspection and criticism of experience" (*Selected Essays*, p. 262).

most incorporeally "on the four Winds," and the seclusion compose a harmonious place apart from the "hunt." The fawn gradually merges, or appears to merge, with the roses and lilies until even its hoof becomes "more soft, / And white, (shall I say then my hand?) / NAY any Ladies of the Land."

But attributing "virgin Limbs" to it and comparing the lilies on which it lies to "whitest sheets" are her own interpolations. Through all the nymph's remarkable description runs an underlying incongruity between dream and reality; beginning the poem with a simple statement of fact ensures our awareness of the discrepancy. While in her dream the fawn barely touches earth, in reality it lies bleeding; the red of the rose-stain can no more replace real blood than the fawn has replaced Sylvio. It is a beautiful fiction, but a fiction, that "*Had* it liv'd long, it would have been / Lillies without, Roses within." For the nymph, however, the transformation of the dual nature of the wild hunt and tame love into the mono-virginal garden was nearly complete when the "wanton" troopers rode by. Strongly fortified by the dream, she converts even the marks of death into symbols. Despite the irremovable stain of the slaying, purity becomes her sole concern and an Elysium of "Swans and Turtles," "milk-white Lambs, and Ermins pure" helps her set aside the difficult conflict of mercy and justice, forest and garden. The last ceremony is to "bespeak" the grave and then, she believes, to die.

The statue she desires will be an accurate mirror of herself, but she perhaps speaks more truly than she knows when saying, "I shall weep though I be Stone": the conflict of cold passivity and warmth will continue.[47] The "white thought in a

47. The statue image may have been suggested by Ariosto's *Orlando Furioso* as well as by the Niobe myth: when Ruggiero sees Angelica bound to a rock in Britain on the Island of Tears, the home of a savage people, he could have "thought she was a statue, made of alabaster . . . if he had not seen, among fresh roses and white lilies, unmistakable tears making the unripe apples dewy" (X.96 ff., trans. Allan Gilbert, New York, 1954).

white shade," as Allen appropriately phrases it, like the Mower's original quest for an impossible innocence, is a rejection of the traditional pastoral compromise. As an artist, she does not consciously embrace and reorder life, despite her obvious creative powers. But human tears will wear away the stone anyway, marring, or rather making more realistic, the art that will adorn the garden. Thus, what she means to be a simple shrine Marvell makes a symbol of her dilemma. If Shakespeare's Hermione is a statue coming to life, the nymph is life wishing to become a statue. And one can easily believe that, while fully aware of the tragedy of the violated garden—as the poet of "The Coronet," the mower poems, and "Upon Appleton House" would be—Marvell means to imply that it would be better if the red were not missing. The suggestion at the beginning that the nymph is faced with a problem she cannot solve except by leaving the world is now less obliquely made. The focus remains upon her dilemma and her failure. If the religious allusions suggest an Atonement that might have solved the dilemma, it is not the business of the poem to explore them; rather, Marvell examines the way of innocence, which, even in its retreat to a garden of surpassing beauty, is inevitably vulnerable to whatever wantonness happens simply to be "riding by."

The pastorals I have examined might be said to be studies in partial and oblique perspectives. The mower poems and "The Nymph" explore through limited personae an inability to reconcile love, art, and death with the quest for ideal being. The "elementary link" of men to nature proves too strong: the nymph ironically becomes the deodand she fears justice will demand, sacrificing herself, in imagination at least, upon the altar of chastity. "Clorinda and Damon" and "Bermudas," brilliant in their way, are perhaps too dependent upon a particular view of nature and religious experience to carry, now, the conviction they might conceivably have had in Marvell's day. The structure of "Upon Appleton House," despite the richness of certain passages and the ambition of the poem as a whole, is loose and its book of creatures restrictive in symbolic mode.

"The Garden" goes beyond these poems in bringing together similar elements of Marvell's sensibility. It combines pastoral themes with the modes of religious meditation, satire, and the philosophical lyric, and in doing so undertakes formal difficulties that seem imposing from any angle we approach them. The mood of "Gestimmtheit" or "letting things be," in Heidegger's phrase, has to prevail through difficult philosophical distinctions, through awareness of the absurdities of man's chase after nymphs and social position, and above all, through awareness of the "fall," the effects of which permeate every moment and activity of the garden. The response of modern readers to the poem, however, testifies that it is essentially one thing, not a composite of several—in fact, the structural and stylistic problems of fusing these elements are solved with such skill that they could be overlooked altogether or, as has happened more often, be understood in partial and simplified ways with a corresponding reduction in the scope and meaning of the poem.[48]

As Lovejoy has pointed out, Christian-Platonists from Au-

---

48. Critical simplification is not an unmixed evil if it leads to something we might otherwise not have observed. Criticism of "The Garden" often appears to be in conflict—and is, if taken from a strictly partisan point of view—but it illuminates various aspects of a complex poem. See Rostvig, "Andrew Marvell's 'The Garden': A Hermetic Poem," 65–76, and *The Happy Man*, pp. 254–66; Milton Klonsky, "A Guide through the Garden," *58* (1950), 16–35; Legouis, "Marvell and the New Critics," *RES*, 8 (1957), 382–89; Wallerstein, pp. 319–34; M. C. Bradbrook and M. G. Lloyd Thomas, "Marvell and the Concept of Metamorphosis," *The Criterion*, 18 (1938–39), 236–54; M. C. Bradbrook, "Marvell and the Poetry of Rural Solitude," *RES*, 17 (1941), 37–46; Harold Wendell Smith, "Cowley, Marvell and the Second Temple," *Scrutiny*, 19 (1953), 189 ff.; Empson, *Pastoral*, pp. 119–32.

gustine to Ficino and the Cambridge Platonists attempt without complete success to reconcile opposing attitudes towards created plenitude. And we have seen that Marvell, like the Cambridge group, both rejects lower links in the great chain for the autonomy of the soul and yet in other poems embraces them, for themselves and as symbolic media or *vestigia dei.* Because it is not ontologically existent, not something constructed out of real materials by a "skillful Gardner," a strictly Neoplatonic garden of Ideas avoids the problem: the mind intuits its ideas without issuing outward among "each kind." It is a retreat *from* the world to a similar but exalted ideal construction rather than a withdrawal *within* the world. As Paul Henry writes, a Platonic "anchoritism of the soul and of God excludes at once all sacramentalism and all true history of becoming. The latent actuality of salvation and the cold transcendence of God make it impossible, in terms of Plotinian Socratism, to conceive of any genuine doctrine of grace."[49] But pastoral as such, as we have seen, is not ordinarily inhospitable to such doctrine. The difference would seem to be of some importance to an understanding of "The Garden": if the nymph's garden and the Mower's meadow are insecure places because Platonic, Christian, and pastoral elements cannot be harmonized, the "garden" is secure because they can be— though Juliana and the wanton troopers are locked out to begin with. The reconciliation is not easily brought about, but perhaps for this reason the poem surpasses most of Marvell's other lyrics in both intensity and ambition.

As a form of pastoral idyll as well as a lyric, "The Garden" begins by closing off a secluded place from the world of "uncessant Labours" where one labors to gain only a "short and narrow verged Shade" and where the only rewards are social.

49. *Plotinus: The Enneads* (London, 1956), p. xxxvii; cf. Emile Brehier, *The Philosophy of Plotinus* (Chicago, 1958), pp. 55–56.

Dasein—a "being *there*" or projected being—becomes "a prey to the things in the world . . . alienated to its own authentic possibilities."[50] This is not a garden of either middle class enterprise or courtly decadence. Both Puritan industry and the cavalier pursuit of nymphs are excluded; the gay, soul-making, solitary wanderer is shut in:

I

How vainly men themselves amaze
To win the Palm, the Oke, or Bayes;
And their uncessant Labours see
Crown'd from some single Herb or Tree.
Whose short and narrow verged Shade
Does prudently their Toyles upbraid;
While all Flow'rs and all Trees do close
To weave the Garlands of repose.

As in the strange economics of the exchange of kids and lambs in the first idyll of Theocritus, the inter-twisted puns of the first stanza reflect the sophisticated toil that occupies the social poet. For industry one is rewarded prudently, that is, with the niggardly providence of the Puritans, whereas the rewards of the garden are abundant, absorbing the poet into them. To become reconciled with nature, the poet must become thoroughly vegetative. Instead of twisting the "Palm, the Oke, or Bayes" into man-made rewards, he must temporarily abandon his claims to civilized culture. Nature thus absorbed in repose is protective, but twisted into laurels is a netted snare (a "toil") which "upbraids" vain labor and leads to labyrinthian "mazes."

Up to this point there is little to which Plotinus might not agree: "Human beings, when weak on the side of contemplation," he writes, "find in action their trace of vision and reason: their spiritual feebleness unfits them for contemplation; they

50. Heidegger, *Existence and Being*, p. 42.

are left in a void, because they cannot adequately seize the vision; yet they long for it; they are hurried into action as their way to the vision which they cannot attain by intellection" (*Enneads* III.8.4). But the emphasis upon absorption rather than transcendence is not precisely Neoplatonic, and it is upon this note that the poem will end. Even before that, however, the goddesses descend, to be incarnated in the plants, instead of beckoning the wanderer upward out of himself:

II

Fair quiet, have I found thee here,
And Innocence thy Sister dear!
Mistaken long, I sought you then
In busie Companies of Men.
Your sacred Plants, if here below,
Only among the Plants will grow.
Society is all but rude,
To this delicious Solitude.

Society's rudeness is doubly expensive because it lacks both the civility a city culture might be expected to have and the solitude required for quiet and innocence: the garden is paradoxically social, society primitive. (The garden as society-in-solitude is presented more clearly in the Latin version:

O! mihi si vestros liceat violasse recessus
Erranti, lasso, & vitæ melioris anhelo,
Municipem servate novum, votoque potitum,
Frondosæ Cives optate in florea Regna.)

The word "delicious" and more explicitly amorous phrases in the next stanza introduce an erotic aspect of that "society" that has proved especially perplexing to critics: "No white nor red was ever seen / So am'rous as this lovely green." As Lawrence Hyman writes, we have no difficulty in understanding why the garden is beautiful, restful, and innocent, "but why is it also sexual!"[51] His answer, like that of Miss Wallerstein and Miss Røstvig, is that Marvell identified himself with the androgynous Adam, who had plants before Eve. Hyman adds that the identity is not complete and that Marvell describes the garden after as well as the garden before the fall, contrasting the two in order to show the superiority of the latter. The garden is "primarily" the "happy Garden state"; though falling on grass is a reminder of "falling into carnal sin" in one sense, "the sexual connotations of the images . . . are perfectly innocent" in the transmuted experience of the androgynous Adam.[52] Miss Røstvig makes the "Hermaphrodite man" still more central, finding that in Hermetic philosophy he is described in the same way Marvell conceives of him, especially in connecting the rejection of Eve with the rejection of matter.

The myth of androgynous Adam seems unquestionably involved in the poem, but we should not take Marvell too solemnly and narrowly. In finding a considerable amount of satire in the poem, Frank Kermode provides a useful corrective.[53] More important, however, the dualism of mind and matter is evident without Hermetic philosophy, and the central paradox of the poem, the annihilation of "all that's made" combined with praise for the created, amorous garden, remains unsolved. "Bi-sexuality" is a metaphor for a unity Adam lost when he became mortal rather than a central theme; far from reversing the "history of man" and "ending where the whole process began: with pure mind,"[54] the poem ends very much in time and in the midst of fertile "industry."

It seems unlikely that the immediate background of the third stanza is either Hermes or the French libertines so much

51. "Marvell's 'Garden,' " p. 13.

52. Ibid., p. 18.

53. "The Argument of Marvell's 'Garden,' " *Essays in Criticism*, 2 (1952), 225–41; cf. Empson, pp. 119 ff.; Truesdale, p. 312; Greg, p. 130.

54. Rostvig, p. 75; cf. Klonsky, p. 35.

as common pastoral works such as *As You Like It* and the flood of love verse in the renaissance in which lovers in their "uncessant Labour" are caught in the throes of love and retreat to the forest only to carve sonnets on trees.[55] Marvell's concern for the trees is no doubt genuine but the tone is ironic; the apostrophe, "Fair Trees! where s'eer your barkes I wound, / No Name shall but your own be found," is not so much Hermetic as common-sensical and satiric. The serious contest of the stanza is simply that between love for a certain kind of nature and a heated chase in which the woods are violated for the sake of temporary gains. Cavalier abandon is now the threat rather than Puritan industry, not prudence but imprudence. As the Mower and Adam both come to realize, the psychology is comparatively simple: the presence of woman in paradise ends the "repose" necessary for regaining harmony with primal nature and for regaining self-orientation. Making the forest or garden an enclosed place frees the female principle from the termagant dangers Marvell associates with nymphs. (As he knew from reading Hermetic material, it was traditionally thought of as a creative womb or *prima materia* (*hyle*), into which the gods—Mercury, Apollo, Christ—descend.)

The mythological framework within which the contest is presented is also traditional, but rewritten to suggest the purposeful motive of the gods:

IV

When we have run our Passions heat,
Love hither makes his best retreat.
The *Gods*, that mortal Beauty chase,
Still in a Tree did end their race.

55. Cf. Edward's love sickness, e.g. in *Edward III*. Edward asks Lodwick, who is to supply rhymes for his outpourings, to sit by him in "the summer arbour": "Since green our thoughts, green be the conventicle / Where we will ease us by disburd'ning them."

Apollo hunted *Daphne* so,
Only that She might Laurel grow.
And *Pan* did after *Syrinx* speed,
Not as a Nymph, but for a Reed.

As in the descent of the sacred plants, quiet and innocence, and
in the retreat of the poet to the garden, the gods thus embrace
the plants. The passionate chase for mortal beauty and the god-
vegetative identity in which it ends do not make reeds sensual;
they simply make nymphs harmless. The incongruity is that
one should race so hard to reach a tree that has no intention of
running off anyway: all violence ends in simple repose.
Whether the gods anticipated that it would or not is question-
able, but the contrast between harem and the hushed, sacred
place is both a reproach to the libertine and an invitation to a
better life. To a degree unusual in Marvell the relationship between innocence and sensuality is explicit: "*When* we have run
our Passions heat," we may enter here, but not before. Further,
the erotic chase of Apollo and Pan ends in art as well as in vegetable love, Pan's reed being an instrument for pastoral song
and Apollo's laurel being a reward that "grows" naturally, not
a manufactured, "upbraided" palm. The heterosexual dangers
of the mower poems and "Upon Appleton House" are thus
circumvented by a combination of belittling farce and transcending, compensatory pleasure.

Marvell's further absorption into nature in stanza five repeats the imagistic action of these myths. He too becomes
"vegetable"—and with cavalier abandon, but abandon rendered
harmless by the garden and complicated by his self-conscious-
ness. His return to boyhood includes an element of the ridicu-
lous and a further suggestion of eroticism purified:

v

What wond'rous Life is this I lead!
Ripe Apples drop about my head;

The Luscious Clusters of the Vine
Upon my Mouth do crush their Wine;
The Nectaren, and curious Peach,
Into my hands themselves do reach;
Stumbling on Melons, as I pass,
Insnar'd with Flow'rs, I fall on Grass.

As the next stanza makes clear, this is not a happiness of the mind, which "mean while" does something else; it is a truancy of animal spirits suddenly freed from "passions heat" and "uncessant Labours." Nature traditionally obliges the moods of the pastoral wanderer in his seclusion, either weeping or rejoicing with him; and so nature reaches out to be "eaten" and does most of the acting. The poet, first moving among the trees and then rooted in the flowers, becomes one with the innocent grass. For all its sensuous abandonment, the stanza has an intensifying suggestion of a harvest ritual in which each item performs its final service. Yet this suggestion and the hint of more serious falls of the flesh only test the strength of innocence and quiet and show them to be durable. The snares here, like the passion of the gods, are perfectly harmless, though the poet knows of the dangers he avoids.

But man is not merely a companion of curious peaches, however passionate his friendship with them may be; he shares characteristics with plants but also possesses a mind. In the pastoral elegy, the difference may only intensify sorrow: "When the mallows and the fresh green parsley and the springing crumpled anise perish in the garden," Moschus writes, "they live yet again and grow another year; but we men that are so tall and strong and wise, soon as ever we be dead, unhearing there in a hole of earth sleep we both sound and long a sleep that is without end or waking."[56] But in a poem of pastoral success, the difference forces the poet to greater self-

56. *The Greek Bucolic Poets*, trans. J. M. Edmonds (Cambridge, Mass., 1912).

realization. The self is defined by its integration into and transcendence of nature rather than by dialectic against it, though there may be dialectical skirmishes against certain aspects of man's natural rudeness. If the entire man withdraws into the garden and finds pleasure there, only the mind can withdraw further, into a garden of its own creation:

VI

> Mean while the Mind, from pleasure less,
> Withdraws into its happiness:
> The Mind, that Ocean where each kind
> Does streight its own resemblance find;
> Yet it creates, transcending these,
> Far other Worlds, and other Seas;
> Annihilating all that's made
> To a green Thought in a green Shade.

Though the soul, as distinguished from the mind, also separates itself from the body and sits in the boughs and sings,[57] it reflects the various light of the natural world in its "silver Wings." The mind's withdrawal is more complete: "annihilating" and "transcending" are concurrent acts, perhaps because in the very act of annihilation the mind discovers its essential being—that which it *is* in itself as distinct from what it *operates on*. Though like the sea in containing all things in its dissolving unity, it is capable also of making other worlds and seas.

In the shift from the passive "wond'rous Life" to creation, the active will, previously abandoned for "repose," is restored: cognitive and conative faculties reinforce each other. The in-

---

57. Cf. A. H. King, "Some Notes on Marvell's Garden," *English Studies*, 20 (1938), 120. For the distinction between mind and soul, see Plotinus, *Enneads* IV.1.1, IV.2.1; Aquinas, *Summa theologica*, Q. 78, art. 1; Ficino: "for the soul lives the life of a plant when it serves the body . . . the life of an animal, when it flatters the senses; the life of a man, when it deliberates through reason on human affairs": *Theologia Platonica*, XII.3 in Josephine L. Burroughs' trans., *JHI*, 5 (1944), 236–38.

tellect and will must act simultaneously upon the ideas (*rationes*) of "things intellectually known," Ficino says: "The intellect . . . can take on the spiritual forms of all things and become all. In this manner the universe, under the concept of being and truth, is the object of the intellect; and similarly, under the concept of goodness, is it the object of the will."[58] Whereas in Ficino the will "moves soul and body to action in order that they may approach the desired objects," Marvell might seem to have willed only annihilation: like the sea at low tide (as Empson points out), the mind pursues the way of chastity in a world nothing enters unasked. And yet it does so with pleasure rather than in dialectical combat, and even in doing so it resurges and creates, withdrawing and simultaneously embracing everything: the paradoxes of Christian Platonism and of pastoral are fused with deceptive ease. It perhaps embraces the "made" world and discovers kinship with each kind (as each kind in turn discovers its true reflection, its "straightened" idea, in the mind) *because* it can always annihilate and create freely. It is both slayer and maker, mirror and oceanic vessel. Green thought in green shade sums up brilliantly the correspondence of inner and outer, the pastoral ambiance that leads to transcendence, the forceful vagueness of what is created in thought, the implications of growth and renewal, the impregnating force of reason in the womb of nature.

After the extreme point of withdrawal, Marvell shifts to the soul in its absorption of the garden. The soul gains freedom by casting the body's vest aside, but its perch in the tree is a limited—and again pleasurable—form of transcendence, a little above the roots and grass that trip up the body, but not entirely disengaged. While preparing for "longer flight" it adds experience of the beautiful to the mind's experience of the true.

58. Cf. *JHI*, 236–38 and *Epistolae*, II.1 in *The Renaissance Philosophy of Man*, trans. Burroughs, pp. 200–01.

The three stanzas that comprise the center of the poem are suspended as body, mind, and soul seek their respective functions, the body (or perhaps more exactly, the vegetative soul) being engrossed in the garden as such, the mind (rational soul) transcending it, and the "sensitive" soul reflecting it. The activities of the sensitive soul are described last, I think, because the movement is toward mediation and harmony. Like Yeats' golden bird on the bough in Byzantium, the soul-bird is emblematic of the artist, who belongs to two worlds, the ideal one created by the mind and the sensible one experienced by the body. Each is necessary to full enjoyment of the garden. (Likewise, even the fraternity with vegetation that Marvell experiences in the "wond'rous Life" would seem in retrospect to depend upon the mind's possession of each "kind" within itself, the enjoyment of sensuousness upon knowledge of spiritual freedom and harmony.) "Singing" thus becomes the natural *act* of the soul, which is guided by the intellect and informed by the senses, however independent its activity may seem in its solo performance. (Augustine writes that of the three kinds of vision—corporeal, intellectual, and spiritual—only the last includes imagination or "phantasy."[59]) Because longer flight is certain eventually, the soul needs no resolve against Created Pleasure; it can safely absorb the real garden. Casting the body's vest aside is simply an act of freedom allowing the phantasy to deal freely with the light "made beautiful

59. *Genesi ad litt.*, XII.6; 7; 24; cf. Aquinas, *Summa theologica*, Q. 78, art. 4. Cf. also Castiglione, *The Book of the Courtier*, IV.67: the imagination is a corporal faculty not wholly purged of material darkness; the level of love on which it operates reminds Cardinal Bembo of "little birds beginning to put on feathers" but too weak for long flight. Renato Poggioli finds the image of the soul in the tree evidence of that narcissistic preening which is common elsewhere in the "pastoral of the self." Thus the "garden" is taken to be an "outdoor boudoir" founded upon a cornerstone of misogyny and misanthropy." "The Pastoral of the Self," *Daedalus, 88* (1959), 694–99.

with innumerable colors."[60] It does not imply that the soul's creative *ekstasis* is in the Plotinian pattern of absolute transcendence.[61]

In turning to general reflections upon garden retreats, Marvell shows further that the annihilation and casting aside are not rejections but preliminaries to emergence. Though it deepens the mood of the wanderer, the myth of Adam is not cause for despair, he finds, because he has already learned not to repeat Adam's mistake:

60. Ficino, *Theologia Platonica*, IX, iii. Miss Wallerstein suggests without elaboration that Ficino's version of the imagination may be involved. While "reason" thinks of a clearer light, it is "phantasy" that absorbs and screens existential light: "The phantasy follows the external senses, the senses the disposition of their own body and of others. . . . When our mind desires to know from teachers of this sort what is the nature of God, the phantasy, a bold enough instructor and workman, contrives a statue, as it were from the five materials which the external senses supply her. . . . Phantasy then offers us a light so clear that no other can seem more radiant; . . . a light diffused almost through the immense inane, which is made beautiful with innumerable colors, and turns in a circle; and by that revolution it sings in the sweetest modes, filling and softening our ears. . . . The body of the world gives us nothing more fair. . . . The phantasy, friend of the senses, creates nothing more sublime. But reason, meanwhile, from the highest watch tower of the mind looks down upon the tricks of the phantasy and speaks forth thus: Beware, little soul, beware the sleights of that sophister. Do you seek God. Receive a light as much clearer than the light of the sun as that light of the sun is more luminous than darkness" (*Studies in Seventeenth-Century Poetic*, pp. 217–18). The similarity between Ficino's definition of "phantasy" and the activities of Marvell's bird-soul is pronounced. The soul's "song" is its highest beauty, a "creation" beyond sensory images but somehow based upon their various light, while the mind knows a still higher light. See also Murray Wright Bundy, *The Theory of Imagination in Classical and Mediaeval Thought* (Urbana, Ill., 1927), p. 129.

61. For previous poems on "ecstasy" see Leo Spitzer, *A Method of Interpreting Literature* (Northampton, Mass., 1949), pp. 1–63. See also Plotinus, *Enneads* VI.1.11: the life of the gods and of godlike and "blessed among men" requires complete "liberation from the alien things that beset us here, a life taking no pleasure in the things of earth, the passing of solitary to solitary."

VIII

Such was that happy Garden-state,
While Man there walk'd without a Mate:
After a Place so pure, and sweet,
What other Help could yet be meet!
But 'twas beyond a Mortal's share
To wander solitary there:
Two paradises 'twere in one
To live in Paradise alone.

Some mention is made, in each stanza after the first, of being "here" or "now" in the garden, but at this point Marvell steps backward and conceives of the particular experience in broader terms. Though keeping paradise to himself might have limited his commitments and preserved the mind's integrity, Adam could not resist abandoning the amorous green for Eve. But if wandering solitary was impossible "there," Marvell is in fact alone now, even though the garden is not "Paradise." (The tonal effect of the contrary-to-fact phrasing of "Two Paradises 'twere in one" is difficult to pin down, since a paraphrase inevitably converts a passing observation into a major qualification of the mood. Ostensibly, the last four lines read: "The androgynous Adam contained paradise within him as long as he did not commit himself to heterosexuality; we could do the same if we could return to Adam's original scene.") Aware of Adam's domestic trouble, Marvell abjures helpmates; the fall is fortunate insofar as it makes latter-day Adams aware of the full value of having "Two Paradises" in one (as the hints of "snares" and the fall onto the grass have intensified earlier sensuous pleasures).

The sun is thus "milder" in contrast to Juliana-Phaeton suns, and "uncessant Labours" are resumed under it in the transforming labor of the industrious bee computing "tyme" in the dial of flowers:

IX

How well the skilful Gardner drew
Of flow'rs and herbes this Dial new;
Where from above the milder Sun
Does through a fragrant Zodiack run;
And, as it works, th' industrious Bee
Computes its time as well as we.
How could such sweet and wholsome Hours
Be reckon'd but with herbs and flow'rs!

One's limited time is thus made fruitful in the garden, which is neither primitive nor excessively trained. Far from destroying the soul, created plenitude is found to enrich it. Higher and lower principles (the Apollo-like sun *in* the flowers), time and eternity are reconciled: the impregnating sun creates the "tyme" in which the bee works. As the sacred plants of innocence and quiet, if below, are harbored in the grosser plants, the *rationes* of a man-made dial are like those of the greater circle of the zodiac. (As Ficino writes concerning human art, man is very much like God: "who could deny that man could somehow also make the heavens, could he only obtain the instruments and the heavenly material, since even now he makes them, though of different material, but still with a very similar order?"[62]) The metamorphosis of the sensual "chase" into a creative, pastoral industry redeems history, transforming time and the "Lucious Clusters" into soul-food, energy for the longer flight. What is "at hand" through the reckoning of the artist is integral to the soul's "being-in-the-world," its *Da-sein,* and thus to its eventual being out of it, which satisfies Marvell as Christian, Neoplatonist, and pastoralist.

62. *JHI,* 5 (1944), 235, from *Theologia Platonica,* XII.3.

4. Love and Time

Now then love me: time may take
Thee before thy time away:
Of this Need wee'l Virtue make,
And learn Love before we may.

("Young Love")

In "The Definition of Love," Marvell, unlike such poets as Dante, Benivieni, or Spenser, was not concerned with the lover's advance on a ladder of spiritual refinement away from the ambiguities of human passion, which distinguishes him from the main line of Platonic love theology. For Marvell, love draws the soul outward in dialectical combat instead of leading it upward as sublimated Eros moving "the sun and the other stars." Since mistresses like Clora (in "the Gallery") resist idealization, love sharpens the conflict of soul and scene, innocence and experience. At one extreme Clorinda may abdicate her role as temptress and sing with Damon of great Pan; at the other, love may be destructive rather than "magnanimous." Love is thus associated with the ambivalent experiences of time and with the violation of reason and the ideal life of the soul. (Apollo's pursuit of Daphne is fortunate only if nymph is metamorphosed to laurel.)

As in the misogynous strain of Sidney's "Leave me O love"

and Shakespeare's "Th' expense of spirit in a waste of shame," Marvell sees love as a threat in a context of larger spiritual and metaphysical matters. He rejects alike the decorums of cavalier love verse, the philogynous idealism of Petrarchan conventions, and the Puritan view of woman as helpmate. Because withdrawal is predominantly auto- and dendro-erotic, he finds it difficult to deal with heterosexual themes without thinking of love as the destruction of the soul's autonomy—except for the dissolving love in which the soul returns to the all-absorbing "sun." Issuance in passion is *self-annihilation*, a kind of symbolic suicide reversing the annihilation of all that's made in the process of *self-discovery*. If the green world is an avatar of creative thought, Juliana evokes masochism and destruction. And because love is thus a slaying, it must be ritualized; the protective strategy is consequently not withdrawal—which is impossible unless the poet becomes an onlooker rather than a participant—but ceremony of some kind. The governing theme is not so much nurture in retreat followed by emergence as the establishing and shattering of civilizing decorum. A huntress like little T. C. is warned to beware playing the game too ruthlessly lest nature retaliate. Nature itself in the love poems (as in the last mower poem) sometimes suggests struggle and the hunt, and sometimes provides an ideal of innocence against which love is reflected. Stating it thus abstractly gives little indication of the complexity and ambivalence of Marvell's attitude toward love and time, but the usefulness of the framework will be borne out, I think, by the connections it offers between what may at first appear to be isolated and puzzling lyrics.

In the service of the Resolved Soul, irony is an instrument that shears off unnecessary connections to the larger world of created and sociable pleasures and thus to time and love: moral concerns are the business of the private world of inner conscience, and the mind's dialectical powers are marshaled behind them. In treating them, Marvell isolates what appear to be strictly personal, interior concerns and hence "almost cries out to be placed in literary histories as a kind of exquisite miniaturist," as John Rosenberg writes.[1] Perhaps for this reason critics often feel "To His Coy Mistress" to be different from and better than the rest of Marvells' poetry. Unlike "The Garden," it does not depend upon philosophical apparatus. It proposes apparently to create something out of the materials of this life rather than annihilating and preparing for longer flight; and the means by which this is to be done are both more universal in appeal and less metaphysically involved than the means at the soul's disposal in other poems. Actually, however, "To His Coy Mistress" is not so radically isolated from the sensibility and values of Marvell's other poems. The difference between it and the others is essentially that, like a negative in which black is white and white black, it reverses the customary strategies. While the Resolved Soul insists upon its integrity and freedom from the world, the proposal to the mistress involves a negation of Platonist assumptions: the lovers are to enter the stream of time, deny providential control of the cosmos, and turn the sun and the emotions loose.[2]

But as in the poems in which Marvell uses a definite persona

1. "Marvell and the Christian Idiom," *Boston University Studies in English*, 4 (1960), 152–53.
2. Cf. Wallerstein, pp. 336–37: "For the seventeenth-century ear the contest in the poem between life and time and eternity was even more sharply defined than to ours; it was just before the dissolution of the world that the Jews were to be converted. That precise religious consciousness, deepening into the somber, inverted religious echoes of the deserts of vast eternity, and, as Mr. Bush has suggested, of the ashes free from lust, and seeing the twofold vision of the lady, the full contrasting image of the chamber and tomb, the tone, the rhythms, which make other *carpe diem* poems of the age . . . seem such dust motes in the sun . . . they give to it an intensity, a seriousness that the most explicit reading of every possible sensual allusion cannot touch."

and in those that manifest divided and complex sympathies, we should, I think, distinguish between the speaker's proposition and the poet's values. In addressing the poem to "his" rather than to "my" coy mistress and in suggesting an under side to much of the imagery, Marvell places the proposal in an ambivalent framework. An unusual deepening of the action and experience of the poem is the result, an ironic division within the total awareness which is not necessarily part of the immediate consciousness of the speaker. This is to say that we should not place undue or oversimplified emphasis upon the triumph of love that the speaker emphasizes. Taking his appeal at face value, critics have seen his proposal as a progressing from "vegetable" love to a "rational" love that can dispel the despair he raises in the mistress.[3] The conditional phrasing

3. See Rufus Putney, " 'Our Vegetable Love': Marvell and Burton," in *Studies in Honor of T. W. Baldwin,* ed. D. C. Allen (Urbana, Ill., 1958), p. 228. Putney adds that the lovers achieve a "renewed understanding of their beauty, their sweetness, their strength, and of their ability to attain happiness despite the tragic ironies of life." F. W. Bradbrook writes that, "vital and dynamic, love is contrasted with the coldness and silence of the tomb where the only movement is that of the worms, and with the dullness and monotony of a humdrum passive life, the iron gates through which love must tear its way. Time and death, the theme of so much Elizabethan and seventeenth-century poetry, are conquered by love." ("The Poetry of Andrew Marvell," p. 197.) Cf. Bradbrook and Thomas: "They are not Joshuas, they are gods," *Andrew Marvell,* p. 46; T. S. Eliot: "It is the theme of *O mistress mine,* of *Gather ye rosebuds,* of *Go lovely rose;* it is in the savage austerity of Lucretius and the intense levity of Catullus. Where the wit of Marvell renews the theme is in the variety and order of the images," *Selected Essays,* pp. 253–54; Legouis, p. 75; John Wheatcroft, "Andrew Marvell and the Winged Chariot," *Bucknell Review,* 6 (1956), 52–53. But see also Anthony E. Farnham, "Saint Teresa and the Coy Mistress," *Boston University Studies in English,* 2 (1956), 227: "With the realization that the ineluctable victory of time annihilates all possibility of earthly joy, happiness must be sought in the only reasonable resolution of the conflict—an urgent and immediate compromise in which time, although not in any way cheated, is put out of mind for as long as possible"; Lawrence W. Hyman, "Marvell's 'Coy Mistress' and Desperate Lover," *MLN,* 75 (1960), 8–10.

of "*though* we cannot make our Sun / Stand still . . ." is thus minimized and love as something that hugs a zest for life to itself is set against a "humdrum passive life" as the only alternative. Though this simplification has its appeal to postromantic readers, the more we consider Marvell's usual attitudes toward time, the more ambivalent the lovers' triumph appears. While the speaker is obviously not a Created Pleasure whose arguments are to be turned inside out to make white once again white, the poem's commitment to love is not unqualified. The *speaker's* main concern is with having too little time and world, but the *poem* also explores the consequences of being trapped in them. (In a sense, of course, too little time *is* too much since time is more prominent as it runs out.) The speaker's come-live-with-me scherzo is interpenetrated with a dirge-like theme mixing a painful sense of loss with exuberance, disappointment with wit.

Perhaps no part of the poem accomplishes this more profoundly than the concluding lines:

> Thus, though we cannot make our Sun
> Stand still, yet we will make him run.

As we have seen, the sun quite often in Marvell liberates the soul by drawing it back to its origins or by distilling essence out of existence, or else the poet seeks protection from it—a symbol, in other words, of providence operating mercifully in time or of a scorching power that burns the self committed too fully to love. (As Damon the Mower discovers, Juliana "makes the Sun / Hotter than his own *Phaeton*.") What does it mean here to make it "run"? Any meaning not consonant with the whole poem should, of course, be disqualified, which rules out, I think, the idea once proposed that the lovers conquer time by propagating a "son." That the poem's simple Hegelian dialectic resolves the tension here also seems open to doubt, since progressing from a thesis ("Had we but World

enough and Time") to an antithesis ("but we do not") to a
synthesis ("therefore, let us do what we can"), whatever it
means in terms of logical structure, does not account for the
wit and ambivalence of the poem. At first glance, in fact, the
lines would appear to deny any kind of symbolic triumph.
With as much pain as joy—and with a suggestion of frenzy—
the lovers can only defeat time by hurrying toward death.[4]
Love is the lowering of the melting point: passion becomes the
god-principle and absorbs the soul, congealed and chill in "On
a Drop of Dew" but now transpiring through every pore. It is
not an intellectual life absorption force but a passional dissolution and tearing.

Consequently, it seems unlikely that the traditional allusions
occasionally found in the sun image are more than peripheral
matters, though they may be useful in bringing out what, even
without concern with traditional symbols, are definite implications of the imagery of the last section.[5] The subjectivity of the

4. Frederick L. Gwynn believes that the sun taken with the image of
time's chariot suggests the ride of Phaeton: see *Explicator*, *11* (1953), no.
7 and cf. *Explicator*, *14* (1956), no. 7, an answer to this position proposed by Lawrence Sasek. If the Phaeton myth is involved, it would probably have carried with it in Marvell's day some of the burden of commentary by Philo and others, who equated the runaway horses with the
passions and the charioteer with reason. See *Phaedrus* 246 A, 253 C–256
D; Philo, *De ag.*, 67–93; Thomas Billings, *The Platonism of Philo Judaeus*
(Chicago, 1919), p. 88; John Carroll, "The Sun and the Lovers in 'To
His Coy Mistress,'" *MLN*, 74 (1959), 4–7.

5. Walter A. Sedlow suggests that the sun image contains an echo of
Psalm 19: "Their line is gone out through all the earth, and their words
to the end of the world. In them hath he set a tabernacle for the sun, which
is as a bridegroom coming out of his chamber, and rejoiceth as a strong
man to run a race. His going forth is from the end of the heaven, and his
circuit into the ends of it: and there is nothing hid from the heat thereof."
He concludes from this that the sun is a symbol of earth and that world
enough and time are therefore finally available to the lovers: "Thus the
lovers' sense of their iron straits becomes the condition of their liberation.
They can force the sun to be his own undoing." See "Marvell's 'To His Coy
Mistress,'" *MLN*, 71 (1956), 6–8. The immediate difficulty is that the

sun image and its connections to the created world of the lovers would seem to be nearer the core of meaning. In its clearest sense, "our" sun is simply elliptical for "our time under the sun"—"we cannot last forever, but we can make our passage interesting." A measure of triumph is undoubtedly intended in this, but the bleakness of the marble vault and the "Desarts of vast Eternity" still hover in the background. Considering the goals of self-creation in other poems, trading the great "ball" of the world for the little ball into which sweetness can be rolled, and the sun for a small share of time and space under it, is to make short if quick gains.

The difficulty, as the speaker makes clear, is that, outside the Platonist framework, time offers no alternative. Though the tax rate is high, the Lady deserves a "state" that stands solidly and has pomp and ceremony; but the great landmarks of time and geography—India and the Humber, the flood and the conversion of the Jews—and the landmarks of anatomy— eyes, forehead, breasts, and, last (to flatter the mistress' idealism), the heart—vanish when one considers one's personal time. For it *is* a personal and not a state issue, the speaker insists. His aim is to destroy the ennobling metaphors Platonic ladies use (with a glance at the court) to ceremonialize passion and convert it into social ritual. If one wants the truth, he proposes, the cosmos is a desert and one's final share in it is very small and worm-infested. The grave has replaced Marvell's fine, private retreats, the desert his sun-controlled tran-

---

literal sun, at least, is not undone; it will survive after the lovers have run their race under it. If the biblical echo operates in the poem, it would seem to be in the other direction: the sun, partly because of the psalm, was too universally taken to be an embodiment of cosmic order not to cause a suggestion of disorder to creep into the image. And the sun, of course, was also taken to represent the Bridegroom (from whom "is nothing hid," the *Sol justitiae*), which suggests an inverted tradition like those of the first and second sections of the poem.

scendence. *In such a world* no defense exists, except to forget time in personal, defiant passion.

In the context of this inversion of customary Marvellian patterns, the vegetable love image is especially resonant, not only because it is an ironic version of dendro-eroticism but also because of the strategic equation within the poem of vegetation and ceremony, which the speaker uses finally to overthrow ceremony for naturalism. Defining "vegetable love" as an "abstract philosophical" term rather than a reference to "erotic cabbages" will not free it entirely of vegetable connotations, I think (even truck garden ones), unless separating the various levels of a phrase will somehow enable us to suppress one or the other of them.[6] E. D. Hirsch, in discussing a proposal to retain them, suggests that it might:

> No doubt, the associated meaning *is* here desirable (since it supports the mood of the poem), but Wellek could not even make his point unless we could distinguish between what "vegetable" probably means as used in the text, and what it commonly means to us. Simply to discuss the issue is to admit that Marvell's poem probably does not imply the modern connotation, since if we could not separate the sense of "vegetative" from the notion of an "erotic cabbage," we could not talk about the difficulty of making the separation.[7]

But distinguishing in this case does not necessarily mean separating, any more than philosophers when distinguishing among rational, sensitive, and vegetative souls mean that man can separate one from the other and remain man. (Man shares with the vegetables, Aquinas writes, growth, generation, and

6. Cf. J. V. Cunningham, "Logic and Lyric," *MP*, 51 (1953), 36; René Wellek and Austin Warren, *Theory of Literature* (New York, 1942), pp. 166–67; Bradbrook and Thomas, *Andrew Marvell*, p. 43; Louis Teeter, "Scholarship and the Art of Criticism," *ELH*, 5 (1938), 183–84.

7. "Objective Interpretation," *PMLA*, 75 (1960), 465.

need for nutrition.[8]) Anyway, the poetry of Marvell has enough amorous green stuff in it to make the argument largely beside the point: the difference between curious peaches and cabbages is very fine. The irony has purchase against the mistress' ceremonies because she wishes to generate slowly and innocently like the plants. But the speaker, too, conceives of love as growing in the sun and growing faster as the sun runs hotter—and unable to grow in the marble vault or in the vast desert. The worm has the last word with man as with vegetation, and time chews on both with its "slow-chapt pow'r," unless they devour it first. Perhaps the implication is also that even if allowed to take its natural course, a pseudo-Platonic love would become "vaster than Empires," as "our" sun, "our" time, and the "one Ball" do, only much more slowly. The speaker simply asks that an expansive wandering over the world in slow time become an intense rolling of strength into a self-contained sphere.

Realization of time's quickness is sprung surprisingly, however, despite the long preparation, the implications of the vegetable image, and the logical anticipation in "*Had* we but world enough . . ." With arguments taken from the Epicureans, the carpe diem tradition, and court wits, and the inverted Christian and Platonic concepts of afterlife, the speaker effectively shatters "quaint Honour" and its idealism. As Donne discovers in "Love's Growth," if love can grow, it can decay; and so the world of expanding time and space can be reversed: the beauty of eyes, forehead, breasts, and "the rest" vanishes, the echoing song is stilled, and the exaggerated efforts at humane manners are dispersed in the desert of the soul, devoured in the body's grave. "Therefore" the soul must be *un*resolved and transpire "At every pore with instant Fires" in an "extasie which doth [not] unperplex."

Both the appeal and the shortcomings of the proposition

8. *Summa theologica*, Q. 78, art. 2.

are suggested by this, "instant" referring not only to the pressure of the moment ("*Now* therefore . . . ," "*Now* let us . . . ," "And *now* . . ."), but also to a quick end to the consuming fires. The tearing of pleasure and the eat-or-be-eaten imagery, of course, stress the violence of passion in time. The soul melts through the body rather than controlling it from within. By their very nature, Marvell indicates, experiences in time and love are subject to these hazards. Humility, transcendence, temperence, and patience—virtues that in other poems are safeguards of the soul against the processes of time—the speaker replaces with our-ness, here-ness, and now-ness. That he shares the dream of an ideal expansive world and unlimited time is implicit in his description of it, despite its absurdity and "quaintness" (some of the irony is self-punitive as well as aggressive); but granted the nature of the experienced world, shattering that dream is a necessity, not simply a lover's strategy: no moral consideration thus broken free from its sustaining absolutes will bear up.

If the triumph is ambivalent, it is also capable of resolving some of the poem's polar tensions. The tension between ceremonial order and a rapacious nature, for example, and the tension in the afterlife between the extremes of the body's vault and the soul's arid desert are forgotten in the fierce common meeting place of willed passion. World and time run together as the sun runs away. If the Christian-Platonist overtones reveal this to be a limited accomplishment, it is perhaps all—the poem suggests—that one can count on here and now. There are no timeless places to withdraw to, no rebirth, no green thought, but the spirit, mistress willing, can create its own way of dying.

Many of Marvell's lesser poems deal with the same subject and are worth investigating in detail both for their own value and for the indirect illumination they provide for "To His Coy

Mistress." "Young Love," for example, one of Marvell's better
minor poems, suggests a way to control love and time before
they gather momentum. It is a *carpe diem quam minimum cre-
dula postero* poem in the same tradition as "To His Coy Mistress," but it overturns the traditional theme: time applies its
pressure not through death but through the very sensual passion that is normally the goal of "come live with me" invita-
tions. The object is to *establish* ceremony and decorum rather
than shatter them. The inversion is the source of much of the
poem's wit, but by itself would not account for the effectiveness of the poem, which derives also from the depth and self-
awareness of Marvell's myths of innocence. Perhaps because
of the combination of wit and emotional intensity which makes
the tonal shifts difficult at times, the poem is surprisingly complex. It is charming and skeptical, graceful and harsh in turn.
The dividing line between ironic self-awareness and cynicism is
very fine. However, in its sharp contrasts lie, I think, some of
the unexpected resources of the poem in repeated readings.

Since it is modeled on "come love me" poems but addressed
to a "little Infant," its rejection of adult love has a double
edge:

I

Come little Infant, Love me now,
　While thine unsuspected years
Clear thine aged Fathers brow
　From cold Jealousie and Fears.

Telling the child of this kind of love is the first step in an education in passion that will be completed more directly later on,
undoubtedly with less ceremony and more earnestness. Young
love, however, is free of worries and can deceive "old Time"
at least temporarily:

II

Pretty surely 'twere to see
　By young Love old Time beguil'd:

While our Sportings are as free
As the Nurses with the Child,

But the beguiling is regarded with mixed feelings. The ambivalence derives partly from the contrast between the wit and the underlying threat, from the implicit acknowledgment of the inevitable sensual sportings to come and the ceremonial game possible despite them. The main point is that instead of deceiving father as older lovers do, they deceive time. Balancing love against time emphasizes the irony of inexperienced youth outwitting its experienced enemy. Yet the supremacy of youthful innocence lasts only a short while; time is beguiled but not defeated, and in a way it *is* the father of young love, as Despair and Impossibility beget love in "The Definition of Love." Without its threat, there would be no invocation, "Come little Infant, Love me *now*." The "need" of time is precisely what forces them to learn love before they may.

Common beauties stay fifteen, Marvell continues (undoubtedly with tongue in cheek, as though to say, "they don't remain young, of course, but they try to"), but childhood beauty more quickly moves one to love it, as the child itself should move swiftly to antedate its destiny before lust sets in. Though in any case time and lust will have their day (her fair "blossoms are too green / *Yet* for Lust"), poet and child can salvage something of value, make virtue "Of this Need." This is not, of course, to make time run faster as in "To His Coy Mistress"; it is to achieve a conjunction of minds before the opposition of the stars can be organized. If fate means well, young love may anticipate it; if ill, "that Ill prevent." But muted undertones of the threat continue to twist the poem in peculiar ways. A strange proposal, at any rate, to put before an "infant," and a strange way to put it: "Now then love me: time may take / Thee before thy time away," the penetration of which is doubly harsh because it may mean, "I may lose you both because you will die and because you may grow up sooner than you should—either way you will not be lovable." "Thy time" emphasizes the inevitability of her being taken away, whether sooner or later. The argument is perhaps stronger than it needs to be, but it is this very strength that keeps the poem from falling into preciousness.

Since Love (Cupid) himself is indifferent to whether the Lamb or the "lusty Bull or Ram" is sacrificed, they can also frustrate "Forraign Claims" by learning a love without aged and "accidental" accompaniments—lust and "cold Jealousie and Fears." By crowning love in the cradle and pledging symbolically that they will place the larger, adult world of "kingdoms" in the service of innocence, they control the future:

VIII

So, to make all Rivals vain
    Now I crown thee with my Love:
Crown me with thy Love again,
    And we both shall Monarchs prove.

As in the repeated phrases of incantation, the words are part of a gesture "now" being completed. The gesture continues the wit and the ironic playfulness, which further intensifies the appeal to "Love me now"; but the uncertainty and the barbs are removed. Though young love cannot, perhaps, endure in a purely innocent way, old and young can have mutual interests —such as their present game—which will influence the future. Since their game is also adult, a monarchial "crowning" of love, in crowning the child the poet beckons it into the kind of game adults play; as the child crowns him in return, she bestows an innocence that disarms his potential cynicism. In both cases the ceremony itself is love's fulfillment.

In "The Unfortunate Lover" the irony and ceremonial formality have another relationship entirely. The misfortunes of love in time are the subject of satire and are exaggerated to the point of grotesqueness; but they are also the subject of a masque-like pageantry that gives them a certain amount of dignity and distance. Partly as a result of the exaggeration, the equilibrium between the fierce hunt and idyllic life, and between seriousness and parody, is upset. Because youthful flames, like summer meteors, soon "lose their light" in the processes of time, the motion of love is downward, toward submergence in time, rather than upward "to make impression" upon it:

I

Alas, how pleasant are their dayes
With whom the Infant Love yet playes!
Sorted by pairs, they still are seen
By Fountains cool, and Shadows green.
But soon these Flames do lose their light,
Like Meteors of a Summers night:
Nor can they to that Region climb,
To make impression upon Time.

II

'Twas in a Shipwrack, when the Seas
Rul'd, and the Winds did what they please,
That my poor Lover floting lay,
And, e're brought forth, was cast away:
Till at the last the master-Wave
Upon the Rock his Mother drave;
And there she split against the Stone,
In a *Cesarian Section.*

The orphan lover who is thus born by "Cesarian" shipwreck into adult love is recognizably Petrarchan with his seas of tears and roarings of the breast. Like Cromwell in "An Horatian Ode," who also emerges in "cesarian" fashion with thunder and lightning, he bursts forth dramatically, though not of his own volition. The garden of the first stanza has the look of genuine Marvellian retreat, but the subsequent imagery is violent enough to suggest a parody of the withdrawal-emergence pattern. The satire is undoubtedly meant to apply only to the storm-tossed lover and not to the yearning for "Fountains cool, and Shadows green"; but whereas "Young Love" succeeds in fusing irony and innocent ceremony, "The Unfortunate Lover" merely juxtaposes them. Stanzas one and two are too radically different in tone to function well together.

"As at the Fun'ral of the World" the lover in stanzas three and four attracts a "num'rous fleet of Corm'rants black" that care for him and fill him with hope and despair until he lies ambiguously between life and death. Yet his situation, despite its grimness, is cast in a once-upon-a-time mode (" 'Twas in a Shipwreck when the Seas . . .") and distanced through witty hyperbole, as in " 'ere brought forth, was cast away" and in the following stanza with its antitheses and paradoxes:

> V
>
> They fed him up with Hopes and Air,
> Which soon digested to Despair.
> And as one Corm'rant fed him, still
> Another on his Heart did bill.
> Thus while they famish him, and feast,
> He both consumed, and increast:
> And languished with doubtful Breath,
> Th' *Amphibium* of Life and Death.

As Bradbrook and Thomas point out, the vigor of the language clashes with the heraldic stiffness of the design, the poem itself being the kind of mobile "masque of Quarrelling Elements" that it describes.[9] The design and the pseudo-mythic atmosphere of the pageant eventually win out, but the victory is costly. Gaining further distance through a heavily satiric irony, the last stanza steps backward from the lurid unreality of the lover's predicament and thus steps free of the ambivalence by dismissing the whole process as too grotesque:

9. *Andrew Marvell*, p. 29.

VIII

This is the only *Banneret*
That ever Love created yet:
Who though, by the Malignant Starrs,
Forced to live in Storms and Warrs:
Yet dying leaves a Perfume here,
And Musick within every Ear:
And he in Story only rules,
In a Field *Sable* a Lover *Gules*.

The lover's unfortunate destiny is to find peace at last only in death and to leave behind only those trappings of love— music and perfume—of which the "Storms and Warrs" have deprived him while alive. The fate of the stars in "The Definition of Love" becomes entirely malignant here, though the malignancy is more grotesque than substantial. If the red ("gules") lover is dressed in his own blood and stands out dynamically against the stormy "Field Sable," his plight is still only "story": he is obviously a paper creature, the artificial invention of a sensibility that obtains perfume out of the dismal storms of love. And this abject Orphan is the only kind of battlefield knight that adult, epic love can create. Though he survives in time, natural lovers "with whom the Infant Love yet playes," who might attract greater sympathy from Marvell, lose their "flame" and leave no impression.   •

"Young Love" and "The Unfortunate Lover" will suffice to demonstrate that themes of love and time are inextricably woven together in Marvell and that heterosexual love (as in Blake) is usually a sign of innocence lost but experience gained, of a commitment to time both rewarding and unfortunate. The demands of adult love and of time appear to make ceremony impossible. This is also true of the contest between epic strife and love untutored by time which underlies "The Picture of Little T. C. in a Prospect of Flowers," "The Gallery," and "The Fair Singer." The surprised note upon which "The Picture of Little T. C." opens is due partly to the fact that it seems astonishing for a creature so potentially dangerous to begin so innocently:

> See with what simplicity
> This Nimph begins her golden daies!

She is a tamer of wildness and a creator of decorum who is like pastoral artists in giving nature its correct form; and she will soon extend her domain, having "conquering Eyes" that will drive like glancing chariot wheels "In Triumph over Hearts that strive." The pastoral shade in which she begins her days must then become the poet's protection.

However, though her glories will be no less glorious for being dangerous to men (who lose whether they yield or resist), her epic renown and pastoral innocence are not entirely compatible. Taming wildness in the garden predicts the taming of Cupid, since both love and nature need instruction from virtue, but in the garden, nature can be "reformed" without violence; in the adult world, violence is inescapable. And even garden arts must be exercised carefully:

> v
>
> But O young beauty of the Woods,
> Whom Nature courts with fruits and flow'rs,
> Gather the Flow'rs, but spare the Buds;
> Lest *Flora* angry at thy crime,
> To kill her Infants in their prime,
> Do quickly make th' Example Yours;
>   And, ere we see,
> Nip in the blossome all our hopes and Thee.

Hence, as Marvell discovers in the example of Thomas Fairfax (in "Upon the Hill and Grove at Bill-borow"), unnatural and self-willed power must not be allowed to enter the garden as it necessarily enters active life. Fairfax compromises by achieving a moderate eminence and by retreating from his own "Brightness" to the "sacred Shade" at the top of the hill, as near heaven as the hill will take him. ("Nor he the Hills without the Groves, / Nor Height but with Retirement loves.") And so T. C. must moderate her ambition. Flora has her own decorum and her own means of retaliation. Beneath the pleasantries of the garden myth lies the threat of death, and this unavoidable fact controls T. C.'s "prospects." "In time" the conquering eyes will have their way; "mean time" the garden must be kept inviolate and the verdant charm of the flowers— which have their own prospects—T. C. must improve only with caution.

The ambiguity of the attitude toward nature, however, and toward T. C. herself, complicates this. Again, the tonal shifts are radical. In a lightly mock epic manner, the first three stanzas submerge admonition in surprised eulogy; the last two stanzas submerge eulogy in irony and admonition. Because T. C. is ideal, she is virtuous (with overtones of *virtù*), but because too ideal for man and possibly even for the garden, she is a virtuous "Enemy." Those who strive for a perfection that human hearts cannot have, the poet warns, run the risk of being broken themselves; and so, while she is unquestionably good, she is not necessarily good for this world, at least not unless she heeds the warning of her tutor. The poet's attitude toward the pastoral retreat and toward youthful innocence is thus twisted by his awareness of the dangers of growing up. He is strangely disarmed and will be passively inert in his retreat ("Let me *be* laid, / Where I may see thy Glories from some shade"). Perhaps as a consequence of the mixture of banter and passivity, he cannot find the proper tone for the admonition:

IV

Mean time, whilst every verdant thing
It self does at thy Beauty charm,
Reform the errours of the Spring;
Make that the Tulips may have share
Of sweetness, seeing they are fair;
And Roses of their thorns disarm:
But most procure
That Violets may a longer Age endure.

Since T. C. obviously cannot perform any of these things, the natural assumption would be that Marvell is taunting her with the limits of her "art."[10] But the mood is more complex than that. As a creature of a kind of Eden, she can in a sense correct the "errours of the Spring." A regenerate force in nature, like Mary Fairfax bestowing straightness upon the woods and sweetness upon the meadows, she can, within limits, make her own garden. (The mind, as "The Garden" says, is an inner world "where each kind / Does *streight* its own resemblance find.") While she remains harmless (which will not be for long), this remains a tantalizing dream on the edge of possibility; it is the dream of the pastoral artist, and at present T. C. is more an artist learning to cultivate nature than future chariot driver. An ideal garden of art despoils the real flowers in order to make them "a longer Age endure." Realization of the limits of art results in the warning to the young beauty of the "Woods" (a more wild and dangerous place than the garden), which replaces the usual pastoral compromise. The final irony is that all T. C.'s creative and corrective powers are subject to the very transience and pain they try to reform: she, too, is a "blossom" who can be "nipped" should she commit the forbidden crime, and nipped by "Flora," a mythological creature, but real enough to strike in protection of her "In-

10. See Joseph Summers, "Marvell's 'Nature,'" *ELH*, 20 (1953), 130 ff.

fants." But the mock heroic tone, the colloquial phrase "nip in the blossom," and the zeugma of "our hopes and Thee" make it difficult to determine with any certainty the final attitude: the poem, suggestive but uneven, lies somewhere between a hopeful vision of a perfect *hortus conclusus* and awareness of its impossibility, between playful eulogy and serious warning. The threat to decorum and ceremony is apparently real but obscure.

In "The Fair Singer" and "Musicks Empire" the main components of T. C.'s ambiguity—the power of art to shape nature and the threatening power over men—are isolated and developed without these complexities. In the first of these, love encircles the free and innocent world of nature and transforms it into a "fatal Harmony." The soul's environment becomes an entangling web and the poet's life in the "wind and sun" is cut off. But if adult love again triumphs over natural innocence and freedom, it does so without the ambivalent relationship of art and nature that brings both into question in T. C.'s case. The singer is paradoxically a "sweet" enemy and the last lines effectively climax a sense of loss that makes the poem more than conventional hyperbole; but nature itself is not ambiguous.

In "Musicks Empire" the situation is simply reversed: nature requires disciplining by art that can "weave" the air. The theme of love, of course, is not directly involved, which means that art itself lacks the inherent threat it has in the fair singer and in little T. C. The terms in which the growth of music is described, however, imply that entanglement in time is not regrettable. "Infant Nature" is wild and jarring until put into order: rather than creating "Fetters" of the elements, music makes a "Mosaique of the Air." As in Dryden's "Song for St. Cecilia's Day," it is art that has raised the world out of chaos:

> First was the World as one great Cymbal made,
> Where Jarring Windes to infant Nature plaid.

> All Musick was a solitary sound,
> To hollow Rocks and murm'ring Fountains bound.

Without harmony, bound to rude winds, "hollow Rocks," and inarticulate fountains, music is a jarring and single-toned instrument. Nature's infancy (and by implication man's) is a primitive state of unrealized potential rather than a state of innocence. Jubal makes "the wilder Notes agree," calls echoes "from their sullen Cell," and builds an organ on the model of their cave, thus imitating nature but improving it. Finally, sounds form families and societies as "Virgin Trebles wed the manly Base,"

> From whence the Progeny of numbers new
> Into harmonious Colonies withdrew.

Only in this social wedding can men sing of their triumphs and only in joining "Heaven's quire" does art fully realize its potential. With his perfected art, the composer may encompass the world:

> V
>
> Then Musick, the Mosaique of the Air,
> Did of all these a solemn noise prepare:
> With which She gain'd the Empire of the Ear,
> Including all between the Earth and Sphear.
>
> VI
>
> Victorious sounds! yet here your Homage do
> Unto a gentler Conqueror then you;
> Who though He flies the Musick of his praise,
> Would with you Heavens Hallelujahs raise.

Though Marvell turns the process to eulogy (perhaps of Fairfax, Margoliouth conjectures), the important point, I think, is that art makes the processes of time worthwhile. Through art one celebrates communal triumphs and links the community to heaven, and, thus attuned to "Heavens Hallelujahs," music justifies the growth from "infancy" to empire and conquest.

The poems we have observed so far reveal that, because Marvell thought of love dialectically, as a threat to the sanctuaries of the self, he could not celebrate it wholeheartedly. "Young Love" and "Clorinda and Damon" circumvent the main difficulties only by making withdrawal unnecessary, while "The Fair Singer" and "The Unfortunate Lover" concede its impossibility. The most rewarding of the love poems, especially "To His Coy Mistress" and "Definition of Love," examine love as a demand for action in the context of the contemplative values of Christian Platonism. The complexity and richness of "To His Coy Mistress" derive partly from the consideration of time and the *act* of love as consolations when that context is invalidated; by balancing conjunction of minds and opposition, "The Definition" makes action unnecessary: arrested dialectic replaces the motion outward to attain the strange, high object.

Yet despite their apparent solutions to the problem of love and their inclusiveness, neither "To His Coy Mistress" nor "The Definition" quite embraces the total complex; both poems appear, in fact, to offer mutually exclusive strategies. What the Christian Platonist required was a form of Beatrice, a sublimated guide to divine Eros able to combine both the celestial and the earthly Venus. The soul's emergence outward, its "transpiring at every pore," could then be its upward "dissolution."

The time of Henrietta Maria and Anne Hyde undoubtedly offered less inspiration for that solution than the period of Laura or the Fairy Queen. But in one poem, "The Gallery," Marvell nevertheless discovers an alternative in the controls of art, perhaps the only alternative capable of both protecting the soul and fulfilling the demands of love and time. In the context of his other poems on love, it is a meaningful though generally ignored poem that brings together nearly all of Marvell's recurrent themes—art, pastoral nature, love's savagery, and the soul's quest for unity, for example—and makes what would appear to be a proposal unique in renaissance and seventeenth-century love poems. It grants that the processes of time twist love into something unnatural, but it finds a restoration of young love still conceivable. The speaker's strategy is to convince Clora of this: everything depends on her. Hence, the poem is cast in the dialectical form of the temptation poem. The "great *Arras*-hangings" are designed to show Clora love-tyrants set opposite "harmless Loves," and vultures of prey opposite halcyons of calm; and one final portrait depicts what was the beginning and what ought to be the end of love, thereby offering a chance for wholeness. The poet attempts to make a single gallery out of "several lodgings." He invites Clora to come and look at the results with the hope that if she sees the integrity of the gallery and her own place in it as the potential bestower of unity, they can find their common being; the soul can be made one despite its love.

Though the portraits contrast sharply, the careful symmetry with which they are arranged is a sign of the soul's unity within its dialectic and of its eventual success. The main burden, however, falls upon the final stanza; in revealing the beginning of love at the end it transcends the love tortures learned in the passage of time. And so Clora may be convinced and reformed. But before that time, the exaggerations of the earlier portraits have a dramatic educational function to perform, namely, to show the cruel mistress to herself and to suggest a cure:

I

Clora come view my Soul, and tell
Whether I have contriv'd it well.
Now all its several lodgings lye
Compos'd into one Gallery;

And the great *Arras*-hangings, made
Of various Faces, by are laid;
That, for all furniture, you'l find
Only your Picture in my Mind.

II

Here Thou are painted in the Dress
Of an Inhumane Murtheress;
Examining upon our Hearts
Thy fertile Shop of cruel Arts:
Engines more keen than ever yet
Adorned Tyrants Cabinet;
Of which the most tormenting are
Black Eyes, red Lips, and curled Hair.

The black eyes will be transformed into the "look" of the last
portrait in which love, caught at the innocent moment when
the poet was first taken, was not yet an emotional labyrinth;
the "curled Hair" will be transformed into hair which "hangs
loosely playing in the Air," and the "cruel Arts" into the
"tenderness" of the shepherdess. In the meantime, the portrait
set directly against these images from the "Tyrants Cabinet"
promises something more supernatural than this, with a suggestion of the Song of Songs and the coming of the Bridegroom, more flattering than concessions to mere dominance in
love:

III

But, on the other side, th' art drawn
Like to *Aurora* in the Dawn;
When in the East she slumb'ring lyes,
And stretches out her milky Thighs;
While all the morning Quire does sing,
And *Manna* falls, and Roses spring;
And, at thy Feet, the wooing Doves
Sit perfecting their harmless Loves.

If this is an impractical dream, it is also a paradigm for love,
something human love cannot be, despite the sensuousness of

the vision, but something it would do no harm for Clora to try to be more often. At this point it serves merely as an antidote for the opposing portraits, an image of *la belle nature* unable to drive out consciousness of *la nature existante* of Clora's grim personality:

IV

Like an Enchantress here thou show'st,
Vexing thy restless Lover's Ghost;
And, by a Light obscure, dost rave
Over his Entrails, in the Cave;
Divining thence, with horrid Care,
How long thou shalt continue fair;
And (when inform'd) them throw'st away,
To be the greedy Vultur's prey.

The "Unfortunate Lover" is recognizable here (as other Marvellian lovers are in other stanzas). Breaking into Arcadia, death and time become even more formidable enemies than the arts of the "Inhumane Murtheress." With the lover already dead and the mistress dying, birds of prey have their hour, picking at the bones in which Clora may divine her own fate with "horrid Care," as she has so carefully determined the fate of her lover. This raving in the "light obscure" is the reward of the arts of love, which, as the arts of the soul reveal, lead from the "Tyrants Cabinet" to the Cave of Despair. The mythic endurance of Venus and the calmness of the halcyon (stanza V) on the other hand, like the pastoral Canticle of the third stanza, offer an alternative. All violence is stilled: the sea has only motion enough to bear the "Ambergris" and the air only enough to convey perfume, while Clora herself merely "sit'st a float."

Finally, then, the last portrait merges the static and innocent beauty of the Venus-Aurora queen with the action of the enchantress, presenting enough motion to be interesting but not enough to be dangerous·

VII

> But, of these Pictures and the rest,
> That at the Entrance likes me best:
> Where the same Posture, and the Look
> Remains, with which I first was took.
> A tender Shepherdess, whose Hair
> Hangs loosely playing in the Air,
> Transplanting Flow'rs from the green Hill,
> To crown her Head, and Bosome fill.

Only a slight hint of disorder remains: instead of resting in the languid pose of Venus and letting the sea transport her, or "slumb'ring" in a Bowre of Bliss, Clora herself, hair "loosely" playing, gathers the flowers from the green hill. Through her Perdita-like gestures, the green is "transplanted" to her, becoming a symbolic crown for the head and filling the bosom: she fuses Marvell's trees and nymphs. This original posture still "remains," despite what has happened in time. The soul's dialectical art catches and holds the one image behind the thousand and more forms Clora presents to the world. It shows that she may be humanly changeable and not lose the ideal image of herself; and so the poet, absorbed in her and in his representation of what she essentially is, may indeed make one gallery well "contriv'd." Instead of going out, he beckons Clora in.

5. *Providential Politics*

PERHAPS THE MOST persistent of the problems that confronted Puritans of various sects in civil and political matters
was that of initiating public, reformative action within the
terms of an essentially private religious experience. Given the
emphasis upon the individual conscience and inner light, it
was inevitable that grounds for the revolution be searched for
in principles of personal freedom and guarantees of religious
rights rather than in principles of equality and class privilege.
Whatever the implications of class struggle in the war, the
feeling that a London merchant, as a religious man, had a
right not to be interfered with was very strong and very effective in converting passive resistance to action; his concern with
enterprise included free trade in words and dogma. For the
bond that held the revolutionary party together, at least in
initial stages, was essentially without a specific dogma or set
of class principles. Later it became the difficult task of Cromwell, Ireton, and others in the center between levelers and
Presbyterians to prevent the establishment of rigid dogma
where the principle of no principle was to be the byword. As
Cromwell made clear to those pushing the army complaints in
the Putney debates, the Puritan was to consult inner conscience
rather than a public manifesto before carrying on public ne-

gotiation, though the difference between consulting God in private and making "appearances of religious meetings covers for designs" against the opposing party might be hard to see: one the strategy of the saint, the other of the Machiavel.

The Puritan became a more spontaneous protestant when the sanctity of the conscience was openly violated; he was never so quickly vociferous as when his ears were in danger. Give him a dialectical opponent and the gate was immediately opened for his emergence, sermon, sword, or polemical tract in hand. While the Lady sits imprisoned by Comus, she is aggressive even in defense; though "chained" in body, she can think—and say—whatever she likes:

> *Comus.* Nay Lady, sit; if I but wave this wand
> Your nerves are all chain'd up in Alabaster,
> And you a statue. . . .
>
> . . . .
>
> *Lady.* Fool, do not boast,
> Thou canst not touch the freedom of my mind
> With all thy charms, although this corporal rind
> Thou hast immancl'd, while Heav'n sees good.
>
> (559–65)

Since even a Platonist-Puritan cannot last forever glued to a foreign seat in a hostile forest, she wants to be rescued. But because Comus is conceived dialectically, the issue against him is clear and the Lady is never in great danger.

Such Puritans as Lord Brooke, John Smith, Peter Sterry, and John Milton (ordinarily), however, found the integration of the contemplative and active lives far more complicated. Since there are not Sabrina-remedies for all occasions, the very rebellion that makes a pragmatist of the idealist threatens to extinguish his idealism in the ensuing violence. In civil matters where one's opponents are seldom so obligingly evil as Comus, the result of abandoning traditional restraints in the purely antithetical pattern of response is that, after the main enemy is defeated, another appears, perhaps from one's own party, and so on ad infinitum until one has turned against everyone and maintains his own sect alone. Though the army paper is "plausible," Cromwell finds, for example, "How do we know if, whilst we are disputing these things, another company of men shall [not] gather together, and put out a paper as plausible? . . . And not only another, and another, but many of this kind."[1] Once the revolt on individualistic, as opposed to class, principles begins, where does it end?

A further complication lay in the belief in providential history, which encouraged the dialectical reaction if one's side was winning and, as the royalist broadsides reveal, ironic debunking if not. That Thomas Fairfax should have looked upon the "fatal day" of Charles' beheading with mixed feelings and with some theology is indicative of the problems which that event, especially, forced upon all but very ardent Independents: "Oh let that day from time be blotted quite," Fairfax writes; yet "if the power divine permitted this / His will's the law and ours must acquiese."[2] As this demonstrates, the conflict between expediency and idealism was removed only in a somewhat perfunctory manner by submission to providential will. Colonel Goffe at the Putney debates illustrates what the doctrine became in the hands of those less deliberative than Fairfax. The quest for freedom involves rigorous struggle against the world and in that struggle it is sometimes necessary for the government to shake loose its burdens, with assistance from God operating through pre-elected saints. "God does seem evidently to be throwing down the glory of all flesh," he continues, "and the greatest powers in the kingdom have been shaken. God hath thrown down the glory of the King and that

1. *Puritanism and Liberty*, ed. A. S. P. Woodhouse (University of Chicago Press, 1951), p. 7.
2. *The Poems of Thomas Third Lord Fairfax*, ed. Edward Bliss Reed (New Haven, 1909), pp. 281–82.

party. . . . There are two ways that God doth take upon those that walk obstinately against him; if they be obstinate and continue obstinate he breaks them in pieces with a rod of iron; if they be his people and wander from him, he takes that glory from them and takes it to himself."[3]

Though reducing the classes to three—the godly, those who had been godly but strayed, and the ungodly—is satisfying and convenient, a permanent government cannot be founded on such antithetical strategy. In attempting to deal with the world, one is either regimented or broken, and in either case freedom is lost. It requires little reading between the lines, however, to see that in Colonel Goffe's account regret is mixed with a certain amount of exaltation. Joshua Sprigge supplements Goffe's remarks with a thought that lay in the minds of many committed Puritans:

> It is God's design, I say, to bring forth the civil government, and all things here below, in the image and resemblance of things above; and whenas those things that are but of [a temporary] and representative nature have clashed with that which hath been their end . . . it hath been the ruin of all states . . . .
>
> Now, my Lord, God having thus taken us apieces, and that righteously, because our government did not stand in God in its pattern, why, he hath only by his providence now brought forth the government of the sword, being that which we are only capable of. . . . Magistrates and all the powers of the world, unless they were in the immediate hand and guidance of God . . . will dash against this stone.[4]

The possibility of making the world below conform to the world above again involves losing spiritual freedom: when the state is left to its own devices, it is eventually dashed against the providential rock. In terms of the withdrawal-efflux pat-

3. *Puritanism and Liberty*, p. 20.
4. Ibid., pp. 134–35.

terns I categorized earlier, Sprigge advocates both despising the world in such a way that it may be subsumed as a dialectical opposite of the spirit and then, having annihilated a sufficient portion of the commonwealth, embracing the rest as an *extension*. He is simply adding the antithetical pattern to the Elizabethan theory of correspondences between "above" and "below" and applying them both to the current political situation. The negative side of Puritan politics, corresponding to the way of chastity is in a sense the saint's defense of his perimeters with the moral sword; the positive side is his attempt to construct a government below "in the image and resemblance of things above."

Despite the apparent compulsiveness of the antithetical strategy, however, active battle of this kind against ungodly magistrates did result in a degree of freedom both for the saint in his saintliness and for others as well. In A. S. P. Woodhouse's words, "First the principle of segregation [i.e. segregation of saint and unregenerate man]; then, after that is enforced, the power of analogy: on these two things the democratic influence of Puritanism chiefly depends."[5] But for those who were less partisan, a further difficulty lay in distinguishing here and now the elect from the unelect, the regenerate freed through "right reason" and the indwelling spirit, from those freed through simple lack of conscience or license. Which group in the actual kingdom adheres to the pattern of "things above"? And saints, like other members of the commonwealth, belong to the order of nature as well as to the order of grace, so that their own concept of the double law, human and divine, can become self-divisive as well as politically schismatic: the wrangle is internal as well as external.

When he turned to such political matters, Marvell in his "quest for unity," like Milton, Sterry, Smith, and others, tried

5. Ibid., introd., p. 86.

to reconcile philosophical and religious principles with action, virtue with *virtù*.[6] If the reaction of the saint or mystic was to reject the scene altogether (as Vaughan and Traherne tend to do) and the reaction of the strongly partisan members of either side was to pummel half and treat the other half as extension, Marvell was clearly not quite at home in either party. He could not reduce either side to pure antithesis, and, on the other hand, he could not subsume a scene at war as an extension of self or divine principle, as he could the garden and sacred grove. (The war is purged from "Upon Appleton House," "The Garden," and "Upon the Hill and Grove at Billborow" in order to make possible an unqualified celebration of the Fairfax family and the garden scene.)

These difficulties are reflected in the ambivalence of "An Horatian Ode" and are further compounded by Marvell's apparent distaste for Cromwell as God's vicegerent, which might be seen as analogous to the struggle between soul and scene in other poems. "The First Anniversary" explicitly treats the

6. Cf. Joseph Mazzeo, "Cromwell as Machiavellian Prince in Marvell's 'An Horatian Ode,' " *JHI*, 21 (1960), 1–17. Mazzeo's reading of "Cromwell as a Machiavellian prince" with more *virtù* than virtue is fresh and provocative. The result of his analysis, however, is to make Marvell inconsistent not only in matters of party allegiance but in fundamental ways of regarding his times. See Hans Baron, "Marvell's 'An Horatian Ode' and Machiavelli," *JHI*, 21 (1960), 450–51. See also Cleanth Brooks, "Literary Criticism," in *English Institute Essays* (1946), pp. 127–48 and "A Note on the Limits of 'History' and the Limits of 'Criticism,' " *Sewanee Review*, 61 (1953), 129–35; Douglas Bush, "Marvell's 'Horatian Ode,' " *Sewanee Review*, 60 (1952), 363–76; R. Wallerstein, *Studies in Seventeenth-Century Poetic*, pp. 279 ff.; L. D. Lerner, in *Interpretations: Essays on Twelve English Poems* (London, 1955), pp. 59–74; Lawrence W. Hyman, "Politics and Poetry in Andrew Marvell," *PMLA*, 73 (1958), 475–79; John Wheatcroft, "Andrew Marvell and the Winged Chariot," *Bucknell Review*, 6 (1956), 22–53; James F. Carens, "Andrew Marvell's Cromwell Poems," *Bucknell Review*, 7 (1957), 41–70; John M. Wallace, "Marvell's Horatian Ode," *PMLA*, 77 (1962), 33–45.

scene as an extension of divine principle operating *through* Cromwell:

> [Mean]while indefatigable Cromwell hyes,
> And cuts his way still nearer to the Skyes,
> Learning a Musique in the Region clear,
> To tune this lower to that higher Sphere.
>
> (45–48)

Making Cromwell's role as mediator clear in the later poem, however, does not necessarily result in poetic gains. Though the commitment in Marvell's subsequent eulogies suggests Milton's faith in Cromwell and in the rightness of the wars (without stating it quite in Milton's terms, of course), Marvell is not at his best in primarily eulogistic modes. With Milton, both poetics and politics were otherwise, since he did not find, between providence and the political arena, a significant gap that might make one doubt whether God is represented by one or another party, or perhaps none: "I am of the opinion, Salmasius, and always have been that the law of God does exactly agree with the law of nature, and therefore, If I have shown what by God's law is established with respect to kings ... I have at the same time ... shown what is most agreeable to the law of nature."[7] In his public declarations at least, Milton believed Cromwell's rule to have come from the rule of sanctity within as well as from genius and military force. The ideal of continuous reconciliation, asserted in Marvell's line "tune this lower to that higher Sphere," is always available to the Miltonic saint who is a true imitator of Christ, as such communication with heaven ought to be, a contemporary writes, to anyone who "hath an enlightened conscience carrying a more bright and lively stamp of the kingly place and power of the Lord Jesus. ... Such a man may be called *micro-*

7. *Works*, gen. ed. F. A. Patterson (New York, 1932), 7, 267.

cristus, the epitome of Christ mystical."[8] But that Marvell's milieu presented him with this possibility was not enough; in "An Horatian Ode," at least, he had to convince himself and his audience that Cromwell could in fact tune nature and grace, that he "knew" as well as "acted." The Platonist concept of the inspired man and the Reformation ideal of the man who acts had to be synthesized before he could endorse the new order with its violent treatment of royalist institutions.[9]

Seen with these problems in mind, the strategy of "An Horatian Ode" becomes clear, at least in broad outline. Marvell can celebrate Cromwell's return only after finding the warrior's emergence justification for his own as state poet. The Cromwellian myth must enable him to expel apathy and feelings of revulsion towards the chaos of the times and to discover grace awakening nature. Only then can the kind of freedom exist that allows one to follow the soul's promptings into action without reservation, even though action may involve regicide. The common task of poet and subject is thus to adjust to an active life of turmoil and violence. Languishing numbers come to mind because the poet himself is involved in the celebration. The reticence of mood implies that there is more to the sudden emergence of the "forward youth" than the mere exigencies of the times: these serve merely to force the poet to confront problems already latent in the conflict between a life of retirement and a life of action. The hour demands that he forsake what is both his protection and his spiritual shadow, that he leave the "muses dear" and face the crumbling of an old and once secure order; until he does so, panegyric is impos-

8. *Puritanism and Liberty,* p. 248.

9. Cf. Lord Brooke, *The Nature of Truth,* p. 34; Whichcote, *The Work of Reason,* ed. E. T. Campagnac, p. 51; and John Smith, *The True Way,* p. 82.

sible. The nature of the shift to Cromwell (line 9) shows that the warrior's course from the garden to the battlefield is representative of the emergence problem (which is further confirmed by Cromwell's private history, lines 29–36). His issuance is dynamic and fearless, like Caesar's entrance into the world; but such *virtù* has its frightening aspects when viewed against traditional moral and religious values and compared to normal ways of being "born." Ignoring distinctions between the emulous and the enemy, he splits the world that has nurtured him: anything that encircles or obscures him is as inimical as direct opposition. This is "Courage high," no doubt, but courage is not an unmixed good.

The struggle of the old, accepted forms of order against the dynamic destructiveness of Cromwell becomes increasingly marked in the rending of "Pallaces and Temples" (king and church). Only by adding divine force to his own does Cromwell exceed the limits of such mortal honor as Caesar gained and break through the laurels that circumscribe and reward ordinary human effort. He does not cease being human, of course ("And, if we would speak true, / Much to the *Man* is due"); but his alliance with angry heaven is the basis for his destruction of the natural order. Heaven's "three-fork'd" lightning, like a trident of the gods, shatters institutions without regard for their merit and usefulness. The burning and rending threaten hierarchy and subordination in the onrush of events. While " 'Tis Madness to resist or blame / The force of angry Heavens flame," it is also difficult to accept it.

However, the force that lies behind Cromwell is not as clear as Joshua Sprigge might have wished, which is again an indication of Marvell's reluctance to identify too quickly with the subject. On the one hand providence is against Charles but on the other its operation is not entirely clear. It functions in the poem as in history—inscrutably and pervasively—to be experienced in the events themselves, rather than perceived or talked about directly (as Shakespeare's impolitic Richard II unfortunately believed it could be). Those most qualified to govern may be "microchrists" or embodied lively images of the "kingly place"; inner and outer governance may be reconciled through them to the image of divine governance as it exists above; but one has only visible action to judge by.

Still, the providential force that lies immediately beneath the surface undeniably exerts pressure. The clash of spirits continues to direct the poem, Cromwell's spirit against Charles' and angry heaven's against a recalcitrant nation being "taken apieces." It is difficult to follow the poet's own feelings through the succession of images, and if we stress one side or another too strongly we destroy the balance. The vacillation becomes more pronounced as the poem progresses, the syntax more difficult to construe. We cannot be sure where Marvell tends to draw the line, but the hints of dispraise which Cleanth Brooks points out are clear enough. Only by arbitrarily constricting the language can we remove its dyslogistic implications (as in the subjunctive, "*As if* his highest plot / To plant the Bergamot" and in the "wiser Art" of the Hampton Court episode, in which plotting is shown in its Machiavellian operation). Though one need not cease believing in the saint simply because he is now and then human, a saint might be expected to move by divine impulsion rather than pre-planned maneuvers. It is not entirely clear whether the Promethean Cromwell has the flame as a gift or has taken it, but the fact remains that in the fierce relationship of Fate to England, ancient rights are shattered. Certainly justice, in purely human terms, has a case against him.

In all this, however, Marvell keeps celebration uppermost, if not pure. He is maneuvering for a more complete endorsement of Cromwell, not because he wishes to reduce the scene to its acceptable parts or create antithetical enemies but because worthwhile reconciliation of above and below comes only through those who have valor and make themselves conduits of Fate's electrical charge: one must conceive within himself a new order closer to the laws of providence before the works of time are found lacking; the flame must be self-engendered as well as derived from above. The conflict reaches its crucial point in the episode of the King's (supposed) escape to Carisbrooke and the execution:

> And *Hampton* shows what a part
> He had of wiser Art.
> Where, twining subtile fears with hope,
> He wove a Net of such a scope,
> That *Charles* himself might chase
> To *Caresbrooks* narrow case.
> That thence the *Royal Actor* born
> The *Tragick Scaffold* might adorn:
> While round the armed Bands
> Did clap their bloody hands.
> *He* nothing common did or mean
> Upon that memorable Scene:
> But with his keener Eye
> The Axes edge did try:
> Nor call'd the *Gods* with vulgar spight
> To vindicate his helpless Right,
> But bow'd his comely Head,
> Down as upon a Bed.

The intangible fears and hope that Cromwell conjures with spiritual mastery and "wiser Art" are a strong, invisible net bringing Charles to ruin. As the contest between King and axe brings the unpleasant facts of regicide prominently to Marvell's mind, the poet must go one way or the other. Under the circumstances, it would be understandable if the poet went back to the "shadows." But while the "bloody hands" reveal the harshness of the "murder," they also applaud the "Royal Actor." The emotional intensity of the play is such that one *forgets* whose side he is on. Though the wiser art and the plot have already predicted the stage image, it now comes forward prominently to convert the memorable "scene" to a milder kind of reality, less final, less historical. Marvell makes no attempt to avoid the brutality of the scene; in fact, no less than the execution would do: it becomes ritualistic and purifying. The executioner-audience demands the performance for its own catharsis. (Death as nightly ceremony supplements this with an old figure beautifully turned, the act of putting the head under the axe "as upon a Bed" being more courageous than merely going to death "as to sleep.") The superb performance of the royal actor "adorning" the tragic scaffold thus paradoxically shows Cromwell to be right, with respect both to the man and to his fated (providential) course. Charles as well as Cromwell has a way of fulfilling destiny. And as he in his deeper wisdom or "keener Eye" searches for the cause of the execution—spirit against saintly axe—and becomes resigned, the poet dissolves the division in his own loyalties: in the "bleeding Head" the "happy Fate" of the government is foretold—"This was that memorable Hour / Which first assur'd the forced Pow'r." Thus, "born" to this fate, the King (as Yeats' poem has it in another connection)

> too, has resigned his part . . .
> He, too, has been changed in his turn,
> Transformed utterly:
> A terrible beauty is born.

His fall suggests that of the royal oak in "Upon Appleton House," which drops "content / Viewing the Treason's Punishment" (stanza 70), and then "serves to feed the Hewels young," those moral guardians of the forest and of the future "Farfacian Oak."

Hereafter, the mood is more fully explicit and less complex as Marvell casts his lot with the new republic. The reminders of violence such as the bleeding head and the image of the hunt are marks of a fully recognized "terrible beauty" and so no longer evoke the kind of ambivalence that characterizes the first half of the poem. The government can be called what it is, a "forced Pow'r," and the future can be foretold in the divinely terrible sign that frightens even its "Architects."

The reaction to the Irish campaign, from which the poem takes its name, is thus purely eulogistic. Since Cromwell's hand had been unusually heavy at Wexford and elsewhere, there would be reason to expect irony. But brutality was a commonplace during the wars. Cromwell himself, whom Marvell later describes quite unambiguously as one whose tenderness extends to all, whose deep soul flows through every channel and to whom kindly nature loves to lose itself, wrote after Drogheda: "Their officers were knocked on the head; and every tenth man of the soldiers killed. . . . I am persuaded that this is a righteous judgment of God upon those barbarous wretches, who have imbrued their hands in so much innocent blood; and that it will tend to prevent effusion of blood for the future."[10] That Marvell's previous reticence does not intrude here, testifies to the strength of his affirmation. For the lines cannot be taken ironically without totally inverting the eulogy:

> So much one Man can do,
> That does both act and know. . . .
> How good he is, how just,
> And fit for highest Trust. . . .

Further, Cromwell not only connects heaven and earth by acting and knowing, but is also extremely *submissive*, hence the image of the falcon within easy call of the falconer, perched on its "green Bow." He may be sketching the character of the benevolent prince, but the important point would seem to be that prince and saint are now the same, as the bird is a medi-

10. *Oliver Cromwell's Letters and Speeches*, ed. Thomas Carlyle (New York, 1899), p. 60.

ator between war and peace, and possesses, besides, the royal
and aristocratic virtues so admirable in Charles. As the poet
finds the vigorous force of Cromwell directed strictly to the
benefit of England, the idiom of personal concern gives way
to public declamation:

> What may not then our *Isle* presume
> While Victory his Crest does plume!
> What may not others fear
> If thus he crown each Year!

The poet's voice returns strongly here and proceeds confidently
to adopt the tone of sage political adviser to one of the age's
more astute politicians. The voice of public celebration and
eulogy is thus combined with the poet's personal endorsement.
The urbanity is a mark of release, and the irony is directed
against a common enemy. The remaining uneasiness is caused
by fears for the strength of the regime rather than doubts of its
rightness, and it defers to the spirit of exhortation.[11] By implication, politician and poet are identified in the arts of war, as
in the "Arts of Peace" before the "unused Armour" had to be
taken down, thanks to the wiser art of Cromwell as tragic
playwright. Though the "Spirits of the shady Night" may be
not only the rebellious angels of Montrose in the north but
also some less definite trouble of the poet who prefers to sing
"in the Shadows," force—and "art"—may ward them off.

It seems likely that even before the Restoration Marvell was
coming to accept as inevitable the separation of the providential universe from the naturalistic world of seventeenth-
century philosophy and science. His advice to Samuel Parker,
who would make the breaking of every human law as grave

11. L. Proudfoot finds an "admonition" in the concluding lines: "Marvell: Sallust and the Horatian Ode," *N&Q*, *196* (1951), 434; Cf. G. M.
Trevelyan, *History of England* (New York, 1954), 2, 214.

as transgressing against God's decrees, perhaps comes from his own experience: "Take heed of hooking things up to heaven in this manner; for, though you look for some advantage from it, you may chance to raise them above your reach, and if you do not fasten and rivet them very well when you have them there, they will come down again with such a swing, that if you stand not out of the way, they may bear you down further than you thought of."[12] A spirit of religious tolerance rare in his time is revealed in his prose tracts arguing for indulgence of nonconformity. This tolerance and the principle of moderation in spiritual matters is not, of course, entirely new in his writing. "Upon the Hill and Grove at Billborrow," for example, had cast a very transparent allegorical veil over Fairfax' tolerance, which seems "as for a Model laid":

I

See how the arched Earth does here
Rise in a perfect Hemisphere!
The stiffest Compass could not strike
A line more circular and like;
Now softest Pensel draw a Brow
So equal as this Hill does bow.
It seems as for a Model laid,
And that the World by it was made.

II

Here learn ye Mountains more unjust,
Which to abrupter greatness thrust,
That do with your hook-shoulder'd height
The Earth deform and Heaven fright,
For whose excrescence ill design'd,
Nature must a new Center find,
Learn here those humble steps to tread,
Which to securer Glory lead.

12. *The Rehearsal Transpros'd*, ed. A. B. Grosart (London, 1873), 1, 407.

Fairfax' refusal to endorse extreme measures—the leveler's "Plain" or the saints' "hook-shoulder'd height"—has provided a "Northern Star" for "weary Seamen" in England's tormented seas.

Tolerance and skepticism are more pervasive later, however, though paradoxically the commitment of the political poems through the 1650s appears increasingly strong. The "sacred Shade" that lies between heaven and the top of the hill gives way to the commons, "green" to public thought. To follow Marvell through the transition is to see his poetic mode gradually alter. Spheres are no longer "tuned" nor is the world subsumed after withdrawal: it is exposed in its corruption through satire and lacerated, though incapable of being purged. Briefly, the lyric poet adopts the modes of the Augustan satirist, which do not suit Marvell as well as they do Dryden or Pope. Although the satires are frequently effective, they are uneven as total poems.[13] (I shall return to them in the next chapter.)

13. Ephim G. Fogel in "Salmons in Both, or Some Caveats for Canonical Scholars," BNYPL, 63 (1959), 223–36, 292–308, regards "The Last Instructions to a Painter" highly, but in distinguishing the poem from the second and third advice poems is led to overstate its merits, I think: "This original, superbly integrated poem, longer than any other now known to be Marvell's, is entirely worthy of him. It commands with complete sureness a remarkable range of effects." It is "distinguished by its deep and principled criticism of the health of 'our Lady State' " (p. 301). This position is reinforced by John W. Wallace in "Andrew Marvell and Cromwell's Kingship: 'The First Anniversary,' " ELH, 30 (1963), 209–35, whose perceptive description of "The First Anniversary" does much to justify a re-evaluation of it. One should distinguish between rhetorical organization and poetic quality, however. For example, to prove that it was "altogether appropriate for Marvell to terminate his poem with an address delivered by a foreign king" is not to demonstrate the effectiveness of the passage as poetry. It is not organization or principle that Marvell's late poems lack but a linguistic and imagistic stock capable of integrating local politics with the universal ground claimed for them. The strain is felt in texture rather than structure.

Contrary to first appearances, even "The First Anniversary," which seems pure eulogy in linking politician and providence, has weakened the case for Cromwell as vicegerent. Images are used primarily to express subscription to, rather than exploration of, Cromwell's struggling government, similar to Dryden's figure of the circle, for example, in "A Poem upon the Death of His Late Highness, Oliver, Lord Protector":

> How shall I then begin, or where conclude,
>   To draw a Fame so truly Circular?
> For in a Round, what Order can be shew'd,
>   Where all the Parts so equal perfect are?

The comparison is a matter of rhetorical strategy rather than an integral part of an analogical system.[14] The central concern of Dryden's stanza,

> He fought, secure of Fortune, as of fame;
>   Till by new Maps, the Island might be shown,
> Of Conquests, which he strew'd where-e'er he came,
>   Thick as the *Galaxy* with Stars is sown.

is very similar to that of Marvell's lines,

> When for his Foot he thus a place had found,
> He hurles e'r since the World about him round;
> And in his sev'ral Aspects, like a Star,
> Here shines in Peace, and thither shoots a War.
>   (99–102)

Marvell's metaphor is in some ways more impressive, more metaphysical (especially in the play on "Aspects"), but it is governed by the same decorums of public celebration. The cosmic Cromwell is an exaggeration rather than a social myth, though the exaggeration itself sometimes contributes to the wit of the poem, as in the compressed vigor of "shines" in peace, "shoots" a war.

14. Cf. lines 325–42 and Carens, pp. 55, 57.

The sustaining principle of the state as Marvell now conceives of it is a law of *concordia-discors*. The Amphion myth renders the principle in musical terms and the architectural imagery develops it in more detail.[15]

> The Common-wealth does through their Centers all
> Draw the Circumf'rence of the publique Wall;
> The crossest Spirits here do take their part,
> Fast'ning the Contignation which they thwart;
> And they, whose Nature leads them to divide,
> Uphold, this one, and that the other Side; . . .
> While the resistance of opposed Minds,
> The Fabrick as with Arches stronger binds, . . .
>
> (87–96)

Cromwell's importance is that of a skillful conductor who can make all instruments of the orchestra harmonize despite their natural anarchy. "All matter yields and may be rul'd" through a prudent partitioning of stresses. He thus overcomes the divisive tendency of the sects by converting their wrangle to dialectical cross-buttressing. The commonwealth is the fixed center; the "crossest Spirits" are the interlocked periphery whose resistance fastens the structure tight. Without transforming the threats and counter-thrusts of "Nature" into something more amiable to the soul and without purging hostile elements, Cromwell disciplines their energy. The relation of art and nature in pastoral poems Marvell simply recasts in political terms, with Cromwell as the "soul" of the commonwealth, the Orpheus of human nature.

The wit of the passage quoted reveals something of Mar-

15. Cf. Pope's "Ode for Music on St. Cecilia's Day" (1730 version) and Dryden's "A Song for St. Cecilia's Day"; also Denham, "Cooper's Hill," lines 203 ff. (1642), and "Windsor Forest," lines 11–16. See Earl Wasserman's reading of these poems in *The Subtler Language* (Baltimore, 1959). For a just estimate of Marvell and Dryden as satirists, see Reuben A. Brower, "An Allusion to Europe: Dryden and Tradition," *ELH*, 19 (1952), 38–48.

vell's own delight in the spectacle. But in other parts of the
poem the praise is less compressed; the tension between the
poet and the myth is different from what it was in "An Horatian Ode." Slothful kings, the Roman church, and dissenters
within the state provide momentary foils against which Cromwell can prove himself. The subtle dialectic of the lyrics is
transformed into a cruder polemic:

> Till then my Muse shall hallow far behind
> Angelique *Cromwell* who outwings the wind;
> And in dark Night, and in cold Dayes alone
> Pursues the monster thorough every Throne:
> Which shrinking to her *Roman* Den impure,
> Gnashes her Goary teeth; nor there secure.
>
> (125–30)

The polemic of satire is not so much part of one complex texture as an intermittent element in the total calculated argument. The strategy is to transfer to Cromwell whatever prestige
the king-sun image, Amphion myth, angelology, and scriptural
parallels will afford. Even the traditional lament of the pastoral
scene makes its linguistic contribution (in the passage concerning Cromwell's coach accident):

> Thou *Cromwell* falling, not a stupid Tree,
> Or Rock so savage, but it mourn'd for thee:
> And all about was heard a Panique groan,
> As if that Natures self were overthrown.
> It seem'd the Earth did from the Center tear;
> It seem'd the Sun was faln out of the Sphere:
> Justice obstructed lay, and Reason fool'd;
> Courage disheartned, and Religion cool'd.
>
> (201–08)

Forced as the conventions are, however, less exaggeration
might have been less effective; the kingly pageantry of the
poem with its compensatory rhetoric is pushed one step further
than necessary, as though to indicate, "I am aware of the ex-

aggeration; but it can't hurt if we pretend in common that Cromwell is 'a greater thing, / Then ought below, or yet above a King.' Our pretense may help to make it so." The unstated advice is to join the pageant because the alternatives are dire: the scene is punctuated with anti-maskes or invective opposites —religious chatter, chaos, floods, and so forth—among which Cromwell's accident is only one indication of the general mortal peril. Hence the reader is implicitly urged to recognize the hyperbole if he wants to, but to identify anyway with the god of nature (Cromwell-Amphion-Pan); the alternative to Pan is panic—the fallen sun, darkness, and floods all over again. The pun on "Panique" is a signal to the reader, purposely incongruous in a straightforward universalizing of sorrow for the injured "shepherd," that the poet is not deceived by the rhetoric, and neither should we be. It would be impossible to demonstrate that this double awareness, of the exaggeration and yet of the necessity behind it, is always there when the polemic thickens; but the poem has too much wit for us to suppose that Marvell was unaware of the cost of the eulogistic decorum he set for it. In any case, behind the rhetorical inflation and its occasional mockery is the continual suasive pressure of the prestige myths. The Amphion myth and the king imagery, for example, unobtrusively but effectively reinforce the hyperbole of mourning rocks and fallen sun behind the "honest" recklessness of "stupid," "savage," and "Panique." The *display* of absurdity in these words helps protect the images with a shield of irony so that, when he puts aside inflationary modes, Marvell can exploit them in serious analyses of political and philosophical problems (lines 1–6, 131–58, 324–42, for example).

Even so, the "universal" images cannot be kept untarnished. When Marvell turns to polemic in satire proper, the wit operates without such demanding restrictions and there is less linguistic discomfort in associating England with the universal ground. The withdrawal-emergence pattern in "The Character of Holland" (1653), for instance, is freely converted to partisan use and made to lend some of its natural inevitability to a military maneuver. It suggests a positive English norm against which the Dutch, whose retreat reveals a profound disharmony with nature, can be judged:

> A wholesome Danger drove us to our Ports.
> While half their banish'd keels the Tempest tost,
> Half bound at home in Prison to the frost:
> That ours mean time at leizure might careen,
> In a calm Winter, under Skies Serene.
> As the obsequious Air and Waters rest,
> Till the dear *Halcyon* hatch out all its nest.
> The *Common wealth* doth by its losses grow;
> And, like its own Seas, only Ebbs to flow.
> Besides that very Agitation laves,
> And purges out the corruptible waves.
>   And now again our armed *Bucentore*
> Doth yearly their *Sea-Nuptials* restore.
>
>   (124–36)

The English retreat is a simultaneous flowing, purgation, and halcyon hatching or rebirth, the Dutch retreat a banishment to prison. Danger is wholesome for the English because it results in a regrouping of forces, as the fleet awaits the spring when it will emerge enlarged and prepared for action. The interplay of "above" and "below" is likewise simplified and converted to a useful satiric norm:

> For now of nothing may our *State* despair,
> Darling of Heaven, and of Men the Care;
> Provided that they be what they have been,
> Watchful abroad, and honest still within.
>
>   (145–48)

While "*Jove* governs in the highest Sphere, / Vainly in *Hell* let *Pluto* domineer"; there is no destroying the state as long as the agitation of its enemies only laves and purges what is corruptible. The violence of history only strengthens the commonwealth.

In "The First Anniversary" (written about two years later), however, Marvell is both more encompassing and less consistent. At times Cromwell's "tuning" of heaven and earth is deceptively easy. Cromwell composes an "attractive Song, / Into the Animated City throng" after learning "a Musique in the Region clear," as though art were strong enough to organize the city without reference to a rural retreat: his "sacred Lute creates / Th'harmonious City of the seven Gates" (lines 65–66). His art has the appearance of being a fusion of integrative and oppositional motives (the personal concern of providence, *therefore* his retuning of the government; the resistance of divisive human nature, *nonetheless* the power of his "Lute"). But even so it is not a final ground ensuring that the soul can safely engage history:

> Hence oft I think, if in some happy Hour
> High Grace should meet in one with highest Pow'r,
> And then a seasonable People still
> Should bend to his, as he to Heavens will,
> What we might hope, what wonderful Effect
> From such a wish'd Conjuncture might reflect.
> Sure, the mysterious Work, where none withstand,
> Would forthwith finish under such a Hand:
> Fore-shortned Time its useless Course would stay,
> And soon precipitate the latest Day.
> But a thick Cloud about the Morning lyes,
> And intercepts the Beams of Mortal eyes,
> That 'tis the most which we determine can,
> If these the Times, then this must be the Man.
> (131–44)

The glance outward, from the celebration to the "useless course" of time and "the mysterious Work" that never seems finished, reveals a nostalgia for the old kingship and the blended hierarchy that extends from the people to "one with highest Pow'r," and then to "High Grace." Present knowledge is limited by "thick Clouds," and even if reclamation were possible the result would be the "foreshortening" of time rather than its use. Cromwell is now a "sober Spirit," a "small cloud" which, though pushed by winds of heaven's "higher force," is from a different world than is the "lightning," a world of greater common sense and less magnitude. Though he brings the fertile storm to a thirsty land, he loses "all delight of life" in "Resigning up" his "Privacy so dear, / To turn the head-strong Peoples Charioteer" (lines 220 ff.). Though he may yet "be the man," these are not the times.

The imprisonment of the times, in fact, is the opening and dominant concern of the poem:

> Like the vain Curlings of the Watry maze,
> Which in smooth streams a sinking Weight does raise;
> So Man, declining alwayes, disappears
> In the weak Circles of increasing Years;
> And his short Tumults of themselves Compose,
> While flowing Time above his Head does close.
>
> (1–6)

The mind is no longer, as in "The Garden," a sea-like mirror reflecting the macrocosm, or a creative instrument capable of transcending the sea altogether. Time is comprised of tumults rather than "wholsome hours"; there is too much of it rather than too little. The soul does not enjoy the various light but rises momentarily and is then engulfed. The nostalgic tone is not only not quite compatible with the celebration of the year's achievements but is evident generally in the best parts of the poem. The hyperbolical praise of Cromwell as the one man who "the force of scatter'd Time contracts" seems less effective poetically than the statement of the problem itself.[16] And the hyperbole is not consistent in this regard; while Cromwell "shall one day kill" our "Sins" and even now stands with poised sword (line 148), he cannot subdue a world so "counter-poised" as this one:

> For the great Justice that did first suspend
> The World by Sin, does by the same extend.
> Hence that blest Day still counterpoysed wastes,
> The Ill delaying, what th'Elected hastes;
> Hence landing Nature to new Seas is tost,
> And good Designes still with their Authors lost.
>
> (153–58)

The "Elected" are no more effective in hastening the "blest Day" (when time will end) than the unelected in delaying it: it remains "suspended" between them. Thus the flood of Noah (the first suspension of "the World by Sin," as Margoliouth points out) is experienced anew in modern time-flooded circumstance, and without a "green, yet growing Ark" in which to take "Sanctuary"; the day is wasted, and not only good designs but even their authors are lost. The rhythm of withdrawal and efflux becomes an endless fluctuation of "flood" and momentary respite.

With Cromwell's death in 1658, Marvell's original political-cosmic scheme deteriorates further; the occasion lends itself to poetry of a much more oratorical ordonnance than that of either the "Ode" or "The First Anniversary." The thought is still intriguing that Cromwell has been a mediary like the "sacred oak, which shoots, / To Heav'n its branches, and through earth its roots," but the protective oak is itself the victim of "angry Jove's" lightning; and the gulf between Crom-

16. Cromwell's "yearly" healing of these waters, even if taken at face value, has limitations (line 402), the full implications of which are revealed in the poem on his death; cf. Carens, p. 70.

well's new abode and the poet's old prison is found to be impassable:

> Thou in a pitch how farre beyond the sphere
> Of humane glory tow'rst, and raigning there
> Despoyl'd of mortall robes, in seas of blisse,
> Plunging dost bathe and tread the bright abysse:
> . . . .
> For we, since thou art gone, with heavy doome,
> Wander like ghosts about thy loved tombe;
> And lost in tears, have neither sight nor mind
> To guide us upward through this region blinde.
>   (287–90, 299–302)

This gulf is partly rhetorical, the result of the eulogistic decorum, but that, too, is significant. Generic forms become more important structural guides in poetry, as here the exalted state and the depressed state have less dialectical interplay and perhaps therefore more rhetorical comfort for the mourner. Cromwell's "seas of bliss" transcend time but exist only "beyond the sphere / Of humane glory." While Cromwell walks on the water, those who remain below are entirely lost in "flowing time."

If there is any justice in these conclusions, the common description of the change between the "Ode" and "The First Anniversary" as a growth in which the half-formed political views of the former find mature, philosophical justifications in the latter is open to question. We might say, rather, that Marvell's political position began to weaken soon after it solidified and was never more forcefully put than in the "Ode," while other concepts, more pragmatic but incompatible with it, occupied his thought from about the mid-1650s onward. The later concept of the state could not, I think, engage the full range of his dialectical powers or serve the same kind of poet.

The eleventh-hour transfer of political aspiration to Richard ("Upon the Death of O. C.," lines 305 ff.) is futile and points to what has been happening generally throughout the last two poems on Cromwell. The predominant impression of the poems is that of a tired rhythm of tension and relaxation, of asserted faith in Cromwell and recurring pessimism. The "foul rag-and-bone shop" of the kingdom, at least, if not of the heart, will serve as a substitute for vanishing symbols.

6. From Lyric to Satire

To ALEXANDER POPE belongs the last significant triumph of
the old order that sustains much of Marvell's poetry, a triumph
of strategic inversion, however, in which the analogies between
divine and human creativity (as Aubrey Williams has shown[1])
are revealed in disintegration. The anti-logos, the "uncreating
word," engulfs poet and song, microcosm and macrocosm in
"eternal Night":

> Yet, yet a moment, one dim Ray of light
> Indulge, dread Chaos, and eternal Night!
> Of darkness visible so much be lent,
> As half to show, half veil, the deep Intent.
> Ye Powers! whose Mysteries restored I sing,
> To whom Time bears me on his rapid wing,
> Suspend a while your Force inertly strong,
> Then take at once the Poet and the Song.
>   (*Dunciad*, IV.1–8)

Only enough world and time exist to expose "the deep Intent"
of the Goddess Dulness before time's "inertly" strong wings
bear all away. The "*Vis inertiae* of matter" (as Pope glosses
line 7), the ally of time, overwhelms the brooding, creative

1. *Pope's Dunciad: A Study of Its Meaning* (Louisiana State University
Press, 1955), pp. 131 ff.

Spirit; coincident with the conquest of space and time by the Goddess (and of Westminster by Whiggery), symbol and metaphor are destroyed and the muses are chained in "tenfold bonds." Darkness as a dialectical enemy becomes an anti-creative power; its deep intent and mystery are inversions of the inscrutable divine purpose.

The old integrated cosmos thus offers a perspective for judging duncery rather than a symbolism and concept of order suitable for lyric poetry. Along with Denham and Waller, Marvell foreshadows the shift. When the new goddess of poetry "to pure Space lifts her ecstatic stare," she will run "round the Circle" and find it "square." And so the disaffection of the Restoration court is exposed by recalling a more just and symmetrical cosmic order. The fragments that the crowd of scribblers bears to the great Queen in the *Dunciad* will be handed down partly from the "Drunkards, pimps, and fools" of "The Last Instructions to a Painter," just as the dunces' religious and philosophic disorientation will result partly from taking the "high Priori Road" (IV.471) of seventeenth-century empirical thought (Pope stipulates that of Hobbes, Spinoza, Descartes, and "some better reasoners"). Correspondingly, the concept of self as "microcosm" in such lyrics as "The Garden" shifts to a concept of self as a complex of egocentric impulses in satire: the "scratching Courtiers" who find themselves listed in "The Last Instructions," like the dunces, quaff the cup of self-love and bring "a total oblivion of the obligations of Friendship, or Honour; and of the Service of God or our Country" (Pope's note to the *Dunciad* IV.517). The self-worship and social anarchy, the anti-platonic atomism and anti-pastoral blight, and above all the divine-human disjunction of the dunces and courtiers—in sum, the anti-culture of the new monarch "Anarch"—are seen in the mirror of a once meaningful cosmic order and its poetic decorums.

Since Pope and Marvell both think of pastoral as a vital part of the tradition, pastoral imagery provides a useful touchstone in tracing the movement from lyric to satire. In place of the pastoral song of Orpheus, which moves through "the vast void" of nature gathering "together the seeds of earth and air and sea, and withal of fluid fire," Pope will find "the bousy Sire" piping, not creative tunes, but "seeds of fire," or *semina rerum,* atoms of a mechanistic philosophy.[2] The decorum of nature "methodized" will be submerged in an antipastoral swarm of "Locusts blackening all the ground, / A tribe, with weeds and shells fantastic crowned." Each will bear some "wondrous gift," a "nest, a Toad, a Fungus, or a Flower"; but the flower will be no more or less impressive than the other items on the list. And such a loss of basic discrimination, Marvell indicates, is a tendency of his times. In "The Last Instructions," for example, when the Dutch admiral De Ruyter invades "our Ocean" and sees himself in its idyllic mirror, he undergoes a change of face, but the change of heart and values that should accompany it is lacking:

> The Sun much brighter, and the Skies more clear,
> He finds the Air, and all things, sweeter here.
> The sudden change, and such a tempting sight,
> Swells his old Veins with fresh blood, fresh Delight.
> Like am'rous Victors he begins to shave,
> And his new Face looks in the *English* Wave.
>
> (529–34)

Archibald Douglas, on the other hand, the "loyal Scot" (lines 649 ff.), is totally transfigured by the idyllic myth-making process, which, Marvell indicates, can retain much of its influence if taken meaningfully. Young and unhardened, a companion of the nymphs as yet untried by "loves Fires," Douglas attains heroic stature by trial in pastoral fires of war. When his ship is burned,

2. *Dunciad,* IV.494; cf. Virgil's sixth eclogue (alluded to by Pope), in *Virgil's Works,* trans. J. W. Mackail (New York, 1950), p. 279.

Like a glad Lover, the fierce Flames he meets,
And tries his first embraces in their Sheets,
His shape exact, which the bright flames infold,
Like the Sun's Statue stands of burnish'd Gold.
Round the transparent Fire about him glows,
As the clear Amber on the Bee does close:
And, as on Angels Heads their Glories shine,
His burning Locks adorn his Face Divine.
But, when in his immortal Mind he felt
His alt'ring Form, and soder'd Limbs to melt;
Down on the Deck he laid himself, and dy'd,
With his dear Sword reposing by his Side.
And, on the flaming Plank, so rests his Head,
As one that's warm'd himself and gone to Bed.
His Ship burns down, and with his Relicks sinks,
And the sad Stream beneath his Ashes drinks.
Fortunate Boy! if either Pencil's Fame,
Or if my verse can propagate thy Name;
When *Œta* and *Alcides* are forgot,
Our *English* youth shall sing the Valiant *Scot.*

(677–96)

Marvell may have in mind as one object of satire the sensual pastoral love lyric of the Restoration (an inverted variation of the old *pastourelle*) in which the knight leaves his station momentarily to achieve the willing nymph. Douglas restores the mythic dimension of pastoral by fleeing "loves Fires" and reserving himself for the "other Flame" (line 660). In any case, Marvell links Douglas with pastoral imagery as part of the total image of heroism, which makes him a "Sun" to illumine future times. As a pastoral myth, Douglas offers a moment of clarity in an otherwise discouraging history. And as a "glad Lover" with "secret Joy" and a "calm Soul," he achieves a strange but convincing fulfillment in lying on the warm bed, the "dear Sword reposing by his Side." His love for "our Lady State" has an inherent grace beyond military or cavalier exploits. Like the composed death of Charles in "An

Horatian Ode," his death suggests a kind of providential violence in history; and as Marvell indicates to his readers at court,
such a death can be educating for those who wish to save the
state. Like Charles' act of lying down beneath the axe, his is
passive, both a suicide and a symbolic unmanning. Like Alcides, whose mortal parts were burned on mount Oeta while
his soul was taken to Jupiter in a chariot, he burns himself,
and "precious life . . . disdains to save." It is a revealing account because heroism is seen as the highest and most excruci-
ating self-annihilation. The sword "reposes" as Douglas melts
into the "sun" that the lovers in "To His Coy Mistress" would
make "run" as they melt in passion. But if Douglas' flame has
no issue except his own symbolic transcendence, it is more
intense than passion's: by melting in the transparent flame, he
becomes "Divine." He has no enemy to use his sword against
but needs none. His symbolic transcendence is ambiguous,
however: though he has his transparent, luminous moment,
his "relics" sink downward in "the sad Stream" that drinks his
ashes. Like the Nymph's weeping statue—a combination of art
and non-life in the midst of holocaust—his reward is to be only
the verse that will "propagate" his name.

The Douglas passage, revealing as it is, is isolated and almost self-sustaining (it was published as a separate eulogy);
it is not closely integrated with what goes before and is only
spasmodically related to the remaining three hundred lines.
The "line of wit" has not evolved far enough for the satiric
poet to manipulate the old symbols freely, as Pope will; Marvell develops them for their own sake in a tone and mood
different from that of satiric sections. The withdrawal-emergence pattern becomes an alternation of heroic passivity and
aggressive satiric fervor. The active voice of "The Last Instructions" aims particular verbal missiles at particular people, who
are too numerous and too variable in their sins to compose a
single, dialectical enemy. Because Douglass lives in another

world from Henry Jermyn and Anne Hyde, Marvell can find no way to hold everything together in one mood, except insofar as the voice of scorn and the voice of eulogy are brought together in the concluding admonition. For Marvell does make application of the Douglas myth, inflamed "Like the Sun's Statue" in its burnished gold, in the final instructions to the King; the pastoral theme is made to serve as a corrective formula. The spots on the "Sun," he warns Charles II, can still be removed but only if the monarch is fully monarchical. The chief faults lie in the court, not in the kingship, and so the infection might yet be cured. "Bold and accurs'd" differently from Douglas, whose curse is a test of his boldness, the courtiers

> The *Kingdom* from the *Crown* distinct would see,
> And peal the Bark to burn at last the Tree.
> (But *Ceres* Corn, and *Flora* is the Spring,
> *Bacchus* is Wine, the Country is the *King*.)
> (971–74)

In the ambiguity of "country," Marvell suggests that natural simplicity and civil order may be joined, and must be if the "country" is to be saved. The monarch, like Douglas, must be infused with the basic sanity and order of nature; the task of the satiric poet is to supply the impetus for such infusion:

> And you, *Great Sir,* that with him Empire share,
> Sun of our World, as he the *Charles* is there.
> Blame not the *Muse* that brought those spots to sight,
> Which, in your Splendor hid, Corrode your Light;
> Kings in the Country oft have gone astray,
> Nor of a Peasant scorn'd to learn the way.
> (955–59)

It is better, Marvell adds, for poetry to "live in Cloysters Lock, / Or in fair Fields to rule the easie Flock" than to criticize un-

justly a just king; but corruption makes necessary a reinstate-
ment of goals and values that can inspire men like Douglas.
Hence the King must identify himself with the country, just
as the mythic goddesses Ceres and Flora are identified with
corn and spring; if he does not, if crown and king are parted,
the bark will be pulled from the tree and destructive fire ap-
plied to the green world itself. The country will indeed be lost.

If the Mower against gardens believes that "Luxurious Man"
has seduced the world, closing "Nature . . . most plain and
pure" in "dead and standing" pools of air, Marvell as satirist
finds that rust, powder, and earthquake do not destroy "an
hollow Isle" so effectively as "scratching *Courtiers* undermine
a *Realm*" (scratching in the sense both of physical vulgarity
and of social and economic climbing). The painter's court,
like Pope's court of dunces, finds the worth of true nobility submerged in the money-consciousness both of the rising city
classes and the decaying gentility. Hence the courtiers

> through the Palace's Foundations bore,
> Burr'wing themselves to hoard their guilty Store.
> The smallest Vermin make the greatest waste,
> And a poor Warren once a city ras'd.
>
> (979–82)

The "country" saviors are the old garden-wanderers of the past,
born "to Virtue and to Wealth" (983). Through virtue they
are free in conscience; wealthy, they are not bound to "stealth"
by want. They alone unite inner and outer worlds:

> Whose gen'rous Conscience and whose Courage high
> Does with clear Counsels their large Souls supply;
> That serve the *King* with their Estates and Care,
> And, as in Love, on *Parliaments* can stare . . .
>
> (985–88)

Their "supply" is soul-store; their "love"—like Marvell's during his last twenty years—is the parliament of "our Lady State."

Except for such moments as the Douglas episode and a few other scattered passages, however, pastoral themes and patterns did not offer Marvell a comprehensive satiric structure or method. He was not ready to make pastoral a medium for social criticism in the manner of Crabbe, or even to convert it into a Wordsworthian anti-urban mode.

In addition, many of the metaphors of the integrated system of nature, art, and grace were themselves not in keeping with the straightforward good sense required of a satirist. Swift, in fact, finds those very Neoplatonic and emblematic concepts of nature that comprise Marvellian pastoral legitimate objects of satire. The pseudo-symbolic theater of oratory in *Tale of a Tub*, for example, exposes the presumption of seeking correspondences between inner and outer worlds. The emblem-pulpit of the "modern saints" is so spiritualized and refined "from the dross and grossness of sense and human reason" that no relation to "sense" remains.[3] The pulpit is made of rotten wood because, being rotten, it gives light in the dark; and it is "full of worms" because "a head full of maggots" invariably accompanies such inner enlightenment and self-concern. The emblem-world and the language of symbolism are thus associated with the products of Grub Street. The hack writer withdraws into his quasi mysticism only to emerge with an armload of manuscripts confounding spirit and matter and mixing together mechanistic spirit jargon and secret symbols.

---

3. The satiric method of Marvell's prose tracts, however, probably had some influence upon later satire; the double-edged raillery of Swift in the *Tale of a Tub*, for example, may be indebted to *The Rehearsal Transpros'd*. See Ronald Paulson, *Theme and Structure in Swift's Tale of a Tub* (New Haven, 1960), pp. 39–48.

In thus shifting from traditional symbols to good sense, Swift avoids the problem of combining them that Marvell's satire encounters. If Marvell advises Charles II to seek the pattern of successful kingship in the example of the "sun," Swift finds absurd any concept of nature "fashioned" upon such a tailor-made universe:

> What is that which some call land, but a fine coat faced with green? or the sea, but a waistcoat of water-tabby? Proceed to the particular works of the creation, you will find how curious Journeyman Nature hath been, to trim up the vegetable beaux; observe how sparkish a periwig adorns the head of a beech, and what a fine doublet of white satin is worn by the birch. To conclude from all, what is man himself but a micro-coat, or rather a complete suit of clothes with all its trimmings?

Swift disarms with one stroke both the artificial man of the periwig and the nature lover of a certain breed. Enthusiasm for creating "far other worlds and other seas" in green thought had obviously waned. Marvell's poetry was too dependent upon it to treat it lightly or discard it.

But in turning from the *Tale of a Tub* to such poems as "Bermudas," "The Garden," and "Upon Appleton House," which depend most heavily upon Christian-Platonist attempts to define nature in terms of a benevolent "Journeyman," we do not find them greatly damaged, perhaps because even here the ironist adumbrates the sanity and judgment of the age of reason. Irony and satire could be used as muted elements within other strategies. The self-awareness of Marvell's best lyrics disarms Swiftean criticism. The multiple perspective of his irony and the singleness of the Christian-Platonist quest for unity complemented each other. Even those poems that find temporal existence useless to the self-contained soul say much that is meaningful about it, and those that for perhaps the last time in the lyric use the old metaphors for self-definition do so with a judgment and skill *"comme on ne fait plus à Londres."*[4]

4. T. S. Eliot, "Andrew Marvell," *Selected Essays*, p. 263.

Bibliography

THE FOLLOWING list includes the major criticism of Marvell's poetry through 1962 and primary and secondary works cited in the text or useful as seventeenth-century background.

GENERAL

Allers, Rudolf, "Microcosmus from Anaximandros to Paracelsus," *Traditio*, 2 (1944), 319–407.

Anderson, Paul Russell, *Science in Defense of Liberal Religion*, New York and London, 1933.

Archbishop of York, "Back to Unity," *UTQ*, 4 (1934), 1–10.

Armstrong, Arthur H., *The Architecture of the Intelligible Universe in the Philosophy of Plotinus*, Cambridge, 1940.

Aubrey, John, *Aubrey's Brief Lives*, ed. Oliver Lawson Dick, Ann Arbor, Michigan, 1957.

Baker, Hershel, *The Wars of Truth*, Cambridge, Mass., 1952.

Barker, Arthur, *Milton and the Puritan Dilemma, 1641–1660*, Toronto, 1942.

Battenhouse, Roy W., "The Doctrine of Man in Calvinism and in Renaissance Platonism," *JHI*, 9 (1948), 447–71.

Bernard of Clairvaux, *The Twelve Degrees of Humility and Pride*, trans. Barton R. V. Mills, New York, 1929.

———, *Vita et res gestae*, Migne, 185:240.

Bethell, S. L., *The Cultural Revolution of the Seventeenth Century*, London, 1951.

Blanchet, Leon, *Campanella*, Paris, 1920.

Böhme, Jakob, *A Dialogue between a Scholar and His Master concerning the Supersensual Life* (1624), London, 1912.

———, *Signatura Rerum, or the Signature of All Things*, London, 1651.

Boyce, Benjamin, *The Polemic Character, 1640–1661*, Lincoln, Nebraska, 1955.

Brathwayt, Richard, *Essays upon the Five Senses*, London, 1625.

Brooke, Robert Lord, *The Nature of Truth* . . ., London, 1640.

Burke, Kenneth, *A Grammar of Motives*, New York, Prentice-Hall, 1945.

Campagnac, E. T., ed., *The Cambridge Platonists*, Oxford, 1901.

Cassirer, Ernst, "Giovanni Pico della Mirandola: A Study in the History of Renaissance Ideas," *JHI, 3* (1942), 123–44, 319–46.

———, *The Platonic Renaissance in England*, trans. James P. Pettegrove, Austin, Texas, University of Texas Press, 1953.

Collingwood, R. G., *The Idea of History*, New York, 1956.

Collins, Joseph B., *Christian Mysticism in the Elizabethan Age*, Baltimore, 1940.

Craig, Hardin, *The Enchanted Glass*, New York, 1936.

Cromwell, Oliver, *Letters and Speeches*, ed. Thomas Carlyle, 4 vols. New York, 1899.

Cudworth, Ralph, *The True Intellectual System of the Universe*, 2 vols. London, 1839.

Dawson, Christopher, *Progress and Religion*, New York, 1938.

De Pauley, W. C., *The Candle of the Lord: Studies in the Cambridge Platonists*, London, 1937.

Digby, Kenelm, *Of Bodies, and of Man's Soul*, London, 1669.

Diodati, John, *Pious Annotations upon the Holy Bible*, London, 1648.

Douglas, Andrew Halliday, *The Philosophy and Psychology of Pietro Pomponazzi*, Cambridge, Cambridge University Press, 1910.

Eckhart, *Meister Eckhart*, trans. C. de B. Evans, London, 1924.

Edwards, Jonathan, *Images or Shadows of Divine Things*, ed. Perry Miller, New Haven, Yale University Press, 1948.

Fairfax, Thomas 3d Lord, *The Poems*, ed. Edward Reed, New Haven, 1909.

Fane, Mildmay, *Rare Poems of the Seventeenth Century*, ed. L. Birkett Marshall, Cambridge, 1936.

Fanfani, Amintore, *Catholicism, Protestantism, and Capitalism*, New York, 1939.

Ferguson, Wallace K., *The Renaissance in Historical Thought*, Boston, 1948.

Ficin, Marsile, *Commentaire sur le banquet de platon* (*In Convivium Platonis*), trans. Raymond Marcel, Paris, 1956.

Fuller, B. A. G., *The Problem of Evil in Plotinus*, Cambridge, 1912.

George, Charles H. and Katherine, *The Protestant Mind of the English Reformation, 1570–1640*, Princeton, 1961.

George, Edward Augustus, *Seventeenth Century Men of Latitude: Forerunners of the New Theology*, London, 1909.

Gilson, Etienne, *Études sur le role de la pensée médiévale dans la formation du système cartésien*, Paris, 1951.

———, *The Philosophy of St. Bonaventure*, New York, 1938.

Glanville, Joseph, *The Vanity of Dogmatizing*, London, 1661.

Goldstaub, Max and Richard Wendriner, *Ein tosco-venezianischer Bestiarius Herausgegeben und Erläutert*, 1892.

Goodwin, John, Ἀπολύτρωσις Ἀπολυτρώσεως, *or Redemption Redeemed*, London, 1651.

Grierson, H. J. C., *Cross Currents in English Literature of the Seventeenth Century*, London, 1929.

Haller, William, *Liberty and Reformation in the Puritan Revolution*, New York, 1955.

———, *The Rise of Puritanism*, New York, 1938.

Haydn, Hiram, *The Counter-Renaissance*, New York, 1950.

Herbert, Edward, of Cherbury, *De Veritate*, trans. Meyrick H. Carre, Bristol, 1937.

Hermetica: The Ancient Greek and Latin Writings . . . *Ascribed to Hermes Trismegistus,* ed. Walter Scott, 4 vols. Oxford, 1924.

Hooker, Richard, *The Works,* ed. Rev. John Keble, 3 vols. Oxford, 1887.

Hugh of St. Victor, *De bestiis,* Migne, 177:21 ff.

Hugo, Herman, *Pia Desideria,* trans. E. Arwaker, London, 1690.

Huizinga, J., *The Waning of the Middle Ages,* London, 1924.

Hulme, Edward Maslin, *The Renaissance,* New York, 1915.

Hulme, T. E., *Speculations,* ed. Herbert Read, London, 1936.

Inge, William Ralph, *The Philosophy of Plotinus,* London, 1918.

Itrat-Husain, *The Mystical Element in the Metaphysical Poets of the Seventeenth Century,* Edinburgh, 1948.

Jones, Rufus M., *Spiritual Reformers in the 16th and 17th Centuries,* Boston, 1959.

Jung, C. G., *Symbols of Transformation,* trans. R. F. C. Hull, Bollingen Series XX, New York, 1956.

Kermode, Frank, "Dissociation of Sensibility," *KR, 19* (1957), 169–94.

Kristeller, Paul Oskar, *The Philosophy of Marsilio Ficino,* New York, 1943.

———, *Studies in Renaissance Thought and Letters,* Rome, 1956.

——— and John Herman Randall, Jr., "The Study of the Philosophies of the Renaissance," *JHI, 2* (1941), 449–96.

Lievestro, Christiaan T., "Tertullian and the *Sensus* Argument," *JHI, 17* (1956), 264–68.

Lipsius, Justus, *De Constantia,* trans. John Stradling, New Brunswick, N.J., 1939.

Lovejoy, Arthur O. *The Great Chain of Being,* New York, Harper, 1960.

———, *Essays in the History of Ideas,* New York, 1960.

MacKinnon, Flora Isabel, *The Philosophy of John Norris of Bemerton,* Baltimore, 1910.

MacLean, Kenneth, *John Locke and English Literature of the Eighteenth Century,* New Haven, 1936.

McNeill, John T., *The History and Character of Calvinism,* New York, 1954.

Mahood, M. M., *Poetry and Humanism,* New Haven, Yale University Press, 1950.

Maritain, Jacques, *The Dream of Descartes,* trans. Mabelle L. Andison, New York, 1944.

———, *True Humanism,* New York, 1938.

Martz, Louis L., *The Poetry of Meditation,* New Haven, Yale University Press, 1954.

Marvell, Andrew, *The Complete Prose Works,* ed. A. B. Grosart, 3 vols. London, 1873.

Merlan, Philip, *From Platonism to Neoplatonism,* The Hague, 1953.

Messenger, Ernest C., *The Reformation, the Mass, and the Priesthood,* 2 vols. London, 1936.

Miller, Perry, *The New England Mind,* Vol. I: *The Seventeenth Century,* Cambridge, Harvard University Press, 1954.

Mitchell, W. Fraser, *English Pulpit Oratory from Andrewes to Tillotson,* London, 1932.

More, Henry, *A Collection of Several Philosophical Writings,* London, 1662.

———, *Enchiridion ethicum* (the English translation of 1690), New York, Facsimile Text Society, 1930.

———, *The Philosophical Poems,* ed. Geoffrey Bullough, Manchester University Press, 1931.

Muirhead, John H., *The Platonic Tradition in Anglo-Saxon Philosophy,* New York, 1931.

Nelson, Norman, "Individualism as a Criterion of the Renaissance," *JEGP, 32* (1933), 316–34.

Nemesius, *The Nature of Man,* trans. George Wither, London, 1636.

Nicolson, Marjorie, *The Breaking of the Circle,* Evanston, Ill., 1950.

———, "The Early Stage of Cartesianism in England," *SP, 26* (1929), 356–74.

———, *Mountain Gloom and Mountain Glory,* Ithaca, N.Y., 1959.

——, "The Spirit World of Milton and More," *SP*, 22 (1925), 433–5?,

Norris, John, *Collection of Miscellanies*, London, 1717.

O'Brien, Gordon Worth, *Renaissance Poetics and the Problem of Power*, Chicago, 1956.

Panofsky, Erwin, *Meaning in the Visual Arts*, New York, 1957.

——, "Renaissance and Renascences," *KR*, 6 (1944), 201–36.

——, *Studies in Iconology*, New York, 1939.

Paracelsus, *Selected Writings*, ed. Jolande Jacobi, trans. Norbert Guterman, Bollingen Series XXVIII, New York, 1951.

Pauck, Wilhelm, *The Heritage of the Reformation*, Glencoe, Ill., 1950.

Pawson, G. P. H., *The Cambridge Platonists and Their Place in Religious Thought*, London, 1930.

Petersson, R. T., *Sir Kenelm Digby*, Cambridge, Mass., 1956.

Phile, Manuel, "Versus de animalium proprietate," *Poetae bucolici et didactici*, Paris, 1862.

Physiologus latinus, versio y, ed. Francis J. Carmody, University of California Publications in Classical Philology, *12* (1933–34), 95–134.

Pico della Mirandola, *A Platonic Discourse upon Love*, ed. Edmund G. Gardner, Boston, 1914.

Pinto, Vivian de Sola, *Peter Sterry: Platonist and Puritan*, Cambridge, Cambridge University Press, 1934.

Pliny, *Natural History*, Cambridge, Mass., 1947.

Plotinus: *The Enneads*, trans. Stephen MacKenna, London: Faber and Faber, 1917–1930.

Pomponazzi, Pietro, *Tractatus de Immoralitate Animae*, trans. William Henry Hay II, Haverford, Pa., 1938.

Poulet, Georges, *Studies in Human Time*, New York, 1956.

Powicke, Frederick J., *The Cambridge Platonists*, London, 1926.

Praz, Mario, *Studies in Seventeenth-Century Imagery*, 2 vols. London, 1947.

Proclus, Diadochus, *Proclus' Metaphysical Elements*, trans. Thomas M. Johnson, Osceola, Missouri, 1909.

Quarles, Francis, *Emblems Divine and Moral*, London, 1858.

Rollins, Hyder E., ed., *Cavalier and Puritan: Ballads and Broadsides* . . ., New York, 1923.

Ross, Malcolm Mackenzie, *Poetry and Dogma: The Transfiguration of Eucharistic Symbols in Seventeenth Century English Poetry*, New Brunswick, N.J., Rutgers University Press, 1954.

Rous, F[rancis], *The Mysticall Marriage*, London, 1631.

Rump: Or an Exact Collection of the Choycest Poems and Songs Relating to the Late Times . . . *1639–61*, 2 vols. London, 1662.

Sensabaugh, G. F., "Platonic Love and the Puritan Rebellion," *SP*, 37 (1940), 457–81.

Smith, Harold Wendell, "The Dissociation of Sensibility," *Scrutiny, 18* (1952), 175–88.

Smith, John, *Select Discourses*, ed. Henry Griffin Williams, Cambridge, 1859.

Smith, Norman Kemp, *New Studies in the Philosophy of Descartes*, London, 1952.

Spitzer, Leo, "Classical and Christian Ideas of World Harmony," *Traditio 2, 3* (1944–45), 409–64, 307–64.

Sterry, Peter, *The Rise, Race, and Royalty of the Kingdom of God in the Soul of Man*, London, 1683.

————, *The Appearance of God to Man in the Gospel*, London, 1710.

Theologia Germanica, trans. Susanna Winkworth, London, 1873.

Thorndike, Lynn, "Renaissance or Prenaissance?" *JHI, 4* (1943), 65–74.

Troeltsch, Ernst, *Protestantism and Progress*, trans. W. Montgomery, London, 1912.

Tulloch, John, *Rational Theology and Christian Philosophy in England in the Seventeenth Century*, Vol. 2: *The Cambridge Platonists*, London, 1874.

Tuve, Rosemond, "A Critical Survey of Scholarship in the Field of English Literature of the Renaissance," *SP, 40* (1943), 204–55.

————, *Elizabethan and Metaphysical Imagery*, Chicago, 1947.

———, "Imagery and Logic: Ramus and Metaphysical Poetic," *JHI, 3* (1942), 365–400.

Vane, Henry, *The Retired Man's Meditations*, London, 1655.

Watson, George, "Ramus, Miss Tuve, and the New Petromachia," *MP, 55* (1958) 259–62.

Weber, Max, *The Protestant Ethic and the Spirit of Capitalism*, trans. Talcott Parsons, New York, 1930.

Whichcote, Benjamin, *Works*, 3 vols. London, 1751.

White, T. H., *The Book of Beasts*, New York, 1954.

Whittaker, Thomas, *The Neo-Platonists*, Cambridge, 1901.

Willey, Basil, *The Seventeenth Century Background*, New York, Doubleday, 1953.

Woodhouse, A. S. P., ed., *Puritanism and Liberty*, Chicago, University of Chicago Press, 1951.

Yolton, John W., *John Locke and the Way of Ideas*, Oxford, 1956.

MARVELL CRITICISM

Allen, D. C., *Image and Meaning: Metaphoric Traditions in Renaissance Poetry*, Baltimore, Johns Hopkins University Press, 1960, pp. 93–153.

———, "Marvell's 'Nymph,' " *ELH, 23* (1956), 93–111.

Bain, Carl E., "The Latin Poetry of Andrew Marvell," *PQ, 38* (1959), 436–49.

Baron, Hans, "Marvell's 'An Horatian Ode' and Machiavelli," *JHI, 21* (1960), 450–51.

Bateson, F. W., *English Poetry*, London, 1950.

Birrell, Augustine, *Andrew Marvell*, New York, 1905.

Bradbrook, F. W., "The Poetry of Andrew Marvell," in *From Donne to Marvell*, ed. Boris Ford, London, Penguin Books, 1956, pp. 193–204.

Bradbrook, M. C., "Marvell and the Poetry of Rural Solitude," *RES, 17* (1941), 37–46.

——— and M. G. Lloyd Thomas, *Andrew Marvell*, Cambridge, 1940.

————, "Marvell and the Concept of Metamorphosis," *The Criterion*, *18* (1938–39), 236–54.

Brooks, Cleanth, "Literary Criticism," in *English Institute Essays* (1946), pp. 127–58.

————, "A Note on the Limits of 'History' and the Limits of 'Criticism,'" *SR, 61* (1953), 129–35.

———— and Robert Penn Warren, *Understanding Poetry*, New York, 1952.

Brower, Reuben A., "An Allusion to Europe: Dryden and Tradition," *ELH, 19* (1952), 38–48.

Bush, Douglas, *English Literature in the Earlier Seventeenth Century*, Oxford, 1945.

————, "Marvell's 'Horatian Ode,'" *SR, 60* (1952), 363–76.

Carens, James F., "Andrew Marvell's Cromwell Poems," *Bucknell Review, 7* (1957), 41–70.

Carroll, John J., "The Sun and the Lovers in 'To His Coy Mistress,'" *MLN, 74* (1959), 4–7.

Chambers, A. B., " 'I Was But an Inverted Tree': Notes toward the History of an Idea," *Studies in the Renaissance, 8* (1961), 291–99.

Colie, Rosalie L., "Marvell's 'Bermudas' and the Puritan Paradise," *Renaissance News, 10* (1957), 75–79.

Corder, Jim, "Marvell and Nature," *N&Q*, n.s. *6* (1959), 58–61.

Cunningham, J. V., "Logic and Lyric," *MP, 51* (1953), 33–41.

Davison, Dennis, "Marvell's 'The Definition of Love,' " *RES, 6* (1955), 141–46.

Duncan-Jones, E. E., "Marvell His Own Critic," *N&Q, 201* (1956), 283–84.

Eliot, T. S., *Selected Essays*, New York: Harcourt, Brace, 1950.

Emerson, E. A., "Andrew Marvell's *A Nymph complaining for the Death of Her Faun*," *Études anglaises, 8* (1955), 105–110.

Empson, William, *Some Versions of Pastoral*, London, 1950.

Everett, Barbara, "Marvell's 'The Mower's Song,' " *CQ, 4* (1962), 219–24.

Farnham, Anthony E., "Saint Teresa and the Coy Mistress," *Boston University Studies in English, 2* (1956), 226–39.

Fogel, Ephim G., "Salmons in Both, or Some Caveats for Canonical Scholars," *BNYPL, 63* (1959), 223–36, 292–308.

Foster, Ruel E., "A Tonal Study: Marvell, 'A Nymph . . .,'" *University of Kansas City Review, 21* (1954), 73–78.

Gwynn, Frederick L., "Marvell's 'To His Coy Mistress,'" *Explicator, 11* (1953), item 7.

Hardy, John Edward, *The Curious Frame,* Notre Dame, 1962, pp. 45–60.

Hecht, Anthony, "Shades of Keats and Marvell," *HR, 15* (1962), 50–71.

Henn, T. R., *The Apple and the Spectroscope,* London, 1951.

Hill, Christopher, "Andrew Marvell and the Good Old Cause," *Mainstream, 12* (1959), 1–27.

————, *Puritanism and Revolution,* London, 1958, pp. 337–66.

Hirsch, E. D., "Objective Interpretation," *PMLA, 75* (1960), 463–79.

Hogan, Patrick G., Jr., "Marvell's 'Vegetable Love,'" *SP, 60* (1963), 1–11.

Hollander, John, *The Untuning of the Sky: Ideas of Music in English Poetry, 1500–1700,* Princeton, 1961.

Hyman, Lawrence W. "'Ideas' in Marvell's Lyric Poetry," *History of Ideas News Letter, 2* (1956), 29–31.

————, "Marvell's 'Coy Mistress' and Desperate Lover," *MLN, 75* (1960), 8–10.

————, "Marvell's 'Garden,'" *ELH, 25* (1958), 13–22.

————, "Politics and Poetry in Andrew Marvell," *PMLA, 73* (1958), 475–79.

Kermode, Frank, "The Argument of Marvell's 'Garden,'" *Essays in Criticism, 2* (1952), 225–41.

————, "Definitions of Love," *RES, 7* (1956), 183–85.

————, *English Pastoral Poetry from the Beginnings to Marvell,* London, 1952.

King, A. H., "Some Notes on Marvell's Garden," *ES, 20* (1938), 118–21.

Klonsky, Milton, "A Guide through the Garden," *SR, 58* (1950), 16–35.

Leavis, F. R., "English Poetry in the Seventeenth Century," *Scrutiny, 4* (1935–36), 236–56.

———, *Revaluation: Tradition and Development in English Poetry*, London, 1936.

Le Comte, E. S., "Marvell's 'The Nymph . . .,' " *MP, 50* (1952), 97–101.

Legouis, Pierre, *André Marvell: poète, puritain, patriote, 1621–78,* Paris, 1928.

———, "Marvell and the New Critics," *RES, 8* (1957), 382–89.

———, "Reply to Dean Morgan Schmitter," *RES, 12* (1961), 51–54.

———, "Réponse à E. A. Emerson," *Études anglaises, 8* (1955), 111–12.

———, "Marvell's 'Nymph . . .': A *Mise au Point*," *MLQ, 21* (1960), 30–32.

Leishman, J. B., *Translating Horace*, Oxford, 1956.

Lord, George deForest, "The Case for Internal Evidence A: Comments on the Canonical Caveat," *BNYPL, 53* (1959), 355–66.

Mazzeo, Joseph A., "Cromwell as Machiavellian Prince in Marvell's 'An Horatian Ode,' " *JHI, 21* (1960), 1–17.

———, "Cromwell as Davidic King," in *Reason and Imagination,* New York, 1962, pp. 29–55.

Mitchell, Charles, "Marvell's 'The Mower to the Glo-worms,' " *Explicator, 18* (1960), item 50.

Nowottny, Winifred, *The Language Poets Use*, New York, 1962, pp. 92–96.

Paulson, Ronald, *Theme and Structure in Swift's Tale of a Tub,* New Haven, 1960.

Press, John, *Andrew Marvell*, London, 1958.

Poggioli, Renato, "The Pastoral of the Self," *Daedalus, 88* (1959), 686–99.

Proudfoot, L., "Marvell: Sallust and the Horatian Ode," *N&Q, 196* (1951), 434.

Putney, Rufus, " 'Our Vegetable Love': Marvell and Burton," in *Studies in Honor of T. W. Baldwin*, ed. D. C. Allen, Urbana, Ill., 1958, pp. 220–28.

Robbins, Caroline, "Marvell's Religion: Was He a New Methodist?" *JHI*, 23 (1962), 268–72.

Rosenberg, John D., "Marvell and the Christian Idiom," *Boston University Studies in English*, 4 (1960), 152–61.

Røstvig, Maren-Sofie, "Andrew Marvell's 'The Garden': A Hermetic Poem," *ES*, 40 (1959), 65–76.

———, *The Happy Man*, Oslo, 1954.

———, " 'Upon Appleton House' and the Universal History of Man," *ES*, 42 (1961), 337–51.

Sackville-West, Victoria Mary, *Andrew Marvell*, London, 1929.

Sasek, Lawrence, "Marvell's 'To His Coy Mistress,' 45–46," *Explicator*, 14 (1956), item 7.

Schmitter, Dean Morgan, "The Cartography of 'The Definition of Love,' " *RES*, 12 (1961), 49–51.

———, "The Occasion for Marvell's *Growth of Popery*," *JHI*, 21 (1960), 568–70.

Sedelow, Walter A., Jr., "Marvell's 'To His Coy Mistress,' " *MLN*, 71 (1956), 6–8.

Sherbo, Arthur, "The Case for Internal Evidence B: A Reply to Professor Fogel," *BNYPL*, 53 (1959), 367–71.

Smith, Harold Wendell, "Cowley, Marvell and the Second Temple," *Scrutiny*, 19 (1953), 184–204.

Spitzer, Leo, "Marvell's 'Nymph . . .': Sources versus Meaning," *MLQ*, 19 (1958), 231–43.

Summers, Joseph H., "Marvell's 'Nature,' " *ELH*, 20 (1953), 121–35.

Swardson, H. R., *Poetry and the Fountain of Light*, London, 1962.

Syfret, R. H., "Marvell's 'Horatian Ode,' " *RES*, 12 (1961), 160–72.

Teeter, Louis, "Scholarship and the Art of Criticism," *ELH*, 5 (1938), 173–94.

Tillyard, E. M. W., *Poetry Direct and Oblique*, London, 1934.

Toliver, Harold E., "Marvell's 'Definition of Love' and Poetry of Self-Exploration," *Bucknell Review*, 10 (1962), 263–74.

———, "Pastoral Form and Idea in Some Poems of Marvell," *Texas Studies in Literature and Language*, 5 (1963), 83–97.

Truesdale, Calvin William, "English Pastoral Verse from Spenser to Marvell," Doctoral dissertation, University of Washington, 1956.

Unger, Leonard, *The Man in the Name*, Minneapolis, 1956, pp. 123–28.

Wall, L. N., "Some Notes on Marvell's Sources . . .," *N&Q, 202* (1957), 170–73.

Wallace, John M., "Andrew Marvell and Cromwell's Kingship: 'The First Anniversary,' " *ELH, 30* (1963), 209–35.

———, "Marvell's Horatian Ode," *PMLA, 77* (1962), 33–45.

Wallerstein, Ruth, *Studies in Seventeenth-Century Poetic*, Madison, University of Wisconsin Press, 1950.

Walton, Geoffrey, *Metaphysical to Augustan*, London, 1955.

Wheatcroft, John, "Andrew Marvell and the Winged Chariot," *Bucknell Review, 6* (1956), 22–53.

Williamson, George, "The Context of Marvell's 'Hortus' and 'Garden,' " *MLN, 76* (1961), 590–98.

———, *The Donne Tradition*, New York, 1958.

———, *The Proper Wit of Poetry*, Chicago, 1961.

Williamson, Karina, "Marvell's 'Nymph . . .': A Reply," *MP, 51* (1953–54), 268–71.

Index

INDEX

Røstvig, 103, 115, 125 f., 129,
138, 142
Rusticity, 107. *See also* Pastoral;
Primitivism

Santayana, 27
Sasek, 157
Satire, 8 f., 53, 107, 109, 166,
196 ff., 204–13 passim. *See
also* Irony; Wit
Sedlow, 157
Shaftesbury, 22
Shakespeare, 13, 32, 37, 137, 143,
153, 187
Shelley, 61
Sidney, 32, 152
Smith, Harold W., 138
Smith, John, 19, 23 f., 26–28,
179, 182, 185
Smith, John, 101
Socrates, 44, 48 ff., 52
Solinus, 115
Southwell, 84
Spenser, 32, 91, 152, 173
Spinoza, 205
Spitzer, 67, 129, 133, 134 f., 149
Sprigge, 181 f., 186
Sterry, 16, 19–22, 25, 65, 86 f.,
125, 179, 182
Stevens, 1, 3
Stoicism, 11, 43, 58, 63
Strabo, 96
Summers, 103, 170
Swift, 37, 39, 211 f.

Tate, 77
Teeter, 159
Theocritus, 140
Theologia Germanica, 15
Thomas, 46, 54, 138, 155, 159,
166
Thompson, 129
Time, 10 f., 25, 36, 59, 76 f., 88,

Time (*cont.*)
125, 150 f., 152–77 passim,
200 f., 204
Traherne, 17, 23 f., 75 f., 84, 87,
123, 183
Trevelyan, 191
Truesdale, 94, 103, 142
Tuckney, 22
Tuve, 46, 77 f., 82

Vane, 19, 24 f., 46
Vaughan, 17, 23 f., 39, 97, 118 f.,
123, 125, 183
Vestigia dei. See Book of
Creatures

Wallace, 183, 193
Waller, 205
Wallerstein, 48, 100, 113 f., 138,
142, 149, 154, 183
Walton, 61
Warren, Austin, 159
Warren, Robert Penn, 46
Wasserman, 195
Webb, 118
Wellek, 159
Wendriner, 116
Whale, 15, 34
Wheatcroft, 54, 155, 183
Whichcote, 15 f., 19, 22, 25, 27,
31, 125 185
Willey, 105
Williams, 204
Williamson, George, 84, 129
Williamson, Karina, 130
Wilson, 103
Wit, 3, 17, 59, 76, 79, 87, 134 f.,
162, 195, 197. *See also* Irony;
Satire
Withdrawal. *See* Humanism
Woodhouse, 25, 180, 182
Wordsworth, 6, 17, 113, 211

Yeats, 93, 148, 189, 203